MUIR
OF HUNTERSHILL

MUIR

OF HUNTERSHILL

Christina Bewley

Oxford New York Toronto Melbourne
OXFORD UNIVERSITY PRESS
1981

Oxford University Press, Walton Street, Oxford OX2 6DP
London Glasgow New York Toronto
Delhi Bombay Calcutta Madras Karachi
Kuala Lumpur Singapore Hong Kong Tokyo
Nairobi Dar es Salaam Cape Town
Melbourne Wellington
and associate companies in
Beirut Berlin Ibadan Mexico City

The publisher acknowledges the financial assistance of
the Scottish Arts Council in the publication of this volume

Christina Bewley,
Muir of Huntershill.
1. Muir, Thomas, b. 1765
2. Scotland — Biography
I. Title
941.107'3'0924   CT828.M78   80–41120
ISBN 0–19–211768–8

Set by Western Printing Services Ltd
Printed in Great Britain
at The Pitman Press, Bath

Contents

List of Illustrations

Map

◇◇

In memory of
my father
Thomas Erskine Muir

Introduction

◇◇◇

Thomas Muir rates a brief paragraph in most British history books covering the latter half of the eighteenth century, favourable or unfavourable according to the author's political viewpoint. His contemporaries labelled him either 'martyr' or 'agitator'. There have been two biographies of Muir. The first, by Peter Mackenzie, was published in Glasgow in 1831. Mackenzie was an ardent campaigner for the 1832 reform bill and his slim book is really a political tract. This is particularly unfortunate as, though Mackenzie was too young to have known Muir or his parents, he did meet friends and relations who could have provided details of Muir's early life which are now unobtainable. Some of Mackenzie's comments are at least based on first-hand descriptions of events. Whether he had received incorrect information or deliberately altered the facts of those episodes, he produced a wildly inaccurate account of Muir's journey through New Spain and barely mentioned his last year as a protégé of the Directory in France. Later historians accepted Mackenzie's version until H. W. Meikle published an accurate resumé of Muir's life in his classic work *Scotland and the French Revolution* in 1912. A short biography by John Earnshaw was published in Australia in 1959. He had unearthed in the Mitchell Library, Sydney, a copy of a rare French book, *Mémoires sur ses Voyages* by Captain François Peron, which described Muir's voyage from Australia to California. Earnshaw also included material on Muir's months in America originally mentioned in an article by J. Jameson and M. Masson, 'The Odyssey of Thomas Muir', in *American Historical Review* Volume 29, October 1923.

One obstacle in attempting a biography of Muir is that there is only scattered, fragmentary material. There are few personal descriptions of him; no details of his mother's antecedents, little information about his family's characters and relationships, hardly any letters from Muir to his relations. There are few family papers because the Muirs were an unlucky family. Thomas had one sister, four of whose sons were killed in accidents. Of her children only one daughter, Louisa, lived to forty. My grandfather was a descendant of one of Muir's uncles, and was only eight when his parents and sisters were lost at sea.

It is also difficult to assess Muir's importance, if any, as a political reformer. The reform agitation of the 1790s was premature, supported by only a minute section of the population, submerged by the French wars. Muir is at most a minor historical figure, but he was active in a decade which spans one of the watersheds of history. The ideas which inspired him found expression in the American and French Revolutions. Some of the doctrines he supported had their origins with the Commonwealthmen; some of the reforms he advocated were not implemented until the 1860 reform bill. Muir has been dubbed a Scottish Nationalist, but this modern term is not really applicable. Muir believed that since Union the English had promoted their own interests to the detriment of Scotland. But he campaigned for a more representative franchise for Scotsmen to elect M.P.s to Westminster, not any form of devolution or separation. It was not until he returned to Paris in 1798, his mind clouded by illness, with an understandable hatred of Pitt's Government, that he supported the French scheme for dividing Britain into three separate republics.

Whether of historic interest or not, Muir's brief life was extraordinarily adventurous, and its pattern has some of the qualities of a Greek tragedy.

As it is such a useful descriptive word on occasion I have referred to Muir and his fellow reformers as 'radical'. They used the adjective in the sense of 'thoroughgoing', 'getting to the root of'. It was not used as adjective or noun in its modern political sense until the nineteenth century. But, though historically incorrect, the meaning of the word is applicable to them. Equally I have quoted their use of the word 'republican'. 'Republic' at that time signified a state governed in the interests of a majority. It could be a monarchy, oligarchy, or democracy.

I would like to thank the staffs of the British Library, the Scottish National Library, Edinburgh University Library, the Mitchell Library in Glasgow, Hammersmith Central Library, the Mitchell Library in Sydney, the Bancroft Library in Berkeley, the Scottish and English Public Record Offices, the *Archives des Affaires Étrangères* in Paris, the Archives of the Indies in Seville, the Clerk of the Faculty of Advocates in Edinburgh, and the Clerk to the General Assembly of the Church of Scotland, for their assistance. I would also like to acknowledge my debt to H. W. Meikle, Marjorie Masson and J. Jameson, and J. Earnshaw, whose research and writings provided much of the material on which this book is based. I should also like to thank Miss Pratt Insh for permission to read her father's unpublished MS. My cousin Philippa Sheepshanks translated the Spanish documents. In particular I wish to thank Richard Brain, without whose expert help this book would never have been satisfactorily completed.

A new world was opening to the astonished sight. Scenes lovely as hope can paint, dawned on the imagination; visions of unsullied bliss lulled the senses, & hid the darkness of surrounding objects, rising in bright succession & endless gradations, like the steps of that ladder which was once set up on the earth, and whose top reached to heaven.

Hazlitt, *Memoirs of Holcroft*

For my part, I started in life with the French Revolution, and I have lived, alas! to see the end of it. But I did not foresee this result. My sun arose with the first dawn of liberty, and I did not think how soon both must set. The new impulse to ardour given to men's minds imparted a congenial warmth and glow to mine; we were strong to run a race together, and I little dreamed that long before mine was set, the sun of liberty would turn to blood, or set once more in the night of despotism. Since then, I confess, I have no longer felt myself young, for with that my hopes fell.

Hazlitt, *Feeling of Immortality in Youth*

CHAPTER 1

Youth

Thomas Muir was born on 4 August, 1765, in a flat above his father's shop on the east side of Glasgow High Street, at that time a picturesque and attractive thoroughfare. His father, James, was a younger son of the 'bonnet laird' (roughly equivalent to a tenant farmer) of Hayston and Birdston farms near Kirkintilloch. James had relations who were prosperous hop growers at Maidstone in Kent, so, as he was unlikely to inherit his father's property, he went into the hop trade. As there were so few opportunities for men in Scotland, there was little social stigma attached to trade. It was as common for a gentleman's son to enter trade as for rich tradesmen to rise out of it. By the time James, aged 39, married Margaret Smith in 1764 he was a successful hop merchant and grocer, owning two adjoining shops with the houses above them.[1] Thomas had one sister, Janet. James and Margaret Muir were both deeply religious, orthodox Presbyterians. They brought up their children in the Calvinist tradition to denounce what they believed wrong, to uphold principles at whatever cost, to help the weak and suffering. From the Covenanters James and his son also inherited a radical turn of mind.*

Glasgow in the second half of the eighteenth century had become a great mercantile centre, importing sugar, tobacco, and other colonial produce from the West Indies and America and re-exporting to Holland and the Baltic. The tobacco trade vanished after the American War of Independence, but the capital which had accrued was reinvested in cotton manufacture. Coal-mines were opened, chemical and soap making started, canals built. Many highlanders and agricultural workers moved into the city and its surrounding villages to work in factories which were springing up. In 1765 Glasgow's population was 28,000, by 1780 it had risen to 40,000, but, until almost the end of the century, it remained a charming, sober, though

---

* The *Dictionary of National Biography* on Muir says that James wrote a pamphlet on Scotland's trade, but this may have been written by a different James Muir.

vigorously expanding city. Industrial slums had not yet appeared and the crime rate was negligible.

Whatever its disadvantages the Act of Union stimulated the Scottish economy and brought it into wider contact with the outside world. The two countries exchanged goods and technological advances, and Scotland could trade abroad on the same terms as England. After the '45, Scotland at last enjoyed a period of peace.

The national income rose rapidly. People were no longer resigned to poverty, nor preoccupied with religious and dynastic squabbles or local feuds. Material progress brought a great change in the spirit and energy of the nation, which in turn produced a cultural renaissance. This was Scotland's golden age, her one brief period of international fame. Scotsmen were among the most brilliant and original minds working in Europe in many fields —philosophy, architecture, history, engineering, economics, medicine, science. There was much truth in Voltaire's sarcastic comment that 'It is an admirable result of the progress of the human spirit that at the present time it is from Scotland we receive rules of taste in all the arts—from the epic poem to gardening.' At Scottish Universities important scientific discoveries, recognition and acclaim for French writers, especially Montesquieu, the lectures of Adam Smith, Hume, and Hutcheson, encouraged an atmosphere of speculation, excitement, intellectual confidence, and the creation of new ideas. The range and vigour of Scottish innovations in all aspects of life greatly impressed other countries. As a result, in the 1770s students came to Scotland from all over Europe to study modern philosophy, political economy, and natural sciences.

Although at this time nationalistic sentiment was not strong, any adolescent Scot would still be affected by the latent hostility and sense of inferiority to the 'auld enemy'. The Scots considered the English arrogant, heartless, unfairly rich. They magnified their own qualities and praised everything Scottish. The antipathy was heartily reciprocated. In the south the Scots, in particular Lord Bute, were extremely unpopular. The English thought them backward, treacherous and poor. There were endless jokes and references in plays to the cunning, cringing, sponging, wily Scot.

When his son was five James Muir engaged a tutor for him, William Barclay, a local schoolmaster. Thomas then learnt the rudiments of Latin in a private school run by Daniel McArthur and entered the junior section of Glasgow University in 1777.* He was an intelligent, hardworking, but not brilliant pupil, winning a prize for good behaviour. Two years later, encouraged by his parents, he began studying divinity. In the eighteenth century a large proportion of students entered the Church, the most certain way of advancement for a young man without influence. The Scottish educational system was remarkably democratic. Though a few aristocrats sent their sons to England, the majority of the upper and middle class, and a number of really poor children, were taught together in schools and universities. Glasgow University had about 800 students and 19 professors. The majority of the students were aged 13–16, because the first years at university were the equivalent of those which would now be spent at school. Students learnt Latin, Greek, logic, history, philosophy, and mathematics; then in their sixth year they attended classes to fit them for professions. About a third of the students came from Ulster and some from America. To save money many walked long distances to the city bringing a bag of oatmeal to eat during the term. The professors were also poor and took in boarding pupils to make ends meet.

The Old College, as the University was then called, stood in the High Street close to the Muirs' home. It was a pleasant collection of stone buildings, mostly dating from the seventeenth century. They were in the Scottish vernacular style with high chimneys and ornamental carving over the windows, built round two quadrangles. There was a clock-tower, a physic garden, a church, with further gardens and fields beyond. After the site had been occupied for four hundred years the property was sold to the City of Glasgow Union Railway Company in 1870 and the university buildings pulled down.

Thomas remained a devout Christian all his life but, after matriculating in April 1782, he decided, instead of entering the Church, to read for the bar. Thomas had been fascinated by Professor John Millar's lectures on law and government. He had shown considerable debating powers in juridical discussions and in college political debates

---

* Mackenzie's *Life*, p. 1, says Muir went to Glasgow Grammar School. David MacArthur taught at the Grammar School later on and this confused Mackenzie (see W. Marshall, *Glasgow Magazine*, 1795). Marshall wrote nearer the time of these events than Mackenzie.

and Millar advised him to become an advocate. Millar was a most remarkable man and made a great and lasting impression on many of his pupils, stimulating them to think independently and helping them to choose vocations. He had been a student of Adam Smith and David Hume. He had originally practised at the Edinburgh bar, but was offered and accepted the chair of Civil Law at Glasgow where he was the first professor to give his lectures in English instead of Latin. He was a brilliant, original thinker, who made Glasgow law school internationally famous. Thomas Campbell the poet describes how his 'students were always in the class before him waiting for a treat. He made investigations into the principles of justice and the rights and interests of society so captivating to me, that I formed opinions for myself, and became an emancipated lover of truth.' Another pupil, Jeffrey, later a judge and co-founder of the *Edinburgh Review*, described his 'magical vitality'. 'No young man admitted to his house ever forgot him. The discussions he led were the most exciting and instructive in which they ever took part.'

Several aristocratic pupils who lodged with Millar, including William Windham and the Earl of Lauderdale, both later Whig politicians, became lifelong friends and disciples. Among his ex-pupils were Edinburgh lawyers who helped bring in the Great Reform Bill. When Melbourne and his brother Frederick were sent, on leaving Cambridge, to lodge with Millar, they were at first amused at the idolatry with which he was regarded by the provincial Scottish and Irish students, but they were converted: 'Millar is a little jolly dog and the sharpest fellow I ever saw.' They were appalled to find that the household studied from morning to night; 'one of Millar's daughters is pretty but they are all philosophers.' In the vacations Melbourne bored and alarmed Lady Holland and Lord Egremont, as all he could talk about were the professor's philosophical ideas. However, when his mother said she was afraid he would become a doctrinaire prig, he assured her that he deplored the ignorant self-assurance of many of the students: 'no place can be perfect and the truth is that the Scotch Universities are very much calculated to make a man vain, important and pedantic. . . . You cannot have both the advantages of study and of the world together.'

Millar extended some aspects of the general eighteenth century criticism of society. His books and lectures ranged over a wide field, the conflicts between different strata of the population, the problem of liberty versus stability, and the ethical principles which should control behaviour. He suggested that a scientific study of society would produce better conditions. He was, in fact, one of the first sociologists. At that time the contrast between areas in different stages of development could be clearly seen in Scotland. Glasgow's economic growth was visibly transforming the life of its inhabitants, whereas feudalism still existed in the highlands.

Millar believed that power was usually manipulated in the interests of a small segment of society, not for the welfare of all. He supported the Americans in the War of Independence and the anti-slavery campaign. He was a staunch advocate of burgh and parliamentary reform and campaigned for church patronage to be taken from ministerial hands. He wanted to improve the lot of ordinary people. He organized reading societies and wrote anonymous anti-Tory political pamphlets. After being appointed Professor, he continued to appear as counsel for poor men charged with crimes before the circuit courts in Glasgow. In 1792 he went to London to meet Fox and other opposition leaders. The majority of educated Scotsmen, who held conservative views, saw Millar's work as a threat to the established order and refused to let their sons attend his classes. He was constantly attacked in the newspapers.

Thomas Muir attended some small tutorial classes of eight pupils which Millar held. Millar used also to invite his favourite and most enthusiastic students to carry on discussions at his house. Thomas spent many evenings there and became greatly attached to him. Millar's son John was a fellow law student. Millar was proud of his family, his university, and his achievements, and quickly retaliated if they were criticized. He taught Thomas to believe in himself and in just causes. Although all this was admirable, the resultant effect on Thomas's character and judgement was in some ways unfortunate.

At the same time as Thomas began studying law, there was a change in another aspect of his life: in 1782 James Muir bought a small property, Huntershill, in the parish of Cadder, an expanding village about ten miles from Glasgow. It consisted of thirty acres of arable land and ten acres of moss.[2] From the gates on the old post road to Edinburgh an avenue led up to the house, an attractive three-storey building of moderate size built in about 1770. It was surrounded by elms and beeches with a superb view south to the Clyde and north to the highland hills. This was a step up the social ladder for the family. Soon Thomas took the extended patronymic customary in Scotland, Thomas Muir, Younger of Huntershill. He became much attached to the place and, though not snobbish, was proud that his father owned an estate.

Thomas had an aptitude for languages and, besides law, studied French, German, and Italian. His father was able to give him a generous allowance and he formed a library containing some rare and valuable books which was housed at Huntershill. Muir lent books freely to friends, neighbours, and artisans keen to enlarge their education. He was an earnest, shy young man but, thanks to Millar's stimulating personality and the camaraderie of student societies, he had shed his reserve by the time he became involved in a typical university controversy.

Although Glasgow University was famous for its liberal teachers, most professors were old-fashioned Tories and strongly opposed change of any kind. This was not surprising since the majority were appointed directly or indirectly by the Crown and the King nominated the Principal. The students had many grievances, as there was a general tendency to disregard student interests. They had one champion – Professor Anderson. He was a difficult man, obstinate and inconsiderate, but a great favourite with the students who nicknamed him Jolly Jack Phosphorous – he does look jolly in his portraits. Anderson could turn his hand to any subject. He had held the chair of Oriental languages, taught French four days a week, and was now Professor of Natural Philosophy. He had created a scandal by voting for himself in the election for this chair. He was not a great scientist, but a capable, energetic teacher, extremely tactless, thriving on controversy. He involved the University in expensive and futile legislation. His experimental course of natural philosophy – 'anti-toga classes' as Anderson called them – was free, open to anyone who cared to attend, so he was instrumental in developing a taste for science among Glasgow's artisans. He had independent means, which enabled him to follow his own inclinations.[3]

Anderson offended the other professors by proposing various organizational and financial reforms. His criticisms were well founded, as the more senior professors were totally unwilling to grant their junior colleagues any share in the management of the University or of its finances, which were most incompetently run.

Finally, in 1784, after much acrimonious squabbling, the Faculty expelled him from all exercise of academic discipline and the privileges of the Senate. The students were most indignant; many were attached to Anderson for his 'abilities, engaging manners and venerable age'. He was 58.

Edmund Burke was Lord Rector of the University at the time. The students passed a resolution asking him to intercede on Anderson's behalf, but he ignored their request. This infuriated them. Normally a Rector was elected for a second year. They decided to take their revenge by not re-electing Burke. The majority of the professors were furious and prevented this by threats and intimidation. The Faculty now tried to abolish the students' power to elect the Rector. So Anderson and the students organized a petition to the Home Office for a Royal Commission to report on the state of the University and the manner in which its funds were applied by the Faculty. Anderson had handbills printed. He invited students to breakfast in relays. His supporters went out canvassing. He collected petitions signed by Scottish and Irish M.A.s, by three-quarters of the students, by Glasgow corporations, merchants, manufacturers, and other inhabitants, altogether over 4,000 signatures. On 24 February 1785 the Trades House of Glasgow passed a resolution, published in the newspapers, saying that for some time there had been divisions among the professors and students, as a result the number of students was decreasing and their education suffering. The Principal of the university, Leechman, aged 79, protested that the allegations were totally untrue and appealed successfully for the repeal of this resolution. A Commission was not set up but Anderson was told he could seek redress through the law courts. Writs and protests flew to and fro. Anderson was so popular with the townspeople that nothing could be done to him, but a divinity student who had been a particularly keen collector of signatures was expelled.

Muir emerged in this fracas as one of the most energetic and admired student leaders. He had a penchant for satirical verse and not only made eloquent speeches and organized meetings, but wrote witty lampoons inciting the students against some of the professors. He was one of the deputation who presented the students' resolution to Burke, and the convenor of a meeting of senior students which decided to publish a pamphlet ridiculing Leechman and his supporters which further exasperated the Faculty. They decided to punish the ringleaders. In the next session, Autumn 1785, a circular letter was sent to all professors saying that they were not to admit thirteen students to their classes, among them Muir, until there had been an enquiry into their behaviour and they had apologized to the Faculty. Some students apologized. Though pressed hard to do so, Muir refused and voluntarily expelled himself from the University. Two students who stood their ground were expelled, one of them deprived of his degree. Anderson took a parting shot at the professors in his will. He left all his property and apparatus to found an educational institute in which 'there were not to be drones or triflers, drunkards or those negligent of their duty'. This was the Andersonian College, now Strathclyde University.

Through Millar, who had defended the students' rights, though more tactfully than Anderson, Muir was offered a place at Edinburgh University, where he studied law for two more years under the Whig Professor John Wylde. Muir must in many ways have enjoyed the move to a more varied, sophisticated environment. At this time Edinburgh was a leading European centre of culture. There were about 1,200 students at the university. Quite a large proportion were dissenters who were barred from Oxford and Cambridge. There was a passion for literary and debating clubs, most of which met in taverns. Benjamin Constant and Jacques Necker said they learnt as much from these societies as from the professors in their days at Edinburgh. Muir already belonged to the Glasgow Literary Society; now, at the Speculative Club, later condemned as a hotbed of radicalism, he learnt much more about political affairs. The lectures of the Edinburgh philosophers, chiefly concerned with moral and social problems, helped strengthen his already strong social conscience.

In November 1787, aged 22, Muir was called to the bar. As part of their final examination students had to write a thesis which was traditionally dedicated to a member of the Law Faculty who had helped them in their studies. Significantly Muir's was dedicated to Henry Erskine, Dean of the Faculty, a man of great charm and intelligence, a Whig and ardent supporter of burgh reform. He was a brother of the Earl of Buchan and of Thomas Erskine, who was to make a brilliant career at the English bar and defend Thomas Paine, among others, in the English courts.

Edinburgh's unusual structure encouraged contact among all

classes of society. Nobles, judges, artisans, labourers, lived together in the tall tenement buildings sharing a common staircase. Advocates and their agents consulted in dark little tavern rooms in the narrow, smelly wynds and closes. Muir had rooms in Carubbers Close near the North Bridge. Lawyers were the cultural élite of Edinburgh. They included many of the most intelligent, able men in Scotland and, as there was no Parliament, were by far the most influential group in the country. Some who did well became landed proprietors. They were drawn largely from the younger sons of the aristocracy, the gentry, and professional men with useful political connections. In 1789 the percentage of lawyers whose father had been a lawyer was 20%, a landowner 41%, a merchant 13%. The profession did their best to exclude those of lowly origin who had a slim chance of success at the bar. Lockhart said they were 'as proud a set of men as ever enjoyed the pleasure of unquestioned superiority'.

Although Muir had no important connections, he obtained quite a large practice and a good legal reputation. He was more successful, sooner, than was usual. Not outstanding, but competent and popular, he had charming and agreeable manners and a generous heart. He proved himself a man of principle, a fluent, sincere and eloquent speaker and 'always showed uncommon zeal and anxiety for the interests of his clients'. He was nicknamed 'the Chancellor' because it had come out that his mother had dreamt that one day he would be Lord High Chancellor of England. Muir preferred to work till about four in the morning and get up late. This led some busybodies to assume he was idle. He was a passionate advocate of Professor Millar's contention that Scottish criminal law was unnecessarily harsh and unfairly biased against humble people. Many young advocates shared his views, but they were frowned on by the majority of senior lawyers who were Tories.

The volume of cases at that date was very small. The records of the courts show that Muir pleaded in a fair number and his practice doubled in the three years from 1789 to 1792. Most of his cases were concerned with business disputes or conveyancing, his clients manufacturers and tradesmen. Through his Glasgow connections he was sometimes retained by Glaswegians to act for them in Edinburgh and he would take the four-in-hand coach from Edinburgh to Glasgow, a fifteen-hour journey, to plead in the Glasgow circuit court. Muir undertook the defence of poor people who, he believed, had been

unjustly accused, usually of theft, occasionally of murder. If they
were penniless he waived his fee. He did not only defend the innocent, however. For instance, Muir succeeded in getting a sentence of
death commuted to transportation for one William Carswell, who
was patently guilty of forgery, on a technicality: he spotted that the
name of one juryman had been omitted from the verdict.[4]

While working in Edinburgh Muir was elected an elder of the Kirk
at Cadder. He corresponded regularly with the Minister on church
matters and, when communion was held, entertained the clergy and
elders at Huntershill. Like many other lawyers, he was able to
develop his flair for public speaking in debates of the General
Assembly. He acted as counsel in various ecclesiastical disputes. One
case concerned Burns's friend the Revd. William McGill of Ayr who
published *An Essay on the Death of Christ*. The conservative
presbyterians in Ayrshire objected because it questioned Christ's
divinity. McGill was arraigned as a heretic. In May 1789 Muir
represented the Glasgow Presbytery when the case was referred
to the General Assembly. McGill apologized, but the general
public were not satisfied. Muir was retained as counsel and
doggedly pursued the case through the church courts again. In May
1791 he appeared once more before the Assembly who dismissed
the complaint.

Another case in which Muir was involved both as elder and lawyer
was concerned with a major controversy of the 1780s. After the '45
the Moderate party dominated the Church of Scotland. Moderate
ministers had become less bigoted, but made little effort to help their
parishioners. They took to farming, studied literature, and cultivated
the gentry. As a result of both the spread of agnosticism and the
conservative theology of the Kirk, many educated people had lost
interest in religion. To attract these back the Moderates rigidly
enforced the law of patronage by which the right of electing ministers
lay with the heritors (landlords) and elders. This strengthened the
power of the lairds and freeholders and meant that few ministers
were elected from the evangelical Popular party, who maintained
that the congregation should have a share in electing their minister.
There had already been two secessions from the Kirk in protest when
in 1781 the Popular party began a campaign conducted from Glasgow for the abolition of patronage. The battle raged for several
years. Finally in 1785 a motion to consider repeal was rejected in the

General Assembly and agitation gradually subsided. Muir followed his parents in supporting the Popular Party.

In 1790 the elders of the parish of Cadder became involved in a dispute with the heritors over the election of a new minister. There were sufficient sympathetic freeholders to ensure that Provan, the minister the congregation wanted, was elected. He had preached and worked in the parish for many years and gained the people's affection. However, local landlords, led by a rich coal-owner, James Dunlop of Garnkirk, tried to introduce 'parchment Barons'* who would vote for the heritors' choice, a young man who was chaplain to an important family in the parish. The prolonged and acrimonious battle which ensued showed that Muir's previous skirmishes with the conservative establishment were not merely undergraduate high spirits, but a sign of the first intimations of those democratic convictions which he was prepared to support with uncompromising persistence. Muir was appointed counsel for the parishioners, and John Millar, (the Professor's son) for the heritors. The case dragged on for several years. It was taken before the Glasgow Presbytery, the Glasgow Synod, the General Assembly, and the Court of Session. Muir contended that the term 'heritor' included feuars, men who held their land in fee. This was finally conceded, the right to vote was granted to more men, and the parishioners' choice was elected.

In March 1791 Muir resigned as a ruling elder;[5] this may have been prompted by the battle over the Minister's election. Muir continued to take an interest in parish affairs, for on 11 June 1792 the Revd. William Dunn of Kirkintilloch, a friend who shared his political views, wrote to say that the elders would like his opinion about celebrating communion at Cadder. Muir replied:

... I wish that gentlemen should be invited whom the people will regard solely as Ministers of religion and not as partisans of any particular party.

There is little information about Muir's first four years at the bar. His greatest friend was Robert Forsyth, a well-connected fellow advocate.† Muir was welcomed into Edinburgh society, gravitating naturally to Whig circles. Through Mrs. Archibald Fletcher, wife of a

---

* See below, p. 18.
† Forsyth's *Principles of Moral Science*, published in Edinburgh in 1809, greatly interested Peacock, whose work – including *Nightmare Abbey* – is full of references to him.

senior Whig advocate, he met Anne Barbauld, the poetess and
educationalist. Daughter and wife of Unitarians, liberal, unassum-
ing, but a brilliant conversationalist, she included William Wordsworth, Fanny Burney, Maria Edgeworth, and Mary Wollstonecraft
among her friends. For the first time Muir went to London, where
she introduced him to leading dissenters. He became particularly
friendly with a young man, Richard Shields, who lived near the
Barbaulds in Hampstead, and the Revd. Theophilus Lindsey.
Lindsey had been a Cambridge fellow and chaplain to the Duke of
Somerset. In 1766 he turned Unitarian and acquired a great reputation in London as a radical preacher and lecturer. Muir also visited a
clever fellow student, James Mackintosh, who had gone south in
1788 and had become a journalist. Through Mackintosh Muir met
Whig politicians and leaders of reform societies who fired him with a
desire to form similar groups in Scotland.

Though there is an unconfirmed rumour reported by Mackenzie
that Muir was hopelessly in love with the daughter of an aristocratic
landowner, nothing else is recounted about his relationships with
women. He does not appear to have had homosexual inclinations.
His closest friends were either married, or married later on. At this
time he was unanimously commended for 'the purity of his life',
which could indicate that he was shy and awkward with young
women. Anne Barbauld and Eliza Fletcher were twenty years his
senior. Later Thomas became so engrossed in political campaigning
that he would have had little time to spare for flirtation. Equally he
may have thrown himself into the reform movement because he had
been jilted. Apparently not highly sexed, hard-working, absorbed in
politics, with the anchor of strong religious faith, if all had gone well
he might have married when successfully established at the bar.

A passport issued by the French authorities in 1793 describes Muir
as 5 ft. 9 ins. tall with red hair and eyebrows, blue eyes, an aquiline
nose, high forehead, round chin, and long, full face. His portraits
vary enormously. In the profile taken from a contemporary miniature he has a handsome, dashing, virile appearance. His face in a
drawing by David Martin is pleasant but podgy. The engraving from
a bust by Thomas Bankes made after his imprisonment when he had
fallen ill, and suffered much, shows a refined, intelligent face, its one
flaw a rather weak chin.

Like many other young men Muir was headstrong, keen to make

changes in the existing order. He was also sober, vigorous, kind, likeable. Vanity was his real failing, which was to increase over the years. Most conceited men fundamentally lack self-confidence. Thomas may well have felt insecure living in a city which traditionally despises men from Glasgow, and competing with advocates almost all of whom came from a higher social stratum than he did. His parents' uncritical love and admiration did nothing to curb his egotism. Still, a promising career lay ahead, and his father could support him in comfort until he earned enough to provide for himself. Great opportunities were arising in Scotland for talented men. His future seemed assured. Events would prove him abominably unlucky.

CHAPTER 2

Origins of the Reform Campaign of the 1790s

To appreciate Muir's decision to campaign for Parliamentary reform it is necessary to give a brief description of the agitation for reform which began in the 1760s and continued intermittently while he was being educated. The latter half of the eighteenth century was a period of intense intellectual activity and optimism, which marked the transition to an industrial society and the increasing wealth of the nation. Some people, in particular the brilliant men who were making scientific, technical, and cultural advances, believed that with increasing knowledge society must change and develop. Most people, however, were traditionalists.

Three groups demanded electoral and economic reform. It provided a useful platform for the patrician Whig party in opposition, who believed the legislature should act as a curb on the executive, but that at present George III with money, patronage, and influence was able to ensure that a majority of M.P.s would support his interests. The squirearchy resented great landowners whittling away their influence, and unnecessary expenses incurred by a corrupt, incompetent administration. Both these groups sought government financial retrenchment, rather than far-reaching constitutional change. The third group made far more sweeping proposals for altering the franchise. It consisted initially of several hundred dissenters, radical politicians, manufacturers, and professional men, few of whom were eligible to vote for lack of sufficient freehold property qualifications. They were influenced by Rousseau and the American colonists. Stimulated by Tom Paine's enormously popular writings their ideas later spread to working men in London and the old provincial cities.

The opposition began a campaign criticizing seven-year parliaments, place-holders, tied votes, and gross corruption at elections. Wilkes's supporters stirred matters up in London, organized public meetings to draft petitions to the King and Commons. In 1776 Wilkes introduced a measure for reform including universal male suffrage, which was treated with total indifference and promptly rejected by the Commons. For the majority of citizens who thought about the matter at all believed that Parliament already represented the nation's interests: land created wealth, so landed proprietors should and did exercise control.

At the same time Yorkshire gentry and freeholders began a movement for municipal reform. Then, exasperated by the expensive failure of the American war, they decided in 1779 to petition the House of Commons to put an end to increasing taxation and squandering of public money by refusing supplies until sinecures and abuse of pensions were stopped. The chief organizer of their movement was Christopher Wyvill, an able, philanthropic, rich landowner. Another leading campaigner was Major Cartwright, also a landowner, with more extreme views, sincere but not highly intelligent. Later he joined the more democratic London reformers and altogether campaigned for over forty years.

In preparation for the 1780 election delegates went to London from twelve counties and six cities with proposals for economic and municipal reform, annual parliaments, and a hundred new knights of the shires. This was the heyday of pamphleteering and shoals of pamphlets demanding reform were issued. The Westminster electors considered a suggestion for M.P.s to be paid wages. The Duke of Richmond, who had been an ardent supporter of the colonists, introduced a measure to give the vote to all commoners and restore annual parliaments. That day the Gordon Riots began from a combination of religious bigotry and the unchecked violence of the more criminal elements in the London mob. The Lords promptly rejected the Duke's proposals. In 1781 the Commons rejected the Yorkshire delegates' petition, condemning their methods of organization and propaganda as dangerous and unconstitutional. But after Cornwallis surrendered at Saratoga, the Government's resignation became inevitable. In 1782 the Rockingham Whigs were able to pass three bills, the most important introduced by Burke, to exclude men who made money from government contracts from the Commons, disenfranchise revenue officers, control the Civil List, and abolish sinecures.

This satisfied the Rockingham Whigs who now manoeuvred to get constitutional reform shelved. So, disillusioned by their lukewarm insincerity, the more advanced reformers turned to Pitt and the Chathamites. Pitt fought the 1782 election as a partisan of reform.

On 7 May his motion for an inquiry into the system of representation was rejected on a free vote by twenty votes. The reformers never did so well again until 1831. The next year Pitt introduced reform proposals in Parliament, the chief feature being the creation of an additional hundred representatives elected by the English and Scottish counties and the metropolis. His bill was rejected by a huge majority. In 1784 Pitt became Prime Minister. In 1785 the efforts of the early reformers failed with the rejection of Pitt's second bill.* More limited than the first, it would have effected modest but useful improvements, disenfranchising some deçayed English boroughs and bringing in some of the newer towns. Because it was Pitt's bill Fox and his followers were unhelpful. It was rejected by 248 to 174. Pitt then quietly dropped the matter.

The Yorkshire agitation was unsuccessful because it was opposed by the majority of M.P.s and the general public were uninterested — there were never more than a few thousand active reformers. Orthodox Whigs were suspicious of the inexperienced reformers with their impractical ideas; they were infuriated by Whig tinkerers. The left wing of the reformers thought the Yorkshire programme insufficiently radical, the right were alarmed by those who advocated more controversial measures. Also the squires and freeholders who formed the basis of the movement were satisfied by Burke's measure which, by cutting the number of pensioners and placemen, reduced the taxpayers' burden.

It is often claimed that the parliamentary machine which existed until 1832 worked satisfactorily; such public opinion as existed was represented, competent men governed, and the nation, by acquiescence, gave consent. Certainly it was easier for an able upper-class young man, or an extremely rich East India merchant, to obtain a seat in Parliament than in the partially reformed Commons of the mid-nineteenth century. Great statesmen had entered the Commons via pocket boroughs but, though a few brilliant men such as Burke and Sheridan could not be prevented from making their mark, commoners were never given high office. The old system had been perfectly satisfactory in a primarily agricultural country; now other forms of wealth and property were becoming increasingly important. New cities such as Manchester had little or no representation. The expanding, educated, prosperous middle classes had no control

* Introduced on 18 April.

over elections. The corrupt electoral system encouraged corrupt and incompetent administration and hampered economic and technical development. Businessmen wanted a voice in government to prevent a repetition of the American fiasco which badly damaged trade.

Among those sections of the population which most bitterly resented the system were the dissenters. Many were rich – bankers, manufacturers, and inventors, whose enterprise was helping create the Industrial Revolution. Oppression had moulded them into an enclosed, slightly self-righteous community. They were unpopular, felt to be alien. The clergy detested their attacks on the established Church. Dissenters had no civil rights – although they had of course to pay taxes – and were excluded from the universities. They represented much that was most admirable in English thought. They believed in the power of reason and scientific progress, the right of freedom of enquiry, and that all men should have equal status in the organization of the State.

Many leading liberal clergy left the Church, became Unitarians and joined forces with the old dissenting sects. Although they were not primarily active politicians, their speeches, sermons, and writings had a tremendous effect, particularly on the growing urban middle classes. The majority of the literary journals were run by dissenters; so was one famous weekly newspaper, the *Cambridge Intelligencer*, edited by a Unitarian, Benjamin Flower. He published the early poems of Coleridge and articles by Anna Barbauld and Christopher Wyvill. Muir corresponded with him.

In England an outsider might be elected to Parliament. In Scotland the few seats were kept firmly in the hands of the establishment. A few grandees owned nearly all the land, and the lairds were at the height of their power. Both parliamentary and municipal representation in Scotland was far less satisfactory than in England. This was partly due to the fact that the Scottish Parliament had not developed as the English had, and partly due to the Act of Union itself. By the Treaty of Union sixteen Scottish peers sat in the House of Lords. In theory they were chosen by their fellows at Holyrood. In practice the government in power sent a list of the peers it wanted to Edinburgh and they were duly elected. Scotland, with a population of 1½ million, was represented in the Commons by 45 members – only one more than sat for Cornwall, which had a much smaller population. Fifteen were assigned to the counties and thirty to the burghs. Edinburgh had a member to itself, but other towns shared members, and some expanding ones, such as Paisley, were submerged in their shires. The franchise was still largely based on feudal law. In the counties the basis of the electoral system was that voters must hold land of the Crown valued at 400 Scots pounds. The freeholders met annually to inspect the electoral roll, and would only add or delete a name if paid to do so. The right to vote depended not only on possession of property, but on direct tenure from the Crown which could convey the 'superiority' of the land. The 'superiority' could become divorced from the effective tenure of an estate and pass into other hands. Since the vote was attached to a 'superiority' and not to a person, it could go to a creditor, a mortgagee, or a woman's husband. This meant that the people who worked the land often had no vote. Also the man who was the tenant of the Crown, the feudal overlord, could parcel out his land in small holdings, each large enough to qualify for a vote, and give it to his nominees for their lifetime. This system led to endless skulduggery. The great county families created fictitious votes for friends who would return members in their interest, and the small proprietors, who were technically sub-vassals and so did not possess the franchise, were deprived of political power. The number of voters in each county was incredibly small. It varied from 12 in Bute to 214 in Ayrshire. In Lanarkshire the 68 voters who did hold land of their own were outvoted by 95 'parchment barons' created by the Duke of Hamilton and the Lord Advocate. By 1780, with a rural population in Scotland of over 1 million, 2,624 qualified electors, half of whom were 'parchment barons', were controlled by about 220 proprietors.

In the burghs the position was equally unsatisfactory. Only the Royal Burghs, towns which had received their charters direct from the King, could be represented in Parliament. Their members were returned by self-elected and self-perpetuating town councils and magistrates. The member for Edinburgh (population 160,000) was returned by 33 voters; Glasgow shared a member with Rutherglen, Renfrew, and Dumbarton. In all about 1,400 men had a share in the burgh franchise. He who bribed most heavily won. It was also very difficult to know what was going on. In England constituents might all be bribed, but they could turn out at election time to heckle the prospective candidates. In Scotland public political meetings were illegal. The pretext was that the Scots could not assemble without rioting; but the cure for that might have been frequent public meetings rather than none. The system led to corruption of every kind. The poor were rewarded with cash, the laird with a regimental commission or a post in the East India Company for his sons. Appeals against electoral malpractice could only be heard by the House of Commons and, because Scottish cases often contained complicated legal points from a different legal system, insufficient time was allotted to them, and attempts to correct abuses failed.

In Royal Burghs the right to elect was vested in town councils, so it was impossible to separate municipal from parliamentary politics. Many burghs were in financial straits because the municipal authorities rented the town lands to themselves and their friends at ludicrously low rates. Common land was sold illegally, fraudulent contracts were passed, streets left unpaved and unlit.

Under this system, from 1770 onwards, one man by patient hard work and tact acquired a political influence in Scotland never equalled before or since. He was Henry Dundas, nicknamed 'King Harry IX', who would later destroy Thomas Muir. Both Dundas's father and his brother had been Lords President of the Court of Session. Although without great intellectual gifts he possessed precisely the qualities needed for success in public life at the time. He was genial, hearty, handsome, kind, tolerant unless his personal interests were threatened, and a superb manager. He had no consistent political creed but he was hard-working, extremely ambitious, and intensely conservative. His vast Scottish correspondence contains not one original idea, not the faintest trace of compassion, idealism or desire to improve conditions in Scotland. He judged everything in terms of power and expediency.

Dundas obtained the support of the Highland chiefs by restoring their forfeited estates. He gained control of patronage at home and employment abroad. He became Pitt's invaluable lieutenant and drinking companion, and was able to provide him with the steady support of almost all the Scottish members and peers during his seventeen-year administration, which began in 1783. Dundas was successively Treasurer of the Navy, President of the Board of Control for India, Home Secretary, Secretary for War, and First Lord of the Admiralty. He opposed the abolition of the slave trade and, in his own interests, was an implacable opponent of reform. His nephew, Robert, loyally carried out his policies in Scotland. Robert Dundas

was an agreeable man and a moderately competent lawyer. Through
his uncle's influence he became Lord Advocate in 1789. He was
popular and conscientious, but weak, cautious, and conservative. At
every crisis he rushed to his uncle for advice.

In August 1782 some Scottish freeholders from country areas held
a meeting in Edinburgh to discuss reform of the county franchise.[1]
Another group, who wanted to reform the Royal Burghs and curb
municipal corruption, had far more widespread influence. They
formed committees in many Scottish towns consisting mainly of
merchants and tradesmen, supported by a few liberal landowners,
minor gentry, and academics, but they remained aloof from the
county reformers. In 1784 a convention of delegates from the burghs
and shires met in Edinburgh and passed resolutions calling for
extensions of the local and parliamentary franchise to all burgesses.
A standing committee, consisting mostly of Whig members of the
bar, was appointed to prepare two draft bills: one to deal with the
internal government of the burghs, the other with the election of
their parliamentary representatives. The movement was moderate,
strictly limited in its appeal, and expressly condemned the proposals
of advanced English reformers for universal suffrage and the ballot.

Glasgow was one of the places where this movement was
strongest. Muir's city lacked political influence and the war with
America had been particularly unpopular there. James Muir was a
keen supporter of the Glasgow Burgh Reform Society. He had sound
personal reasons for this. Although he owned land at Huntershill,
the superiority had long since been given to a nominee of the Earl of
Selkirk, so he had no vote. His cousins in America had far more
control over their government than he had. Nothing is known about
his son Thomas's activities until they begin to be reported in the
newspapers in 1792, but he must certainly have taken an interest in
the burgh reform movement, whose leaders included Professor
Millar and the Whig lawyers whom he most admired, Henry Erskine
and Archibald Fletcher.

Wyvill suggested the Scottish and English reformers should join
forces but the Scots, from a narrow and cautious though idealistic
attitude, were reluctant to do so at the one moment when a combined
front might have succeeded. They believed the changes they sought
were different. They assumed the English movement would succeed,
and that reform would follow in Scotland as a matter of course.

When Pitt's second motion was lost in 1785 both the Scottish landed proprietors and the burgh reformers abandoned the idea of parliamentary reform.

The Burgh Committee had, anyhow, decided it would be best to concentrate on municipal reform. Pitt took no interest in their proposed bill. Dundas said he would oppose it. As no Scottish M.P. would give support, a petition was eventually presented to Parliament by Sheridan. By 1788, 54 Scottish burghs had forwarded petitions. But the defeat of Pitt's bill had in effect put paid to municipal reform, which was too closely connected with parliamentary reform to be considered separately. Besides, each class of Scottish society regarded the other's grievances with indifference. The majority of the upper classes wanted to preserve their influence and the nation's stability, so they supported Dundas and the Tories. The labouring poor were not yet involved; profoundly reactionary, they had shown their latent power by rioting violently against the proposed Roman Catholic Relief Bill in 1779. That bill, as a result, though passed in England, was withdrawn in Scotland. Most freeholders were prepared to make do with the reformation of the counties' electoral rolls in 1790. The burgh reformers continued to agitate but received little support and lacked determination.

There were, however, material reasons for discontent. Prices were rising. Most Scots considered that they were neglected and badly ruled by an alien government. Since Union, taxes were heavier and more efficiently collected. Excise laws were very severe, and unfairly penalized the Scots. Recent economic and social changes had created antagonism between different sections of the community. Wages rose, so manual workers began to assert themselves. Combinations were formed. In 1787 the Glasgow weavers struck, the first time such a protest had been made in Scotland. There was a vague, increasing sense of grievance about political affairs.

Then the French Revolution began. This had an intoxicating effect on liberals and intellectuals. If a country formerly controlled by such a notorious despotism could advance so far so quickly, what could not the British do? In Scotland not only the Whigs but men such as Dr. Robertson, leader of the Moderate church party, and Dr. Adam, Principal of Edinburgh High School, welcomed it. Its impact on young men such as Muir was tremendous; it fired their imagination, created a unique excitement.

Initially the Revolution produced a mood of internationalism; a feeling that everywhere men were struggling for the same ideals. Many Britons who wanted to improve their own Constitution watched with envy and approval. Various clubs sent congratulations to the French Assembly. Among the most influential was the Society for Constitutional Information, founded in 1780 to disseminate reform literature. Its keenest supporter was Major Cartwright; members included Sheridan, the Dukes of Richmond and Roxburgh, Lord Edward Fitzgerald, Lord Sempill, a young Scottish elective peer, and Thomas Paine.

Only one Scottish society sent an address to the Assembly, the Whig Club of Dundee. British societies were in general rather condescending to the French. They declared that Britain had no need to borrow from France; the British Constitution needed only a few minor adjustments to be perfect.

People of all nationalities who could afford to travel crossed over to Paris to watch the great innovations taking place. Among them were several Scotsmen. One was Thomas Christie, son of the Provost of Montrose, editor of the *Analytical Review*, friend of Dr. Johnson. At the request of the National Assembly he translated the French Constitution into English. Another was the irrepressible Professor Anderson.[2] He had invented a shock-absorbing gun-carriage and, having failed to attract the attention of the English Government, took it to Paris. A model was hung in the Hall of the Convention with the inscription 'The gift of science to liberty'. Guns of this type were successfully used by the French in battle.

The dissenters welcomed the Revolution, not realizing at first that it was alien to many of their ideals. They naturally resented the humiliation of being still denied rights now granted to the French. On 4 November 1789, in commemoration of the centenary of the 1688 revolution, Dr. Price a famous dissenting savant, inventor of the sinking fund, delivered a sermon 'On the Love of our Country', a moderate but impassioned plea for equal rights for all, which was to have widespread repercussions.

The Popular party of the Church of Scotland also decided to agitate against the Test Act. At the annual meeting of the General Assembly in 1790 a great debate took place on the motion that the extension to Scotland of Charles II's Test Act was a violation of the privileges stipulated in the Union Treaty. The Moderates and many leading lawyers including Robert Dundas argued that it was not an auspicious moment to put forward such a motion, but it was carried. Muir must have been present at this debate, he probably spoke in it, certainly he would have supported the motion. In the Assembly it was a triumph for the Popular movement, but Parliament rejected their petition in 1791.

Burke, meanwhile, who was violently alarmed by developments in France, had been brooding on Dr. Price's sermon. In November 1790 he published his reply, *Reflections on the Revolution in France*, which was to have a far-reaching effect on public opinion. Burke condemned abstract rights as meaningless and dangerous. Men had no claim to precise equality, but to particular advantages related to the individual's position in society. Liberty meant security of life, property, and opinion. He doubted whether France had obtained this. He feared the deadly iridescence of the Revolution. The *Reflections* achieved rapid popularity in official circles. It provided the first important check to the general enthusiasm for the Revolution and clarified the governing classes' vague suspicions of radicalism. Burke stirred up British xenophobia and dislike of change. His charges were hysterical, inaccurate, and unfair to the idealists who began the Revolution, but he prophesied correctly that it would end in violence and the rise of a military dictatorship.

It was Paine's *The Rights of Man*, however, that was to have by far the greater impact. The first part was published in 1791. Though not in the same intellectual class as Burke, Thomas Paine was a brilliant journalist and his writings reached a very wide public. He expounded the simplest ideas thrown up by the American and French Revolutions in unsophisticated terms which appealed to the ordinary man. He believed that the only rational way of organizing society was to try to make men happy. He failed to see the merits in monarchy or to concede that a corrupt President could be as dangerous as an evil King. He argued that government is derived from the people, can be altered at their will and must be conducted for their benefit through a system of popular representation. He did not believe that Parliament would reform the system on which it flourished. Why should Pitt alter a process whereby he was regularly handed 39 tame Scottish votes? A free political association of the whole nation should elect a general convention to carry out parliamentary reform. To prevent corruption M.P.s should receive salaries. Paine had been in America when the States were drafting the Bill of Rights and their Constitution, with its provision for periodic revision; he appreciated their remarkable achievement. Paine also pointed out that the French Constitution was more liberal than the British, and that it set a precedent for a new one drawn up from first principles. This deeply shocked and frightened many people who had been brought up to revere the British Constitution.

Part I of *The Rights of Man* was received with interest and, though widely criticized, was tolerated. It was Part II, published in February 1792, which caused a furore. It was concerned with improving the conditions of the people of Europe, and contained Paine's only original ideas. Some of his schemes for social reform were far in advance of his age. He advocated allowances for the poor, the aged, and children, free education, and a progressive income tax. Many of his suggestions were moderate, but he advocated some extreme measures – titles and primogeniture should be abolished, and property redistributed. Part II also contained virulent criticisms of the government and abuse of George III (Mr. Guelph), which attracted far more attention than Paine's pension schemes and, in the terminology of the time, was a 'libel on the constitution'. Paine was vain and self-satisfied. He was not a profound thinker, but he popularized the idea that politics were the concern of the common people and the means by which they could alleviate their poverty.

Cheap abridgements of *The Rights of Man* at two pence had an enormous circulation, and in one form or another its sales were said to have reached the staggering figure of one million. (It was the eighteenth-century equivalent of *Das Kapital*.) Paine's violent republicanism was a great help to the Government, who disingenuously maintained that the moderate reformers approved of his ideas.

The Rights of Man achieved rapid popularity in Scotland and was translated into Gaelic. The number of newspapers and periodicals increased enormously. Men with little knowledge of national or foreign affairs were stimulated by events in France. As John Galt described in *The Annals of the Parish*, a book which gives a vivid picture of Scotland at the time,

Men read more, the spirit of reflection and reasoning was more awake than at any time within my remembrance. . . . cotton spinners and muslin weavers, unsatisfied and ambitious spirits, clubbed together and got a London newspaper. They were nightly in the habit of meeting and debating about the affairs of the French.

The Scots had always had close connections with the French and so were more disposed than the English to regard their actions favourably.

Dinners were held annually in both Scotland and England to commemorate the fall of the Bastille. On 14 July 1791 Muir attended a dinner in Glasgow presided over by Lt. Colonel Dalrymple of Fordell and Professor Millar. Toasts included one to *The standing army of France who, in the duties of soldiers, lost not the feelings of citizens* and *May every civil government be founded on the natural rights of man.*[3] Although the implications could not yet have been clear to them, Louis XVI had just been brought back from Varennes – the turning-point of the Revolution. The Lord Provost of Edinburgh sent Henry Dundas, now Home Secretary, lists of the Bastille celebrators, but the authorities were not yet worried and no action was taken.

On the same day a dinner at Birmingham marked a significant setback for the reformers. With the tacit consent of the authorities a mob attacked the homes of dissenters in Birmingham. The magistrates made no attempt to intervene in the rioting which lasted four days. The house of Joseph Priestley – who discovered oxygen – was burnt, his laboratory with all its unique equipment destroyed. These riots were the result of counter-propaganda and the beginning of persecution. From now on 'King and Church' mobs would be encouraged to attack their supposed enemies, the dissenters and radicals.

In April 1792 younger Whigs, including Grey, Sheridan, and Lord John Russell, founded the Society of the Friends of the People. It was an exclusive society with a subscription of two guineas. The members were mostly well-to-do men of liberal principles; their objectives were to restore frequent elections and extend the franchise to all responsible citizens. They expressly repudiated Paine's works. Several Scotsmen joined, including the Earls of Lauderdale and Buchan, Lord Kinnaird, Thomas Erskine, Colonel Norman Macleod of Macleod, M.P. for Inverness, Professor Millar, and James Mackintosh. Grey gave notice in Parliament of his intention to submit a motion for a reform of the franchise. Fox and the official opposition gave him only cold, insincere support.

More plebeian radicals formed societies mainly in the old urban centres such as Sheffield and Norwich. The most important was the London Corresponding Society, founded by Thomas Hardy, a Scottish shoemaker. Members were largely tradesmen, artisans, and mechanics. The society made its first public impact with a series of resolutions advocating drastic reform published in April 1792. Though these societies frightened the Government, only a minute proportion of the population ever became subscribing members. All reformers consistently maintained that Britain wanted reform, not revolution; but they did not conceal their sympathy for French efforts to improve their Government. In Scotland a committee was formed in January to consider how to improve the electoral system. Burgh reform was still a respectable project there and both Robert Dundas and Henry Erskine became members. In March another successful burgh reform meeting was held in Glasgow.[4]

Glaswegians were particularly enthusiastic supporters of the Revolution. A subscription was opened in January 1792 'to aid the French in carrying on the war against the emigrant princes or any foreign power by whom they may be attacked'. It was so popular that £1,200 was said to have been collected.

On 20 April France declared war on Austria. In the deteriorating international situation Paine's writings and the activities of the popular societies caused great alarm. On 21 May the Government issued a proclamation against seditious meetings and publications. This was aimed particularly at *The Rights of Man* and inevitably served to advertise it. Sales soared, people rushed to ask for 'the book that was forbidden to be sold'. In Scotland, outside official circles, the proclamation provoked a storm of disapproval. The press was almost unanimously hostile. Colonel Macleod, an ardent reformer, said:

This set people of all ranks reading and, as everybody in this country can read, people are already astonishingly informed. Farmers, ploughmen, peasants, manufacturers, shopkeepers, sailors, merchants are all employed in studying and reasoning on the nature of society and governmment and, as they reason with great deliberation, they are slow in determining how to act.[5]

Christopher Wyvill wrote:

Paine . . . has excited such fear of revolution among quiet people that will operate against reform measures. . . . Jealous aristocrats have watched the progress of the spirit of Reformation with increasing anxiety. . . . what was aversion to the popular cause soon improved into keen and violent hatred; . . . Exaltation expressed by the people here on the successful efforts to emancipate the French nation and apparent ease with which the transition might be made in this country . . . pushed their panic to its present extremity.[6]

But later even Wyvill became infected with the growing unease:

If Mr. Paine should be able to raise up the lower classes, their interference will probably be marked by wild work and all we now possess, whether in private property or public liberty, will be at the mercy of lawless and furious rabble.

Such fears were ill founded. All over the country corporations and county meetings of freeholders were voting loyal addresses to King George. Talleyrand, on an unofficial diplomatic mission to England, gave a very accurate view on the true state of affairs in a letter to the French Foreign Minister, Dumouriez:

The mass of the nation . . . attached to its constitution by ancient prejudices, habit, comparison of its lot with that of other states, and prosperity, does not imagine anything could be gained from a revolution of which the history of England makes it fear the dangers. The country is solely occupied with questions of material prosperity. The opposition has been weakened by agitation for Parliamentary Reform.[7]

On 8 June the rift in the Opposition was made greater when Lord John Russell and some other members, frightened by increasing hostility, resigned from the Society of the Friends of the People.

◇◇◇◇◇◇◇◇◇◇◇◇◇◇◇◇◇◇◇◇◇◇◇◇◇◇◇◇◇◇◇◇◇◇◇◇◇◇◇

CHAPTER 3

The Reform Campaign

1792 was the climacteric of the reform campaign; it was also a year of great unrest in Scotland. The authorities attributed this to the reformers, but most disturbances were not really about politics. The winter of 1792 was severe, the summer wet and cold, the harvest poor. Food and fuel were scarce; corn prices the highest for a decade. In 1791 a most unpopular Corn Bill had been introduced in Scotland, warmly approved by the landed proprietors, but strongly opposed by the industrial areas, led by Glasgow. Its main feature was giving bounties for export and imposing duties on imports. It was ill thought out and incompetently administered, and it caused great hardship. At Leith and Aberdeen, colliers and sailors went on strike against abominable pay and conditions. In Lanark there was trouble lasting eight days because the magistrates had enclosed part of the burgh moor. In Ross-shire the crofters rioted, rightly fearing that the proprietors were out to replace them with sheep. The tree of liberty, French symbol of *liberté, egalité, fraternité* – spectre of Jacobinism to the establishment – was planted in Scottish towns and villages. It represented a demand for more democratic government, better material conditions, or a combination of both according to the demonstrator. When hungry crowds burnt Henry Dundas in effigy in Aberdeen, Dundee, Peebles, and Perth, the authorities seized on their actions as a useful means of discrediting reform.

Before the King's Birthday on 4 June Edinburgh was flooded with anonymous handbills urging people to demonstrate in favour of democracy. The garrison was reinforced, to the annoyance of the populace, and, after so much advance publicity, it was not surprising that a large crowd collected. When troops were prematurely called out by Sheriff Pringle a furious mob broke the windows of both Henry and Robert Dundas's houses. The Provost attributed the rioting, which lasted for three days, to 'an evil spirit which seems to have reached us, which I was in hopes John Bull would have kept to himself'. In fact, though the urban proletariat took up reform slogans and cheered French victories, though many unskilled labourers read extracts from Paine, the majority were too poor and ill-organized to play any effective part in political agitation. They were, anyhow, far more interested in struggling to improve their living standards. It was the 'middling classes', not the poor, who joined the reform societies.

In the spring of 1792 Anna Barbauld, toasted in Paris as 'Lady Defender of the Revolution' had visited Scotland, staying with Mrs. Eliza Fletcher.* Mrs. Barbauld met Muir again, and her favourite ex-pupil, Lord Daer, a young man of 24, the Earl of Selkirk's heir. He had been at Edinburgh University, then in Paris at the outbreak of the French Revolution. He was a keen reformer, a member of both the Friends of the People and the London Corresponding Society. Mrs. Barbauld may have introduced Muir to Daer. She would certainly have encouraged their radical opinions.

Up to this point Muir's political activities are only a matter of conjecture. From now on they can be pieced together from newspapers, spies' reports, and evidence given at his subsequent trial. In July he defended Lockie, one of the King's Birthday rioters.

By many ingenious arguments and nice reasonings Muir endeavoured to take off the force and application of the proof. He indeed did everything for his panel [the accused] that he could. . . . Mr. Muir stated and admitted the dangerous tendency of mobs, and observed that when they set out on foot in order to obtain redress of grievances, or from any other cause, they defeated the cause they meant to serve.[1]

Lockie was sentenced to fourteen years transportation. This case is a typical illustration of Muir's attitude. He was happy to defend humble men accused of attacking the Government, but deprecated any form of violence.†

On 4 July Colonel Macleod optimistically assured Grey, in London, that Scotland was 'unanimous for Reform'. So many country gentlemen crowded into Edinburgh for a burgh meeting that even Robert Dundas seconded a reform motion.

Some younger men, however, in Glasgow, Edinburgh, Dundee,

---

* For some years Mrs Barbauld and her husband ran a school at Palgrave, Suffolk.

† No one queried the legality of transporting Lockie as they would do later after Muir's trial. Lockie was accused of rioting, not verbal sedition, but the fact that he was subsequently pardoned is perhaps an indication that the authorities had doubts about his sentence.

and Perth, were becoming impatient with the burgh reformers' lack of success. Erskine and Fletcher were approached with the suggestion that the burgh reformers should widen their aims and campaign for parliamentary reform. They refused, believing their efforts should be concentrated on local abuses. So on 26 July the Edinburgh Society of the Friends of the People was founded.[2] Muir's name does not appear on the list of founding members, which included his fellow lawyers Campbell, Forsyth, Millar, and Morthland (another Glaswegian). He subsequently claimed*, however, and was not contradicted, that it was he who had originally suggested forming the Society at a meeting in Fortune's Tavern; though he supported burgh reform he had greater faith in the wider reform of Parliament. As the burgh movement was run by senior Whig lawyers, Muir may have felt that the new Society would provide a better opportunity of making his mark; besides, most young men would find the broad issues of Parliament more interesting than the intricacies of municipal intrigue.

Though much less extreme in its views, the Edinburgh Society resembled the London Corresponding Society rather than the London Friends of the People in the composition of its membership and its structure: it was to have local branches. Captain Johnston, an ex-army officer, was elected President, Lord Daer and Colonel Macleod joined, but members were mainly schoolmasters, shopkeepers, shoemakers, tailors, tanners, and brewers. Muir was one of the two men chiefly instrumental in formulating the rules and organization of the society. The other was William Skirving, a Fifeshire farmer. He had originally studied divinity at Edinburgh University. He was interested in the theory of farming and wrote agricultural pamphlets. Like other small farmers he supported reform because they had no say in government, and the Excise and Corn laws were particularly harmful to them.

Henry Erskine and Archibald Fletcher dissuaded many of their Whig friends and legal colleagues from joining, and this greatly restricted the Society's strength and influence. Erskine believed circumstances were not propitious. If the leaders persisted, hopes roused would be dashed and they would lose authority before reform became practicable later. Erskine was to some extent correct. On the other hand, if more men of standing like himself had joined the

---

* At the first General Convention of the Society.

parliamentary reformers, they would have carried more weight and the government could not have clamped down on them so severely.

In the summer recess Muir went home to organize the movement in the west. Colonel Macleod visited the Glasgow reformers in August and found them 'strongly disposed to go even further than we wish'. According to Annie Fisher a hostile witness at Muir's trial:

he was much busied about reading and writing. . . . at the time of the harvest circuit he was counsel for two soldiers at Glasgow accused of disloyal comments about King George. . . . many country people came about Mr. Muir's father's shop and he would read aloud political works to them in the backshop. . . . his conversation was commonly on political subjects. . . . she heard him read Volney's Dialogue between the Governors and the Governed [a popular French radical work] to his mother, sister and others.[3]

Annie was a servant girl in Muir's parents' Glasgow house. Unfortunately there is no record of what his mother and sister thought about all this.

James Muir described his son as having 'a retiring disposition'.[4] By 1792 Thomas appears to have thrown off his diffidence and become a forceful, self-confident political campaigner, the chief orator among the more advanced reformers. He was no brilliant political theorist, but his energy and passion built up and inspired the Scottish parliamentary reform movement.

When Muir returned to Edinburgh in September he was elected Vice-President of the associated societies forming in and around the city. Correspondence with other organizations was initiated and a letter circulated inviting local clubs to send members to a general convention to be held on 11 December. It was technically illegal to form a national society, so correspondence was the only means by which Societies could join forces; with bad communications it was also often the only means of contact. Muir drew up the plan of internal government of the affiliated societies and helped form committees.

The organization was similar to that of the older Sheffield Societies. As numbers grew, members were divided into small, manageable units. Each group elected one or more delegates to sit on co-ordinating committees. Business was conducted according to rules laid down by the General Committee. The groups met weekly in a coffee house or tavern. A chairman was elected for the duration of the meeting to maintain order and direct business. A secretary was elected for at least three months to deal with minutes and subscriptions. At meetings letters from other branches and pamphlets were read and political literature handed round. This gave the members confidence and furthered their political education. There were speeches, followed by general discussion on policy and administration. It was a practical and effective system. The Societies' activities were directed by the delegates, who were answerable to their constituents, so popular feeling was expressed. There were no large meetings to frighten the authorities.

In a wave of enthusiasm Societies sprang up at Dalkeith, Dunfermline, Dundee, Musselburgh, Strathaven, Stirling and Wigtown; at Perth four groups were formed containing 'some men of standing, mostly weavers'. According to the Whig *Caledonian Mercury*, 30 September 1792:

That keenness of political enquiry which for a long time seemed to be confined to England, has now reached this northern clime and extended its influence with rapid strides, so that it now pervades the whole of Caledonia. Societies are everywhere formed and clubs instituted for the sole purpose of political debate.

A spy reported that the Edinburgh Society had gained another hundred members in three weeks; they included a draper, a gardener, a cabinet-maker, a medical student, a bookseller, and a painter. Captain Johnston, who had become Chairman of the General Association of the Friends of the People, founded the *Edinburgh Gazetteer*, which was to 'attach itself to the parts of the people'.

Muir handed out tracts in the Parliament House and taverns. He was also instrumental in founding a reform society, the Associated Friends of the Constitution and of the People, in Glasgow, on 3 October.[5] Lt. Colonel Dalrymple of Fordell, a cousin of the Earl of Stair, was elected President, Muir Vice President; the Hon. Major Maitland, M.P., brother of the Earl of Lauderdale, Professor Millar, several schoolmasters, and a number of merchants joined. The entrance fee was 6d. plus a quarterly subscription of 3d. This encouraged regular attendance, but did not prevent poor men joining. The society's aims were magnificently comprehensive:

To cooperate with the Friends of the People in London, to enter into every legal and constitutional measure, to obtain a shorter duration of Parliament, to abolish corruption and the pension list, to cut down armaments, democratise town government, secure the election of clergy by the congregation and diffuse political knowledge.[6]

Members had to declare their adherence to the government of Great Britain as established by 'King, Lords and Commons' and swear to oppose all sedition, riot, and disorder. The society published a pamphlet about the inequalities of representation and the merit of abolishing the Septennial Act. Among the benefits expected to result from a 'restoration of the Constitution to its genuine principles' were the end of bribery, the abolition of the East India Company's monopoly, and the introduction of trial by jury in civil cases. At the third meeting of the Association four hundred were present, of whom 121 were new members. Muir made the final speech in which

with much eloquence he pointed out the nature and patriotic views and the benefits to result from these associations. He recommended order and moderation in their behaviour and exhorted the affiliated societies not to admit any person as a member unless recommended by one or more of their committee. He received loud and universal applause.[7]

Largely as a result of Muir's remarkable organizational ability societies were formed in many of the neighbouring towns and villages. He made a propaganda tour, speaking to little groups of weavers and bleach-field workers at Campsie, Kirkintilloch, Lennoxtown, Miltown, and Paisley. They were receptive audiences. Formerly they had worked at home, small communities competing with each other for work. Lately they had begun to move into the factories and mills springing up round Glasgow, which provided far greater opportunities for discussion and mutual stimulation. Quicker methods gave them more free time, but they resented their loss of independence, the harsh factory discipline and strict routine. Muir had 'great presence of mind, ready tact, fluency of language'. He soon became a popular speaker. High-minded, serious, energetic, he took up the cause with an almost religious fervour, keen to convert anyone who would listen to him – but without apparently analysing the nature of his audience. He never comments in his speeches, nor is there any other evidence that he commented, on the work his listeners did, the wages they earned, the conditions they lived in. Nor does he appear to have considered that employers might resent his inciting their workmen to embark on political agitation, an action later pounced on by his accusers. Though he does not seem to have realized the significance himself, this was the first time Scottish artisans had formed societies through which to give their views public expression. Muir was helping to lay the basis of the first working men's political clubs, to create the foundations of a labour movement in Scotland.

Muir's recorded speeches are based on ideas current at the time. He held the 'Norman Yoke' view of constitutional history, then fashionable in progressive circles. The original purity of the Constitution before the Norman Conquest had been lost and must be regained (as Burke and his supporters emphasized the need to uphold tradition, the reformers found it a useful counter-gambit to hark back even further into the past). Muir would quote Blackstone – the only way to obtain reform was by petitioning, the right secured to the subject by the Bill of Rights. He believed Parliament could be over-awed by force of public opinion. He declared that every man should have a vote, but emphasized the importance of responsible behaviour. The authorities believed Muir's private views were far more radical than those he expressed. This seems unlikely. Muir was a middle-class lawyer; he wanted to break the power of the oligarchy which controlled government and to prevent exploitation of the poor, but he expressed strong disapproval of those who wanted 'an equal distribution of property'.[8] He was an ardent disciple of Millar's bourgeois liberalism – equal opportunities for all.

It is difficult to assess how far Muir was impelled by ambition. As he himself said, given universal suffrage he would probably have been M.P. for Cadder. In the political climate of the time, however, Muir would have had far more chance of success in his profession, and influence in the government of his country, if he had suppressed his whiggish inclinations. Muir followed the eighteenth-century tradition that members of the Scottish bar played a prominent part in public affairs. Most advocates were connected with landed families and the higher echelons of Edinburgh society; they knew where their professional interests lay and supported Dundas. Muir, Morthland, and Millar were less constrained to conform. They were Glaswegians with a different background. Among the other leading reformers, Archibald Fletcher was of humble origin, and it is possible that the Erskine brothers' liberal attitude was fostered by the fact that their parents, though aristocrats, were extremely poor. Though Muir's critics said he was rash and foolish, none suggested that he chose reform only as a means to power. Like his friend Forsyth, he was carried away by the enthusiasm generated by the French Revolution at a time when he had sufficiently established himself at the bar to be able to take time off for politics.

Meanwhile the French under Jacobin influence had been adopting a more menacing attitude. The royal family were imprisoned in the Tuileries, the British ambassador recalled from Paris. In September a republic was proclaimed. The massacres of political prisoners which then took place deeply shocked the British and had a disastrous effect on the popularity of the reform movement. Many people believed, quite erroneously, that the mild British agitators were also violent revolutionaries. Outside events caused Muir's campaign to be prejudged and condemned before it had really got started. Muir failed to appreciate the dangers. Daniel McArthur, his former teacher, asked 'If he did not think it a wrong time to insist on reform seeing what had happened in France?' Muir replied:

That he thought it a proper time as the country enjoyed the blessings of peace; that there was no comparison betwixt this country and France; that in France they had sought a revolution, and had brought it about, but that in Britain we wanted no revolution, but only a moderate reform.

In October Henry Dundas, worried by 'the fermentation of the country', travelled north. The Government's alarm was understandable; following the examples in America and France the ordinary Briton was taking to politics. Besides, the authorities were deluged with misinformation. They discounted reports of the inherent dangers of grain and fuel shortages and concentrated on tales of subversive activities. Spies were employed on an unprecedented scale, partly because the regular police force was totally inadequate. They were paid piece rates, so sent in inaccurate and lurid reports which grossly exaggerated the strength and violence of the aims of the Friends of the People. It is not easy now to gauge how far the authorities believed in the conspiracies their agents invented or fomented. Perhaps they frightened themselves with their own fabrications.

Dundas's fears were confirmed by the mounting hysteria, the numerous confidential warnings he received. Sir William Maxwell said his neighbourhood teemed 'with emissaries of sedition', Paine's writings were in the hands of almost every man,

Scots peasants understand nothing of . . . equal representation and other
grievances of which the discontented in a higher rank of life complain. . . .
they may be tempted to unite and risk their necks in the hopes of bringing
about a division of the landed property and of getting 100 acres which they
have been told will fall to the share of each individual.

Another gentleman declared that 'all over Scotland manufacturers
and other workers are poisoned with an enthusiastic rage for liberty
that will not be crushed without coercive measures'. A letter describing a Glasgow meeting illustrates how invariably reform was now
coupled with events in France:

The reformers met last night, all low tradesmen except Professor Millar and
Mr. Muir who, notwithstanding the temperate language of the declaration,
made most inflammatory speeches. . . . The success of the French has had a
most mischievous effect here, [though] did it go no further than give occasion for triumph to those who entertain the same sentiments, there would be
little harm done; for they are very few, and but two or three of any influence
or respectability − but it has led them to think of forming societies for
reformation in which the lower classes of people are invited to enter, and
however insignificant these leaders may be in themselves, when backed with
the mob, they become formidable.

In some respects this information was correct. In spite of all their
efforts the Friends of the People had not yet attracted a widespread
or influential following. But spies' talk of inflammatory speeches
was quite untrue. Even spies' reports show how moderate and careful Muir's language was: 'The Friends of the People should stand
together until a complete reform was obtained. No rash measure
should be taken to effectuate this. . . . They should persevere with
one application after another to Parliament until success was
achieved.' The Kirkintilloch Society passed a resolution of thanks to
Mr. Muir for his 'unrelenting exertion in the case of freedom and
humanity'.

One informer accused Muir of circulating seditious papers. He
forwarded a totally innocuous pamphlet on Scotland's inadequate
representation in Parliament and misleadingly included an anonymous letter dated 'the last year of the French Republic' proclaiming
'Fame sound the downfall of Monarchy and the elevation of Democracy Amen', attached to a boringly sober resolution of the Glasgow
Friends of the People. An indication of the authorities' hysterical
state of mind is that, instead of destroying anonymous letters, they
forwarded them to London.

The most accurate reports were submitted by a spy known in the official files only as J.B. An educated man with a dry sense of humour, he joined the Edinburgh Friends of the People and was never suspected by his fellow members. J.B. had qualms of conscience. He asked that his work should be burnt so that his words 'may not rise up to accuse me on the day of judgment'.

He described many meetings addressed by Dalrymple, Maitland, Millar, Morthland, and Muir. At one over two hundred were present, and a builder presided. Dalrymple, Johnston ('the modern Demosthenes'), and Muir all made lengthy speeches – Muir's in particular was a long one, in which he said that the Excise Law should be revised through Parliament. Judging from both newspaper and spies' accounts Muir was addicted to long speeches. Luckily, as he was a lively and powerful speaker, he does not appear to have bored his audiences. At a meeting of about 300 Macleod made a rousing speech: 'His purse, his sword and his influence were at their service and he would stand by them to the last drop of his blood'.

On 21 November arrangements for a General Convention were ratified. Resolutions were adopted and published in the newspapers:

1. If any member was found guilty of riot or sedition his name would be expunged.
2. Any member unjustly punished by 'the arm of power' should be protected by the society.
3. Two members of each of the nine Edinburgh Societies were to be chosen to draw up an address to Parliament.

The reformers courted publicity as they wanted to influence public opinion; but the very fact that they were sufficiently organized to act in concert, issue pamphlets, and draw up petitions alarmed the establishment.

Dundas energetically roused support for the Government. The Lord Advocate spent £100, the Lord Provost of Glasgow £40 on loyalist propaganda. Their line was that the electoral system might have its faults, after all nothing is perfect, but the reformers were jeopardizing Scotland's new-found prosperity. Constitutional societies were formed with support from the secret service funds. Some rather amusing skits were published which give a good idea of the reformers' earnest, naïve deliberations. The opening scene of *The Scotch Tocsin Sounds* is set at the Jacobin club in Blackguards

Wynd.[9] The President and Vice President are recognizable carica-
tures of Johnston and Muir. A baker rushes in with a rumour that the
French have taken Berlin with 20 sail o' line. All rise to embrace each
other with a civic kiss. A drunken tailor is ejected. The members
stand and chant in unison that everyone will be rich when a reform of
Parliament is obtained.

If only the authorities could have adopted this tone of harmless
ridicule, it would have kept the agitation in proper perspective. But,
as the Glasgow Friends of the People complained, they were determined to prove that the leading men in the Society were really
republicans 'with sinister, secret plans'. Having fewer resources than
the Government, the Friends of the People could only continue to
deny all charges. Dalrymple and Muir protested that their demands
fell far short of what Pitt had advocated a few years previously, that
reform had preceded the French Revolution. They tried to dissociate
themselves from the wild fringe which always bedevils popular
movements, to make clear that they had no links with the Jacobins,
but they were not believed. As Pallain, the French representative in
London, said: 'Paine only is seen in their every action'. Dundas
ordered the letters of Macleod, Johnston, and Dalrymple to be
scrutinized at the Post Office. This was prompted by a report that

Colonel Dalrymple had attempted to inspire republican principles in the
landholders of his estate and, though the most sensible part of the people
looked upon him as a madman, still the mischief was great in distributing
seditious printed books among them as they assembled in great numbers in
the fields and sent delegates from one place to another.

On 19 November the French published a decree of fraternity
offering assistance to all men striving for freedom. This was a disas-
trous blow for the reformers. People who had been horrified by the
September massacres now became obsessed by the fear that the
French would assist a similar revolution in Britain. Manufacturers,
preferring stable conditions to political power, turned to Pitt. In
Scotland almost all the gentry and many others faded away. In
Parliament only a small number of Whigs still supported reform.
Upper-class leaders who stood fast, such as Earl Stanhope and Major
Cartwright, were rather eccentric, their followers mainly urban arti-
sans. As a result they had little contact with men in positions of
authority and did not appreciate the growing antagonism.

November and December were months of intense activity in Scotland. There was hardly a community which was not divided into 'government men or blacknebs'. Dundas had more cause to be alarmed by rioters than by reformers. In the eighteenth century rioting was almost the only means of popular protest. There were unwritten rules. The mob would attack a specific object and depart. Never before had mobs been associated with political slogans. Now, when a Dundee mob threatened to unload a cargo of meal which could not be landed because of the Corn Laws, they cried 'liberty and equality'. When there was a further spate of burning Dundas's effigy, boys shouted 'No King!' At Perth and Dundee the French entry into Brussels on 13 November was celebrated with bonfires, bell-ringing, and trees of liberty. The inhabitants were compelled to illuminate their windows.[10] Worried officials recalled the riots against the Roman Catholic Relief Bill, which had shown how the poor could be organized against the Government.

Events abroad caused Dundas to return to London. On 16 November France, supporting Belgian interests, had thrown open the navigation of the Scheldt. This was a direct challenge to Britain, who had guaranteed the rights of her ally Holland. Dundas now called out the militia in Scotland. To justify this the Government alleged 'rebellion', but would have been hard pressed to prove it. Many responsible Scotsmen thought the Government unnecessarily alarmist. Sir Gilbert Elliott, a typical country magistrate and supporter of Pitt, said, 'The idea of Scottish insurrections . . . is certainly ridiculous to those who live in Scotland and know the truth'. Macleod wrote to Grey:

The conduct of Government seems to be a mixture of timidity and cunning, they are really afraid of insurrections on the one hand and on the other they court and provoke them. On the slightest occasion the troops are put in motion. . . . A few days ago some boys assembled at Dundee to plant the tree of liberty. One of the magistrates immediately announced an insurrection and it was industriously given out here that the inhabitants had risen, seized the Custom House and Excise officers and refused to pay taxes. In consequence the 42nd regiment is ordered to be quartered in Perth and Dundee.

On 21 November delegates from reform societies in and around Edinburgh met to consider proposals for the Convention to be held in the Scottish capital for three days in December. Muir played a leading part in the meetings, at which his friends and fellow advocates James Campbell, Robert Forsyth, John Millar, and Morthland were present. According to the *Caledonian Mercury*,

Muir was proposed as Vice President with many plaudits from the whole convention. Muir said the motion and plaudits had come like a thunderbolt upon him and declined the honour. Mr. Thompson Callender [author of *The Political Progress of Great Britain* *] said his friend declining an office for which he was so well qualified put him in mind of the speaker of the House of Commons declining that office. Mr. Muir then in a handsome speech accepted the office.

As usual much of the delegates' time was spent discussing administration. Muir favoured a scheme for Presidents of established Societies to nominate officers of new ones. Several members thought this would give too much power to individuals, when the principal object of the association was to divide power. Muir then proposed that the matter should be submitted to the Societies. There were heated arguments as to whether the delegates should be permanent or not. Muir always had decided views and expressed them forcibly and at length. He said it was dangerous to entrust men with the power of prolonging their delegation. They might sit to eternity. At the same time Muir said the Convention of Delegates should be permanent and conduct the business committed to them even if the original delegation had been changed. Several speakers, including Forsyth, disagreed with Muir. They were all trying to solve the problem of democratic societies – how to reconcile democracy with efficiency.

New branches of the Friends of the People were still being formed. They passed resolutions threatening to expel members who joined in riots, but to no avail. Thomas Christie and the Revd. Thomas Fyshe Palmer, Unitarian Minister in Dundee, were blamed for instigating the Dundee riot, which they had expressly condemned.

On 1 December a second proclamation against sedition was issued. Almost every city, town, and county returned thanks for the proclamation, some spontaneous, some forced (Henry Dundas had organized the issue of such addresses when he was in Scotland). The creation of loyal associations was encouraged. The best known was that of John Reeves, formed on 28 November in London for 'Protecting Liberty and Property against Republicans and Levellers'. In particular Reeves attacked printers and publicans. Coffee houses

* See below, p. 52.

and taverns were warned that their licences would be withdrawn if they leased their premises for political meetings. Paine's works were destroyed, his effigy burnt.

On 4 December James 'Balloon' Tytler, a well-known Edinburgh chemist and littérateur, editor of a radical review, *The Historical Register*, was indicted for circulating a pamphlet advocating the promotion of reform by passive resistance. The following day the Edinburgh Friends of the People held a meeting to discuss the arrest of two members for distributing some allegedly seditious papers. Muir warned them of the danger from spies and

admonished the people with respect to their behaviour in the present critical situation of affairs and strongly enjoined temperance and moderation. The societies should be careful to attend to the moral and political character of those admitted as members.[11]

Afterwards Muir, Skirving, and others called on the Lord Provost to offer the services of the Friends of the People to co-operate with him and the magistrates in the suppression of popular tumults. The Provost replied that he did not know any 'legally constituted society under that designation, but that it was not from the associations that the magistrates apprehended disorder'.[12]

On 11 December rioters in Manchester, in the name of 'Church and King', attacked and destroyed the offices of the *Manchester Herald* and the Manchester Reform Society. Nonconformists' houses were burnt. For three days the mob looted and rampaged unchecked. Manchester, a centre of liberalism, was cowed.

Encouraged by the authorities a society similar to Reeves's was founded in Edinburgh. Pamphlets were circulated in defence of the Constitution and resolutions left for signature at the Goldsmiths' Hall. This Goldsmiths' Hall Association, as it became called, now emerged as the opponent of the Friends of the People in Edinburgh.

The Friends of the People made further strenuous but unsuccessful efforts to persuade the burgh reformers to join forces with them. Mrs. Eliza Fletcher recalled Mr. Muir's calling on her husband:

I heard them at high words in an adjoining room. Mr. Fletcher told me that Muir quitted him much dissatisfied because he could not persuade him to join the society. . . . 'I believe him to be an honest enthusiast, but he is an illjudging man. These violent reformers will create such an alarm in the country as must strengthen the Government. The country is not prepared to second their views of annual parliaments and universal suffrage.'

Macleod, Dalrymple, and Maitland, however, members of important Scottish families, encouraged Muir to continue campaigning. Regarded by many of their equals as tiresome cranks, they belonged to the hard core of Whigs who believed passionately in reform and saw no reason why it should be delayed by French excesses.

Muir differed in one important aspect from his fellow reformers: he had made contact with the United Irishmen. They were a society formed largely of professional men in Dublin and Belfast who appreciated that trouble with France would provide a golden opportunity to force concessions from the English, called United because Protestants and Catholics had combined to demand a more representative Irish Parliament. Muir wanted to create a united reform movement of the Scots, English, and Irish. Through common friends in Glasgow he had entered into correspondence with two Irishmen. One, Dr. Drennan, poet and fashionable Belfast *accoucheur*, was at first the intellectual leader and pamphleteer of the United Irishmen. A gentle man, he had been educated at Glasgow, then Edinburgh University, where he had come under the influence of Dugald Stewart's philosophic republicanism. The other was Archibald Hamilton Rowan, who, though of far greater wealth and social status, in temperament and character had many affinities with Muir. They became friends. Hamilton Rowan was a huge, powerful, handsome man with beautiful manners. Vain, kind, flamboyant, and brave, he thoroughly enjoyed the position he acquired as champion of the plebs. Fired by the injustices of the way Ireland was governed, he gadded about Dublin in the bright green uniform of the Volunteers covered with republican badges, ready to fight for the underdog, issuing fierce statements, basking in the crowd's applause.

CHAPTER 4

The Convention

The first Convention of the Delegates of the Scottish Friends of the People was held in Edinburgh on 11–13 December 1792. It provided a means for the reformers to meet each other and co-ordinate policy in debate; it was an exhibition of strength and a challenge to the government. Its chief purpose was to arrange for a united petition to Parliament. The designation 'convention', meaning a delegate conference for propaganda, had been used before in Scotland and recently by Wyvill, but it was an unfortunate choice as the French Revolution had given it a more sinister significance. There were about 160 delegates representing 80 societies in 35 towns and villages from the predominantly manufacturing areas which ran from Glasgow north to Dundee and east to Edinburgh. Not all societies could afford to send representatives and the Edinburgh Societies accounted for more than half of those present.

The leaders of the Convention were Daer, Dalrymple, Forsyth, Johnston, Millar, Morthland, and Muir. Macleod was absent as Parliament was sitting. Several other Edinburgh lawyers attended, also Major Maitland, Sir John Allen, 'other members of the gentry and professions and some dissenting clergymen'.[1] The bulk of the delegates were shopkeepers, printers, teachers, and skilled artisans. Muir took a more radical stance than his fellow lawyers and emerged as leader of the smaller, less moderate faction of the conference.

Muir made the introductory speech. Daer addressed the Convention as 'fellow citizens' – a phrase unlikely to calm the authorities' fears. Skirving, hard-working but an appallingly dull speaker, was appointed secretary. He was to remain a staunch campaigner throughout the next dangerous year. Daer and Muir both proposed Dalrymple as Chairman. At first he declined – 'as he was a military man, the Ministry might accuse him of attempting to raise a rebellion' – but finally accepted. Morthland proposed that various resolutions should be placed on the table for consideration on a future day. Muir replied that unless they were considered immediately, they might as well lie on Arthur's Seat.* Although minutes do not convey the flavour or sparkle of a speech, it is clear from frequent comments of 'universal laughter', 'loud applause', that Muir was by far the liveliest, wittiest, and most stimulating speaker. He also appears to have played a somewhat vociferous part in the proceedings.

On the second day Daer, who disapproved of standing committees as giving power to a junta, insisted that, as in the French Assembly, every question should be discussed by the Convention. Muir 'in a speech of some length opposed everything he proposed'. Others supported Daer, including Richard Fowler who commented that 'some people attempted to raise themselves from insignificance by advancing plausible arguments in favour of infamous measures'. Muir did not press the matter and Daer's suggestions were adopted.

Muir produced a printed address from the United Irishmen to the delegates, signed by Drennan and Hamilton Rowan, which he had received just before the Convention. He must already have shown it to some of his colleagues as Dalrymple immediately protested against its being read as he considered it treasonable. Muir 'took upon himself the whole responsibility and danger of the measure', a gesture which would not have had much practical effect. A 'universal cry to hear it' arose, so Muir read it. The address paid compliments to the Scottish nation, compared the inadequate franchise of Scotland and Ireland, and proposed that conventions should be held throughout the kingdom to discuss reform and send a united petition to Parliament from England, Scotland, and Ireland. Muir moved that an answer should be sent. 'We cannot consider ourselves as mowed and melted down into another country. Have we not distinct courts, judges, juries, laws etc. . . ? The people of Ireland *will* a reform. The Scotch *will* a reform.'

Drennan and Hamilton Rowan's intentions were harmless, but their high-flown, bombastic phrases, urging the Scotch and Irish to persevere 'until we have planted the flag of freedom on the summit, and are at once victorious and secure', could be misconstrued and the majority who decided that the letter should be ignored were right. It was a cardinal error on Muir's part to have brought it before the Convention. Just the stuff to make Dundas, who saw, or pretended

* Arthur's Seat, the name of a hill overlooking Edinburgh to the east, is a corruption of the Gaelic *Ard-na-said* – the height of the arrows, i.e. convenient ground to shoot from.

to see, bogey-men everywhere, declare that the Celts were combining with the French to start an insurrection. Muir agreed later that same evening to withdraw the letter and return it to Drennan so that the doubtful phrases could be 'smoothed'.

Among those who supported Muir was the Revd. Thomas Palmer, already viewed with suspicion by the authorities. He was one of the cleverest of the reformers, connoisseur of architecture, painting and poetry, a keen amateur gardener. Born in 1747, Palmer belonged to an important Bedfordshire family. Educated at Eton and Cambridge, appointed a Fellow of Queens', he was set for a distinguished career in the Church when he became disillusioned with its reactionary attitude and began to have doubts about the Trinity. Palmer gave up his living, went to Montrose as a Unitarian minister, then moved to Dundee. He was a first-rate preacher and published Unitarian tracts and reform pamphlets. Latterly he had spent much time in Edinburgh and Glasgow, where he helped found Unitarian societies and became friends with Muir. Palmer held more extreme views than the majority of the reformers. He produced a resolution against the threatened war with France, but Millar and Morthland argued that the Convention was only concerned with parliamentary reform, so it was withdrawn. Like Skirving, Palmer was to remain a reformer when most of the educated leaders gave up.

Morthland moved a series of resolutions drawn up by the committee on the aims of the Friends of the People. More radical members wanted to put in a clause about 'restoring' the Constitution to its supposed former purity. Muir patriotically remarked that in the reigns of Edward I and III 'in Scotland a free man was even more free than in England'. His suggestion that, as in those days, all over 21 should have the vote was greatly applauded. There was much discussion about which words should be used — some might be considered treasonable. Muir cautioned against using the phrase 'source of these abuses'. Unfortunate inferences might be drawn; 'What is the source of these abuses? The royal influence. What! Are you to remove the King? Then, gentlemen, we shall find ourselves in the same predicament with those foolish fellows who got drunk with the soldiers in the Castle the other week and drank "George the III and last" (loud laughter).' (They were now in gaol.)

Finally all agreed that it was better to keep to general terms. Members should petition not as a convention but as individuals.

Muir commented that 'even so they would be known. It would be whispered, it would be spoken of, that they were a representative body from the different associations of Scotland. Mr. Grey . . . will insist that the people are *firm, collected*, and *strong. . . .*'

Muir moved that a permanent Committee of Finance should be set up at Edinburgh. When this had been agreed he then outlined a plan for financing the Societies throughout Scotland. Finance committees in each county would correspond with the Edinburgh Committee which would report to the Convention. Muir, who had done much of the groundwork, was keen to make the movement as effective and efficient as possible. Some members, including Fowler and Daer, were agreeable that finance should be supervised by committees, but not the general policy and conduct of the Societies, as this would give too much power and influence to a few delegates, of whom Muir was one. The more conservative members feared that, if not controlled, hot-heads might lead the Societies into unnecessary clashes with the authorities. There is no evidence that Muir wished to abuse his position or take control from other leaders. He supported democratic methods, but wanted to prevent the cumbersome method of everyone's taking part in all decisions, resulting in nothing being achieved. If Muir and a few colleagues sat on permanent committees they would exert more influence over the movement than they could at meetings of the whole Convention. One cannot judge if the machinery evolved would have worked satisfactorily because the movement was so rapidly broken up by the authorities. But Thomas Hardy remained secretary of the London Corresponding Society for many years without destroying its democratic nature, and there is no reason to suppose that Muir and Skirving would not have succeeded equally well.

On the last day, the petition to Parliament was read and approved. Then came another minor episode which was taken up and distorted by the government-subsidized newspapers. Two members suggested that, to help magistrates suppress riots and tumults, all associates should be provided with a 'Brown Janet', i.e. powder, ball, and bayonet. This was promptly quashed, but rumours were assiduously spread that the Convention was arming for an insurrection.

One delegate said that many burgh reformers now wanted to co-operate with the Friends of the People. Muir, who had been absent defending a client in court, returned in the middle of the discussion. 'He said that he did not know what had been said upon the motion, but, from the little he had heard, he was clearly against it. The Friends of the People could not with any consistency invite a particular class of men to co-operate . . . though he hoped members of the Convention of Royal Burghs would join the associations, as many of them had done, individually'. Clearly Erskine and Fletcher's refusal to co-operate still rankled, for Muir then followed Johnston in retailing details of their obstructiveness. Voting showed that the house was equally divided on the issue, so it was decided to invite them to join as individuals.

John Millar then called attention to an advertisement of the Goldsmiths' Hall Association in the *Edinburgh Herald*, announcing that they had passed resolutions to protect the Constitution and counteract associations for dispersing seditious writings, 'An insidious attempt to discredit the Friends of the People'. Millar suggested that members of the Convention should subscribe to the resolutions which had been left for signature at the Goldsmiths' Hall, signing themselves delegates of the Society of the Friends of the People. The first members to reach the Hall signed the book, later arrivals were refused entry. The Goldsmiths' Hall Committee ordered the delegates' names, including Muir's, to be deleted, and published their reasons for counteracting 'such impudence' in the newspapers. Public condemnation by such an influential body was to have serious consequences for Muir and the Scottish reform movement in general.

At the final evening session they agreed to meet again in April. Muir paid a graceful tribute to the Chairman and congratulated the Convention on

the free spirit of enquiry which had pervaded all their debates. . . . They had not assented to a single clause in their resolutions in compliance to great names. . . . they had not tamely yielded their judgements to those of others. This was the true spirit of liberty. . . .

There was an emotional ending. Fowler suggested that all present should take the French oath 'To live free or die'. The whole company stood, raised their right hands, and swore the oath; this was followed by prolonged cheering. Dalrymple said their impulsive action could be misrepresented and magnified into sedition. They must be careful not to give their enemies any grounds for criticism, so the oath was erased from the minutes, another point later held against the Convention in certain quarters.

In fact the delegates behaved correctly throughout. There was not the faintest suggestion of any clandestine revolutionary inclinations. As Daniel Stewart, Secretary of the London Friends of the People, told Grey:

Many gentlemen of respectability and large property were members. The magistrates of Edinburgh did not molest the convention. The proceedings appear to me to have been such as the most timid supporter of parliamentary reform could not object to.

Though the assembly was small, its members of no great significance, it was a remarkable occurrence, a minor landmark in Scottish history. For the first time shopkeepers and artisans had attempted to take part in the government of the country.

Any claim Muir may have to a small niche in European history, rather than in personal biography, rests largely on the enormous amount of campaigning and administrative work he carried out which resulted in the successful three-day meeting in December 1792 of the Scottish Convention. Muir's evident sincerity, his geniune desire to help the common man, had roused great interest. He was 'indefatigable, by word and deed the champion of reform. He was the movement in the West.'[2] Some reformers blamed Muir for the 'indiscretion of his zeal'. Zeal is essential for anyone who wants to remedy abuses; but he also needs sound judgement. He must have a sense of mission, but this can lead to obtuseness and conceit. Like Paine, Muir was exuberantly and naïvely confident that his ideas would triumph in spite of materially powerful opposition. He believed, as did many others, that a new golden, glorious era was dawning. He did not appreciate that the year 1792, which had begun in a spirit of elation, was ending in an atmosphere of fear and suspicion. Nor, in spite of warnings from older men such as Dalrymple, would he admit that it was unwise to take official note of the United Irishmen's flamboyant letter. In one sense he showed a wider vision in looking across the sea to Ireland; but it was foolish to encourage the Government's fear of a coalition of agitators in the three kingdoms. Like other idealistic young supporters of radical causes, he refused to moderate his campaign when it became unpopular, thinking compromise would be betrayal. He was unable to accept that, in the prevailing climate of opinion, it would be sensible to move carefully.

The growth of political societies had created a genuine dread of revolt among the upper and middle classes. With their full approval the Government now initiated a campaign of intimidation; persecution of booksellers, newspaper proprietors, and leading reformers was to continue for many years. In particular, professional men who associated with plebeian reformers were attacked. Scotland, still partly feudal in outlook and largely controlled by Dundas and his Tory lairds, could offer least resistance to repression, so there it was carried to extreme lengths. Also, the Auld Alliance and past insurrections made Scotland's loyalty suspect. The nation was so overwhelmingly loyal such repressive measures were quite unnecessary; but Pitt, fearing war, wanted to have public opinion firmly on his side.

Parliament assembled on 13 December. The Lord Mayor of London moved an address in the Commons stating that numerous societies had been formed to subvert the Constitution. He was strongly supported. Fox asked, since they claimed an insurrection existed, where was it? On 18 December Thomas Paine, who had fled to France in September, was tried *in absentia* and outlawed.

Towards the end of December the Home Office files are crammed with reports from spies and loyal citizens. A reactionary panic was developing into a witch-hunt. People were only too ready to believe in French plots. 'Jacobin' became a term of abuse. Preoccupation with death, lack of control, and susceptibility to violent stimulation led many eighteenth-century men to drink and to gamble to excess, and may have encouraged many to exaggerate the political situation.

One of the authorities' phobias was that billeted troops would be suborned. On 16 December a rumour ran round Edinburgh that Colonel Macleod's regiment had set out for Scotland to propagate his opinions among other soldiers. Later the Lord Advocate enquired whether Macleod's letters in the *Morning Chronicle* defending the Friends of the People were actionable or contrary to the privileges of the House of Commons, but was told he was unlikely to be successful if he pressed the matter. On 15 December he sent Evan Nepean at the Home Office J.B.'s report of the Convention, endeavouring to obtain a copy of the United Irishmen's letter, 'a treasonable item'. 'The Solicitor and I are resolved to lay Muir by the heels on a charge of High Treason. Dalrymple is frightened out of his wits.' (Certainly from this moment Dalrymple plays no further recorded part in the reform movement.)

Although the authorities were investigating his activities, Muir continued as vigorously as before. At a meeting on 18 December at Portsburgh, with Skirving in the chair, he reiterated that the Friends were emphatically opposed to the division of land.

On 19 December a Mr. Jackson produced before the Sheriff papers 'brought to me near Huntershill'. Muir had asked a farrier who kept a public house on the road to Edinburgh to paste them up, but the smith refused. 'Mr. Muir has taken his revenge by building a smith's shop and public house opposite where all the printed papers of the society are exhibited and distributed.' These papers consisted of a broadsheet containing a few mild comments on Equal Representation, Just Taxation, and Liberty of Conscience; the official *Resolution* of the Glasgow Friends of the People; and the *Declaration of the Rights of Man* issued by the French National Assembly. They were sent by Dundas to Messrs. Chamberlayne and White, a firm of London solicitors, who were legal advisers to the Home Office. Evidently not thinking them actionable, they replied that 'the papers, if prosecuted at all, must be prosecuted in Scotland where they were published'.

On 19 December also, to add to Dundas's alarm, Dublin Castle warned him that a Mr. Archdeacon from London and Mr. Muir from Scotland were expected shortly to establish a more intimate correspondence between the Societies of England, Scotland, and Ireland. On 27 December the Goldsmiths' Association offered a reward of five guineas to the first person who gave information of any bookseller after this date selling or distributing gratis Paine's *The Rights of Man*, or information of any person circulating amongst the working people of Scotland copies of that libel on the Constitution.[3]

Muir, who was to defend Tytler, set out from home on 2 January 1793, to prepare the defence. As he alighted from the carriage at Holytown, a stage from Glasgow, he was accosted by a King's Messenger with a warrant for his arrest. They arrived at Edinburgh about eight o'clock in the evening. Muir was brought before Sheriff Pringle of Edinburgh and Honeyman, Sheriff of Lanarkshire. Muir said he would answer no questions: 'I will not desert in my own case a principle which I have invariably applied to the cases of others'. Honeyman observed that there was a material difference between pleading on principles as counsel and acting on them as a private character. 'There may be a distinction' replied Muir, 'but I know it not. If principles are just, they must be applicable to all cases, and all situations. I have never yet acted on a principle either in public or private, which my conscience or understanding disavowed; and this, surely, is not a time to deviate from them'. Muir was then asked if he had ever given anyone copies of Paine's works, or of *The Patriot*; whether he had been a member of the Convention of the Friends of the People and had there read an address from the United Irishmen in Dublin and moved that the Convention should send them a solemn vote of thanks; whether he had ever given anyone Flower's book on the French Constitution (the Scots authorities considered this a dangerously radical book). He declined to answer. Muir then asked the Procurator Fiscal the name of his informer, as 'he was credibly assured that certain persons had endeavoured to impress the minds of those who might be called as witnesses against him by holding out to them the hope of places and emoluments'.[4]

Robert Dundas told his uncle that *The Patriot* 'appears to be more within the reach of the law than anything I have yet met with. It was circulated from Dundee, to various persons. . . . Honeyman traced a copy home to Muir . . . who had circulated it chiefly in Kirkintil-loch. . . . I have no doubt . . . of such proof as will enable me to bring this ringleader of sedition immediately before a jury'. Three trials were due to begin on Monday, 'the other cases come forward every successive Monday as fast as got ready'. The Lord Advocate asked for cash for himself and Pringle to reward spies and emissaries. Johnston, though closely watched, had not yet brought himself sufficiently within reach. Dundas's effigy had been burnt once more.

Muir was freed on bail and promptly attended a meeting in Edinburgh. J.B. sent in a despondent report. His attitude to the Friends of the People was somewhat ambivalent and he regretted their decline. About a hundred people were present; morale was low. Muir said another association was to be formed, composed of most respectable people of different political views, 'for the preservation of the Freedom of the Press'.* J.B. dryly suggested that, as a Christian, the Lord Advocate would surely approve this society's aims. J.B.

---

* After a preliminary meeting on 17 September 1792, the Society for the Preservation of the Freedom of the Press was officially founded by Thomas Erskine on 18 December 1792.

did not comment on Muir's arrest, but a Tory newspaper, the *St. James Chronicle*, mentioned that 'The Friends of the People are very much astonished at seeing their leader seized in this manner. This gentleman has been named Chancellor of the Commonwealth, so far had matters gone with them.'[5] Discouraged by loyalist opposition the delegates of the Edinburgh Association agreed that they should not use the term 'Friends of the People' in any petition to Parliament 'as this term has become so obnoxious'.

Tytler fled to Ireland, but other trials were held. The three printers who had drunk a toast of 'damnation to all crowned heads' were sentenced to nine months' imprisonment. Thompson Callender, author of an allegedly seditious article published in *The Bee*, fled to America. The bookseller and printer involved were sentenced to three and six months. Another bookseller, John Elder, and William Stewart, a Leith merchant, were indicted for circulating the French National Assembly's *Declaration of the Rights of Man* and demanding reform of the Scottish burghs. Stewart fled and the case against Elder was dropped. The flight of so many accused suggests that they entertained doubts about the impartiality of Scottish judges and juries. In fact the first trials were conducted with moderation and the punishments were reasonable – probably due to the insignificance of the accused. One judge, Lord Henderland, however, discussed transportation as a possible, though previously unknown, punishment for sedition.

Meanwhile, Muir to his sorrow had been abandoned by nearly all his acquaintance. He thought he had made many friends in Edinburgh society and at the Bar who would have stuck by him, but on all sides he was shunned and treated with contempt. Some felt he had gone rather far, others feared arrest on similar charges. He was particularly distressed by the desertion of Forsyth, his companion since student days. Muir was the first to suffer the ostracism which all the Edinburgh Whigs were to endure until the French Wars ended. It was a terrible blow to his heart and his self-esteem.

He decided to go to France to see the Revolution at first hand. He may have intended to stay there till charges against him were dropped and it was safe to return; he may merely have jumped at an excuse to escape from the unpleasantness of life at home. In the event it was to prove another mistake. Muir left on 8 January, having arranged with his solicitor James Campbell to advise him if and

Thomas Muir

Huntershill

Engraving of the bust of Muir
modelled at Portsmouth

Loyalist medal:
'The Three Thomases'

when criminal charges were issued. If Muir had intended to visit Ireland he now abandoned the idea. However, the United Irishmen admitted him to their Society, he 'having taken the test'; Hamilton Rowan signed his certificate.[6] Rowan too had been arrested for distributing seditious papers and released on bail.

On his arrival in London, Muir talked to Fox and was enthusiastically entertained by the Friends of the People, who were depressed by events in France and increasing antagonism at home. On 11 January Muir addressed a meeting of the 'Friends of the Liberty of the Press' at the Freemasons' Tavern. This was attended by leading reformers such as Lauderdale and Thomas Brand Hollis and many M.P.s including Samuel Whitbread, Sheridan, Grey, Maitland, Macleod, and Lambton. According to the Whig *Morning Post* he made a most elegant and forceful speech:

. . . Liberty of the press and speech in Scotland were almost at an end. Spies intruded into all company, sentinels of the Treasury were stationed in every tavern, rewards offered to informers. . . . With respect to loyalty he was not exceeded by anyone if affection to the Constitution were intended, but if the word meant (as he feared at present) an inclination to rivet more tightly the yoke of oppression about the necks of his countrymen, he had but little of it. He loved his sovereign but could not on that account forget the people. Thank God even the Scotch at length began to feel they had rights. . . .

According to a spy his speech was heard 'with murmurs and marked signs of contempt of the agents in power'. Immediately he finished speaking Thomas Erskine moved a resolution to afford the Patriots of Scotland every assistance in the power of the Society.

So much attention from so many leading Whig politicians went to Muir's head. Not only did it confirm his conviction that he had been right and more cautious campaigners wrong, but it encouraged him to overestimate his influence and importance. He wrote to Skirving that, if the authorities did decide to bring him to trial, his stay in Paris would be short as he intended to plead his own cause in person. He would

try what could be done with the Convention to save the life of a certain great personage, and to circulate it as the opinion of the people in Britain that the death of the King would disgrace the cause of freedom for ever.

J.B. reported that some of Muir's friends regretted that he went to France. His enemies said he had gone as an 'Envoy or Ambassador from the Friends of the People to aid the revolution and to lay plans for kindling it in his own country. . . . Chagrined at his late usage, he intended to welcome the miscreants into Britain'. Some believed he had been sent by the republicans of Scotland to hasten the King's execution. Propaganda against the reformers was becoming more virulent. The Lord Advocate wrote to Nepean: 'It is impossible you can touch Muir, who is either in London or . . . gone to France, unless he fails to stand trial, which does not come on until this day three weeks the 11 February'. He was still trying to catch Tytler and suggested advertising a fifty guinea reward in the London papers. Millar and Morthland had persuaded a meeting, 'mostly low people', to reject another resolution of Palmer's against war with France. The Earl of Lauderdale had chaired a county reform meeting. Gloom reigned among the reformers but Daer and Macleod were labouring to keep their spirits up. Dundas had once more been burnt in effigy.

On 18 January Daer wrote to thank Grey for the cordial reception given Muir. He ended with the tart comment

should a case ever occur when a man thus appears before you whose manner even disgusts, and whose conduct cannot be approved of as wise or prudent, I trust the good sense of your Society will recollect only that he is a Martyr or an Envoy from brethren in distress.

Daer said that in England they believed there were more reformers in Scotland and vice versa. Alas there were few in Scotland, but he believed many more would sign a petition. He implored the English Friends of the People to take heart and petition to keep the cause alive. Scotch reformers were more oppressed than in the South. The English must support them, or national divisions would arise.

Daer's letter contains interesting comments on Scottish opinion about Union, much of which is still applicable today:

Scotland has long groaned under the chains of England and knows that its connection there has been the cause of its greatest misfortunes. . . . you may call it Scotland's prejudice . . . but you should at least be aware of how we Scotsmen see it. We have existed a conquered province these two centuries. We trace our bondage from the Union of the Crown and find it little alleviated by the Union of the Kingdoms. You say we have gained . . . commerce, manufactures, agriculture. . . . union gave us little assistance in these except removing a part of the obstacles which your greater power had thrown around us. But, if it did more, what would that amount to, but the common saying that we bartered our liberty and with it our morals for a little wealth? You say we have gained emancipation from feudal tyranny. I believe that had no union ever taken place we should have been more emancipated than we are. Any share of human evil that might have awaited us we are ignorant of, whereas we feel that we have undergone.[7]

Daer complained that the Scots Courts of Law had taken to themselves powers materially affecting the liberty of the subject. 'Our civil establishment distinct, even our greed and national vanity working to retain these offices for natives', so the English remained ignorant of the internal situation in Scotland. 'We have suffered the misery which is perhaps inevitable to a lesser and remote country in a junction where the Governing powers are united but the Nations are not.'

One of the greatest bonds of Union was that the reformers of both nations needed each other. Daer believed parliamentary reform would give the Scots more say in government and 'relieve you of that vermin from this country who infect your court, parliament and every establishment'. But many differed from him. 'We may require to be treated with delicacy and tenderness as a Nation whose temper is somewhat sour, who have sometimes met with insults and always felt the degradation of artificial inferiority.' To judge from Muir's remarks at the Convention and his later attitude he almost certainly shared Daer's views.

CHAPTER 5

France

Muir arrived at Calais on 15 January and posted on to Paris where he put up at the Hôtel de Toulon in the rue des Fosses du Temple. He joined with 'many friends of humanity of every nation and every party' in fruitless efforts to save the King. Louis XVI's execution on 21 January had little immediate effect on the metropolis and Muir was soon introduced to a far more exhilarating, sophisticated society than he had encountered before. The moderate Girondins, mostly lawyers and writers, who were then in power, were internationally minded on principle and welcomed foreigners with enthusiasm. A cosmopolitan, progressive community had developed containing inevitably some cranks and impractical idealists, a few crooks and spies. Desmoulins said such a collection of people had not been seen since the Tower of Babel.

At least 40,000 foreigners were in the city and the British contingent was the largest. Their rendezvous was White's Hotel, later known as the Hôtel de Philadelphia in honour of the American colony who lived in it. The British Club met there, its members, English, Scottish, and Irish, dazzled by the Revolution. They included Lord Edward Fitzgerald, cashiered for presenting an address to the National Assembly and toasting French victories, Jeremiah Joyce, writer, Unitarian minister, and tutor to Lord Stanhope's children, and Nicholas Madgett, whom the British rightly suspected of being an Irish spy. Dissensions broke out among the club members and it was dissolved in February. Some members regarded their native land as the perfect model the French should emulate, others viewed the Revolution as a new kind of religion to be imitated and, if necessary, imposed by force in Britain. Captain Monroe, the British agent left in Paris to keep an eye on events, reported that 'our countrymen who have been endeavouring to ruin their country are now struggling for consequence among themselves.'

There were many descendants of refugees from the '15 and '45 in

Paris; also several Scottish businessmen. Scotland had a long tradition of commerce with France and, in spite of the Revolution, the
policy of increasing continental trade initiated by Pitt was continued.

Muir met another acquaintance in Paris, James Smith, a Glasgow
gunsmith. He had been indicted for sedition as author of an advertisement in the *Glasgow Advertiser* praising *The Rights of Man*. His
counsel advised him to disappear until the court was in a better
temper so he fled to France and was outlawed. Smith sent a letter to
the Secretary of the Glasgow Friends of the People, which was
opened at Glasgow Post Office:

I had the honour to dine with Mr. Maxwell and Mr. Muir. We met him by
mere accident in a coffee house in the Palais Royal. We had all the fashionable dishes, with variety of wines – Burgundy etc. – for 3/6d. All perfectly
quiet here since the death of the King. . . . much safer than Glasgow, no
robberies, or pickpockets . . . women very well dressed.

They had 'been to visit Helen Maria Williams, author of Poems and
Letters from France, also Thomas Christie, author of History of the
Revolution, and his wife. In these houses almost all the great literary
and political characters in Paris congregate. . . .'

Dr. William Maxwell of Kirkconnell was a friend of Burns. Helen
Maria Williams had initially gone to France because her sister married a French Protestant clergyman. She was very pretty, intelligent,
affected but warm-hearted. Her poetry, journals, and travel books
had considerable success. She had been famous in London for her
support of liberal causes and her cultural tea-parties. Horace Wal-
pole referred to her and her friend Anna Barbauld as Deborah and
Jael. Miss Williams enthusiastically adopted the principles of the
Revolution, settled in Paris, and was taken up by Madame Roland.
She and her mother held a Sunday evening salon in the rue du Bac
which was attended by leading Girondists and distinguished foreigners. Her songs were sung after toasts at dinners at White's. She
was the friend, and later became the mistress, of an enigmatic figure,
John Hurford Stone. He was a Unitarian, extremely clever, witty, a
shrewd businessman, a friend of Fox, Sheridan, Price, and Priestley.
Talleyrand was a frequent guest at his celebrated dinner-parties. He
manufactured chemicals in England, went to Paris in April 1792 to
set up a chemical factory, and settled there with his family. Stone was
an ardent supporter of the Revolution. The Girondins thought

highly of him and his advice on English affairs. Stone had dealings
with Margarot, a leading member of the London Corresponding
Society, and, for ideological reasons, plotted against the British
Government. Although he had no connection with Ireland he
became involved in French intrigues with the United Irishmen. In
1795 he and his brother William were indicted for high treason. His
brother was acquitted, but John was convicted *in absentia* and
England barred to him. Stone's wife had been very promiscuous and
he finally obtained a French divorce. He fell in love with Helen Maria
Williams and set up house with her, but there is no concrete evidence
that they ever married.

Muir met Paine, who held court at White's Hotel. He also made
friends with many of the Girondins including the philosopher the
Marquis de Condorcet who called Muir *'le doux Écossais'*.* Muir
was invited to the salons of intellectuals such as Madame Roland.
Here, in contrast to narrow Edinburgh society, aristocrats and men
of humble origin met as equals. He remained an ardent francophile
for the rest of his life.

Muir began writing letters from the moment he arrived in France.
There is no clear indication in his correspondence whether he originally intended to return and stand trial. Cross-Channel posts were
erratic, taking from ten days to two months if they were detained by
the *Comité de Surveillance*. Several of Muir's letters to Skirving and
Johnston took a long time to reach them. To James Campbell:

> I wrote you from Calais and from Paris, and impatiently expect your answer.
> Write me fully about my private affairs, but about nothing else. Whenever
> you or my friends judge it expedient I will immediately return; but I cannot
> leave Paris without regret. I am honoured by the notice and friendship of an
> amiable and distinguished circle; and to a friend of humanity, it affords
> much consolation to find according feeling in a foreign land.

Muir wrote again on 27 January to say he would return whenever
Campbell thought proper, but it would be with reluctance that he
would 'quit Paris for a month or two'. 'Tell Johnston, Skirving and
Moffat no distance of space shall obliterate my recollection of them.'
An odd phrase if he really expected to see them within a few weeks;

---

* Mackenzie says[1] he met Lafayette who referred to him as 'the brave Scottish
advocate'. This is impossible as Lafayette had already fled and been imprisoned in
Austria, though Muir could have met Madame de Lafayette who was still in Paris.

besides Muir must have known his trial would come on before a
month was up.

Campbell, who was clearly fond of Muir, complained in a letter
dated 26 January how hurt he was that Muir had left without saying
goodbye and had written to other friends first. In his opinion it had
been imprudent to go to France. Muir may well have avoided Campbell, knowing he would try to dissuade him from going abroad.
Throughout his life Muir was curiously blind to circumstances and it
is quite possible that he failed to appreciate the construction that
would be put upon his visit to Paris. Campbell reported that about
half an hour before writing he had been served with Thomas's
indictment. His trial had been fixed for 11 February. He enclosed a
letter from James Muir 'who is extremely uneasy'. These letters
reached Mackintosh in London on 29 January and a Frenchman
took them on to Paris. Copies were sent by post to Muir c/o Stone.
Skirving wrote that Johnston was to be charged for publishing too
accurate an account of the judges' comments at the *Bee* trial (Johnston received three months imprisonment) and optimistically
declared that no one believed a jury would convict Muir. On 7
February Mackintosh told Campbell that he had been expecting
Muir daily, but 'I think he is delayed due to the embargo laid on ships
in French ports and so a plea to delay his trial should be entered'.

Even if Muir intended to return, he would now have found it
difficult to do so, for on 1 February France declared war on England.
In the eighteenth century civilians were little restricted by warfare
and could travel freely behind the battle-fronts, but Grenville, the
Foreign Secretary, had passed an order on 8 January by which no one
could enter England unless he had a passport from the Principal
Secretary of State, who could refuse an entry permit on the grounds
that the applicant was a dangerous revolutionary. In retaliation no
British subjects were allowed to travel across France or embark at
ports unless they had a passport from the Department of Foreign
Affairs. Smith wrote that Muir:

will set out the moment he procures his passport, which is now a work of
some difficulty. Mr. Muir makes a great sacrifice in coming back so soon as
he has already made a very great proficiency in the language, has made
valuable and dear connections and is enchanted with the climate.

On 31 January J.B. reported that no letters had arrived from Muir:

'His friends here suspect that their letters to him have been kept up, in order that he may not appear and of consequence be outlawed.' A letter of Muir's dated 13 February was taken to Scotland by a traveller and published on 1 March in the newspapers:

Upon the evening of the 8th I received letters from my father and my agent Mr. Campbell informing me . . . that my trial was fixed for Monday 11th instant. The distance and the shortness of the time could not permit me to reach Edinburgh by that day. War is declared between England and France and the formalities requisite to be gone through, before I could procure my passport, would at least have consumed three days. I will return to Scotland without delay. To shrink from danger would be unbecoming my own character and your confidence. I dare challenge the most minute investigation of my public and private conduct. Armed with innocence I appeal to Justice, and I disdain to supplicate favours.[2]

Muir's trial was postponed to 25 February but, as he did not return, he was outlawed and his father's bail forfeited. Erskine, as Dean of the Faculty of Advocates, raised the question of Muir's membership, and on 6 March it was unanimously agreed that he should be struck off the roll. According to Mackenzie this did not distress him because, if acquitted, he intended to go to America and practise at the bar there. Extraordinary rumours circulated about Muir. Some claimed 'His first visit to his native country will be like that of Coriolanus with an army of the enemy at his back,' others that he had enlisted in the National Guard.[3] His doings were discussed everywhere. People became his enemies through hatred of the opinions attributed to him.

J.B. learnt the contents of a letter from Muir to his father. According to this third-hand report Muir had been commissioned by the seven proprietors of a cotton mill in the West to purchase £50,000 worth of land in France where they meant to set up a factory. 'The whole company with implements were to go over as soon as they could wind up their affairs and establish an extensive cotton factory.' Dundas became greatly agitated but, on investigation, it turned out that the scheme had been shelved till war was over. In the final paragraph of the letter:

Mr. Muir adds that he would have come over and stood his trial and paid any fine, however high, if he had been certain he would not have been condemned to imprisonment or sent to Botany Bay.

If this is correct, Muir had already decided not to return; though it is highly unlikely – albeit prophetic – that he expected to be sent to Botany Bay. On 14 March J.B. reported that Skirving and Campbell had received further letters from Muir saying he would return as soon as he could get a passport, but rumours spread round Edinburgh in April that he was going to America.

At the end of 1792, encouraged by Burke, the Duke of Portland and his friends had agreed to support Pitt and the Tories. The following year some Whigs accepted office. Only Fox with a dwindling group of followers remained in opposition. The war was at first popular and roused the nation's latent anti-gallicism. A great wave of patriotism swept the country. Now that it was inextricably, though unfairly, connected with the French, there was more widespread opposition to reform. What had seemed harmless a year ago appeared far more sinister now. Many liberals were profoundly disillusioned with France and found themselves obliged to defend a republic which had executed its King and confiscated the property of the Church and nobility. Widespread conservative reaction to the violence and aggression of the French Revolution reached such dimensions that burgh and county reform agitation, which had far wider and more influential support than parliamentary reform, was suspended.

A second Convention of the Scottish Friends of the People met in Edinburgh on 30 April. The calibre of delegates was far below that of the previous one. Only about twelve who had attended the first were present. Skirving took part, but none of the Edinburgh lawyers. Extremist, ill-educated members outnumbered the moderates. The proceedings were less orderly, but also less important. Still, the Convention did continue to promote petitions.

The parliamentary reform movement had been struggling against increasing difficulties, but made one concerted final effort. On 6 May Grey presented a petition from the London Friends of the People. This was supported by nearly 30 other associations, of which 13 were from Scotland, including the areas where Muir had been most active, Glasgow, Campsie, Kilmarnock, and Paisley. Macleod's petition from Edinburgh stretched the whole length of the House. Grey asked the House for a committee to consider the petitions, but they rejected his motion by 282 to 41. It had long been evident that Parliament, not surprisingly, wanted no change in the electoral system. The Friends of the People had shut their eyes to the fact, which most politicians appreciated, that the country as well was now against them. This crushing defeat marked the end of moderate agitation for constitutional reform. However, the rebuff did not have entirely the desired effect in Scotland. On 21 June the Lord Advocate complained that he 'had no idea the Friends of the People would have stuck so long and so well together'. In July Professor Millar was said to have drawn up a petition against the war signed by many Glaswegians. J.B. was set to find evidence against Palmer 'that most determined rebel in Scotland', who had taken 'an increasingly important part in the Edinburgh Society since Muir's departure'.

On 4 March David Blair, a naval officer turned Glasgow manufacturer, married Muir's sister Janet. He won his bride in an underhand fashion. Janet had been engaged to a naval officer whose ship was ordered to the West Indies. Blair – a fellow officer – turned up at Huntershill saying that her fiancé had died. He was lying. He wanted to marry her himself. After their marriage the truth came out and caused great misery. Little is known about Blair – whether he liked or disliked his brother-in-law, whether initially he approved or disapproved of reform. He was on the list of prosecution witnesses for Muir's trial but was never called. Blair appears to have prospered, for two of his sons became naval officers, one became a lawyer and another a Captain in the East India Company, while his daughter married – well – the Revd. Laurence Lockhart of Milton Lockhart and Germiston, half-brother of J. B. Lockhart, Sir Walter Scott's biographer and son-in-law. The wedding could have been arranged before Thomas's arrest, or fixed to take place when he would, with luck, have returned to Scotland. Equally, after Thomas had been outlawed and could clearly not be present, his sister may have decided to get married at once.

Muir meanwhile was present during some of the most dramatic months in French history. In March the Convention declared war against Spain. Now almost all Europe united against France; as a result her army was defeated in Belgium. A Jacobin crowd attacked the headquarters of the Girondin press, but a *coup d'état* was averted. Inflation was rampant, arrests were made, lists of suspects drawn up; incipient rioting and looting in Paris increased. On 6 April the Committee of Public Safety was formed. A week later there was an attempt to impeach Marat for issuing a most inflammatory address; on 25 April he was triumphantly acquitted. This led to the downfall of the Girondins and the ascendancy of the Jacobins.

The position of foreigners became more perilous as the political situation deteriorated. Although the mail-boats had been suspended in March, it would appear from external evidence that Muir received a letter from his father telling him that he had been outlawed and advising him to go to America for the time being – where his family had relations and business connections.[4] Muir apparently decided to follow his father's advice. On 3 April he obtained a declaration of residence certifying that he had lived at the Hôtel de Suède, rue de l'Université, since 20 March. On 23 April he received a passport from the Council General of the Commune of Paris, countersigned by the Minister of Foreign Affairs, to travel to Philadelphia. On 4 May he received a passport from the Commissary of the Tuileries section of the Committee of Surveillance. He set off for Havre de Grâce where his passport was given a further endorsement. On 16 May he booked a passage to New York for 900 livres, but because of difficulties with the authorities the ship was delayed.

From a distance Muir heard of the terrifying events in Paris. On 31 May the *sans-culottes* rose against the Convention; surrounded by 80,000 armed men it was forced to yield. Condorcet fled; Madame Roland was arrested; Robespierre and the Jacobin majority took over. On 7 June Robespierre demanded more stringent laws against foreigners. Four days later he proposed that they should be expelled. Later an order was passed ordering their imprisonment. Another American ship, the *Hope*, arrived at Havre de Grâce bound for Baltimore via Belfast. Muir transferred to it and escaped in time.

The ship docked at Belfast on 17 July. Muir set off for Dublin where he was welcomed and entertained by the United Irishmen. He met Curran and spent a week with Hamilton Rowan at Rathcoffey. From Rowan he collected letters to Macleod and Palmer and a large quantity of printed matter. While Muir was in Dublin Captain George Towers, master of the *Hope*, wrote guardedly to Muir's father to inform him that his son was in Ireland. James replied in a state of dismay and agitation:

I am at very great loss how to answer your letter, as it's not understood by me: if it's the Friend that I have, if it's he, I would be overjoyed to see his handwriting, and to know what has become of him these three months. I thought he had been at Philadelphia ere now, where letters are forwarded for him. Mr. John Richardson . . . is to sail in the *Almy* of New York directly, and has two packets of letters and a trunk for him; and there are many letters wrote for him to the first people of America. Once he were there, he'll get letters to General Washington. . . . the loss of this young man has been a dreadful affliction to us. Please give your friend this letter. . . . I hope in a year or two he can return, if he doth not love America; and be so good as cause him write me one line in your letter. You can direct it; and if he does not choose to sign it, you can put your initials to it.

Muir sent a cautious note to Towers from Dublin on 27 July:

This day I received yours and will be down upon Tuesday evening. . . . I am happy to hear my friends are well. I will write them from Belfast.

On 29 July Muir collected a letter from Dr. Drennan's sister to another sister in St. Andrews. The next day the *Hope* crossed the Northern Channel and Muir transferred to a small boat which carried him to Portpatrick. There he was recognized by a customs official, Carmichael, who had once worked as clerk in an attorney's office and seen Muir pleading at the Edinburgh bar. Accounts vary as to what happened next. Muir said that Carmichael was the first to recognize him, that he posted on to Stranraer where he made a declaration and surrendered voluntarily to Ross and a magistrate. According to one version Muir put up at an inn in Stranraer where Mr. Boniface, the landlord, became suspicious and called the local magistrate; according to another Boniface was acquainted with the Muir family, took fright at Thomas's arrival, and sent for the authorities. At Muir's trial the Lord Advocate made much of the fact that he had landed clandestinely. Boniface or Carmichael may have tipped off the authorities, but, as Muir pointed out in his defence, the prosecution failed to call either Carmichael or Ross, although their names were on the list of prosecution witnesses. Muir claimed this was because their evidence could prove that he entered the country openly.[5]

Muir was arrested and on him were found: a red turkey pocketbook which contained letters from Campbell and Skirving which he had received in Paris; his French passports; his ticket for New York; his certificate of election to the United Irishmen and the letters from Hamilton Rowan and Drennan's sister; also his father's and his own letters to Captain Towers, and a vast number of pamphlets, some of which, if he proposed to surrender to the authorities, were not likely to improve their opinion of him:

29 copies of *An address from the Catholic Committee of the United Irishmen exhorting Catholics to co-operate with Protestants to obtain a reform of the franchise*:

5 copies of resolutions of the United Irishmen at a meeting on 15 July 1793;

24 copies of an abstract of the trial of Francis Graham, who had attempted to get a witness to give false evidence against Napper Tandy and Hamilton Rowan;

11 copies of an Act of George III to prevent tumultuous risings, printed in Dublin in 1787;

84 copies of a paper printed at Rathcoffey under Hamilton Rowan's direction including a quotation from Milton advocating unlicensed printing.

At his trial Muir said:

I knew only two ways by which I could possibly return home. The first by way of Hamburg; the second by the longer but more certain circuit of America. I adopted the latter as more safe and less liable to interruption. I found a vessel which was to sail for New York. . . . that vessel by an embargo was detained for nearly three months. In this interval another American ship, the *Hope*, arrived. The Captain was to touch in at Belfast. . . . I immediately embraced this opportunity of returning by way of Ireland, not to implore favour, not to ask protection, but to demand justice. To pass from France to any of the dominions of Britain I had no passport – my passport was to America. After a short passage I was landed in Ireland. There I remained no longer than nine days. I concealed not my name. I appeared publicly. To all I announced my situation and intention.

The true course of Muir's actions cannot be unravelled now. Did he at first intend to return to Edinburgh but was seduced by the charms of Paris into delaying until war provided a valid excuse for non-appearance? Had he arranged with his father to wait in Paris until it was certain he would be brought to trial, in which case he would go to America? His reason for travelling via America rather than Hamburg is very thin. The exchange of letters between Towers and the Muirs carefully concealed Thomas's identity. Muir could have planned to go to Philadelphia, but changed his mind after visiting Dublin. There he found the United Irishmen cheerfully suffering harassment from the authorities. Hamilton Rowan, who had resolutely (or obstinately) ignored all hints from friends at the Castle to move to England, was waiting to be arrested. Fired by Rowan's enthusiasm, and by the atmosphere of heroic sacrifice, Muir may have decided that he too must demonstrate his unwavering support for the cause and fulfil his promise to his fellow reformers that he would return to clear his name. He may have hoped to be acquitted, but decided that it was worth a year or two's imprisonment to become an honourable martyr. The letters he carried indicate that he intended to go to Edinburgh. From Drennan's sister Eliza: 'This letter goes by a gentleman that is to set off for Edinburgh tonight.' From Hamilton Rowan to Macleod: 'Mr. Muir has been so good as to say he would converse with you on this subject, and to him I again refer you for the present state of this country.' To Palmer: 'Mr. Muir is so anxious to get off from Dublin on his road home, that I am the more flattered by the visit he has paid me here. . . . I shall be most anxious to hear from Scotland . . . of the safety of my new friend. . . .'

It is possible Muir planned to visit his family and friends clandestinely; but it would have been difficult for him to move about Edinburgh without being recognized, or to contact Macleod and Palmer, who were watched by spies, without being detected. Besides, if this was his aim, why did he not conceal his arrival in Scotland more carefully? He may have kept the ticket for America to prove – if arrested – that he could have escaped if he wished, but why did he carry his father's letter, the one document which would indicate that he did not intend to return? Conceivably he did not envisage being searched and wanted to keep it as a memento of his father.

The Stranraer Sheriff reported: 'Muir was apprehended here on his way from Ireland. He seems a good deal confused re the idea of Stranraer Jail till he is conveyed to Edinburgh.' Robert Dundas informed Nepean, 'I have little doubt, though he avow his intention of coming home to have been with a view to stand trial, that he is an emissary from France or the disaffected in Ireland.'

Muir's position was now far more serious than when he was charged in January. Deprived of easy contact by the war, Muir would not have realized how much the climate of opinion at home had altered. The majority of upper- and middle-class supporters had abandoned reform agitation; it was now almost entirely carried on by urban artisans. There was general disapproval, even hatred, of anyone with radical tendencies. Reform became synonymous with sedition. Fear, prejudice, government propaganda, war hysteria, ignorance, led to the suppression of freedom of opinion. To people who knew nothing about him Muir had become a symbol of rabid republicanism and treason, a man who had deliberately gone to France and associated with regicides. If he already intended coming

home and wanted a fair hearing he should never have jaunted down
to Dublin. The Irish had always intrigued with the French and, since
war was declared, anyone who belonged to the United Irishmen was
bound to be suspect.

On Sunday 4 August Muir was clapped in handcuffs and leg-irons
and taken by coach to Edinburgh where he was lodged in the
Tolbooth. On 9 August, escorted by a troop of soldiers with drawn
bayonets, he was brought to court – where he petitioned for recall of
the sentence of fugitation imposed when he had failed to appear in
February. The Lord Advocate commented that 'Whatever motive
Mr. Muir had for leaving his country was best known to himself, but
one thing was certain, he left it at a very critical period, and when
there lay against him a very serious accusation;'[6] the sentence of
fugitation, however, could be erased. Muir asked for bail as he
would not be able to prepare his defence in a crowded jail. Not
surprisingly his father's pledge was refused this time, but bail put up
by Campbell and other friends was accepted.

Morthland and Millar asked Henry Erskine to defend Muir. He
agreed, but Muir refused his offer. Another able Whig lawyer also
offered to defend him, but Muir again refused. Erskine later said: 'He
declined my assistance. He pleaded his own cause and you know the
result.'[7] Cockburn, with thirty-five years' hindsight, made the
shrewd comment: 'Muir had the folly to decline, partly from vanity,
partly from despair.' Muir wanted to defend the cause of reform,
Erskine wanted to restrain him from doing so. Muir, who had a good
opinion of himself, may have believed he could conduct his own case
perfectly satisfactorily and wished to shine in court for the last time.
He may also have wished to spare his fellow lawyers from undertak-
ing an unpopular defence which might prejudice their careers. It was
a disastrous error of judgement. No one pleads well in his own cause.
A man whose future is at stake cannot have the necessary detach-
ment to pounce on an advantage or counteract an unexpected attack.
He cannot see the case from other points of view, or consider
impartially what will best sway judge and jury in his favour.

CHAPTER 6

<><><><><><><><><><><><><><><><><><><><><><><><><><><><><><><><><><>

The Trial

A man who was a child at the time later described the day of Muir's trial, 30 August, 1793:

> It took place on a Thursday. It was thundery and exceeding dark, rain fell in torrents. There was but one topic and interest, Muir and the trial. Our house, the city were empty. All had gone to witness it.[1]

The High Court of Justiciary sat in a small dark room with a low gallery at the south-east end of the Parliament Hall. The Great Hall was crowded and the whole of Parliament Square outside. The trial began at 10 a.m. and lasted for sixteen hours.

Robert Dundas, the Lord Advocate, conducted the prosecution. He was a poor speaker of moderate legal ability. Of the five judges Lords Swinton, Dunsinnan, Abercrombie, and Henderland were honest, well-meaning nonentities. They had no experience of political trials, were terrified by what they believed to be the threat of revolution, and dominated by Braxfield, the strongest man on the Scottish bench. He was the model for Robert Louis Stevenson's Weir of Hermiston. His origins were humble; his grandfather had been the Earl of Selkirk's gardener. He was not learned but highly talented, with great powers of reasoning – a profoundly practical lawyer. For many years he had had the largest practice at the bar. A formidable, dangerous man, gross, heavily built with black eyebrows and penetrating eyes, he spoke in a growling voice with a strong Scots accent and deliberately used coarse turns of phrase.

Muir, elegantly dressed, arrived late and was rebuked for keeping the court waiting. The indictment, drawn up by Robert Dundas, had four main charges:

1. Exciting disaffection by seditious speeches, especially at meetings Muir had been instrumental in calling;
2. Advising and exhorting persons to purchase and peruse seditious and wicked publications;
3. Circulating various seditious papers:
   (a) *The Rights of Man*;

(b) Two pamphlets approved by the Friends of Reform in Paisley: *A Declaration of Rights* and an *Address to the People*;

(c) *A Dialogue between the Governors and the Governed*: an extract from Volney's *Ruins, or a Survey of the Evolution of Empires* (this was an abstract and speculative history covering 6,000 years, not alluding specifically to any country, though clearly much of it was about France);

(d) *The Patriot*;

4. Reading a seditious and inflammatory writing in public, viz. the United Irishmen's address.

Selections were quoted from the more extreme passages in *The Rights of Man* and *The Patriot*. *The Patriot* was full of the usual radical jargon,

Rouse then ye Britons! Awake from the slumbering state of apathy in which you have so long suffered yourselves ingloriously to remain! . . . Raise your voice – the voice of the people – and sound in the ears of tyrants and their abettors that you will be free . . .

but its main theme was the injustice of Old Sarum and Septennial parliaments. To conclude the indictment, it was asserted that in January, to evade punishment, Muir had left the kingdom. He had failed to appear to stand trial. Then

having lately in a private and clandestine manner come into this country, by way of Ireland, he was discovered and apprehended.

Under Scots law counsel submits a list of witnesses and a written defence. This Muir had handed in the evening before. The Lord Advocate asked Muir if he had anything further to add to his defence as he would be debarred from doing so later. Muir said no,

. . . he had exerted every effort to procure a more equal representation of the people in the House of Commons. . . . I deny that I ever advised the people to accomplish that great object by any means which the constitution did not sanction. I grant that I advised the people to read different publications upon both sides. . . . I consider the ignorance of the people to be the source from which despotism flows. . . . Knowledge must always precede reformation, and who shall dare to say that the people should be debarred from information, where it concerns them so materially? I am accused of sedition: and yet I can prove by thousands of witnesses that I warned the people of that crime, exhorted them to adopt none but measures which were constitutional, and entreated them to connect liberty with knowledge, and both with morality.

The judges took an exaggeratedly severe view of the charges against Muir, but their comments reflected opinions prevalent at the time. Henderland said Muir was charged with endeavouring to create a rebellion: 'Had Muir observed the situation of a neighbouring country, he would have seen that similar crimes had like an earthquake swallowed up her best citizens, and endangered the lives and properties of all. His actions would introduce levelling principles . . . which had occasioned so much blood more than a century ago.' Swinton said: 'he did not believe that in the memory of man there ever had been a libel of a more dangerous tendency read in that Court. There was hardly a line which . . . did not amount to high treason.'

Muir did not challenge the relevancy of the charges. In Scottish trials the defence could claim that, for example, the acts cited in the indictment did not constitute the crime with which the accused was charged. Normally there were long arguments about this. In general Muir adopted the wrong attitude. He conducted his defence with spirit, vigour, dignity, and intelligence, but he made one or two important mistakes of which this was the first. The Government wanted to make an example of him. Instead of concentrating on demolishing the prosecution's case, based entirely on circumstantial evidence, Muir played into the Court's hand by emphasizing that he was a reformer and making political speeches.

Now came the impanelling of the jury. A disadvantage for the accused of Scottish courts at the time was that the judges really selected the juries themselves. The Sheriffs of the three Lothians, standing officers of the Crown and creatures of Dundas, sent in lists of 45 men. From these 135 the justiciary clerk, appointed by Braxfield, chose 45, of whom the court picked 15. Peremptory challenge was not allowed. The jurors could only be challenged on grounds of insanity, outlawry, deafness, or dumbness. On this occasion care had been taken to choose jurymen who belonged to the Goldsmiths' Hall Association. Two of the jurors had signed the Association's notice offering a reward for evidence of anyone's circulating Paine's work. The second man, called Captain John Inglis, a naval officer, said 'that he was a servant of the government. That he did not consider it proper that Mr. Muir should be tried by a jury composed of servants of government and he begged leave to decline being a juryman.' The court told him there was no impropriety in his serving. After Braxfield had selected the first five jurymen, he asked Muir according to custom if he had any objection. Muir 'protested against their sitting

on his trial because they belonged to an Association who had publicly judged and condemned him without knowing him.' The court
unanimously rejected his objection. Muir made the same objection
to all the other jurymen and offered to prove his point. 'I demand
justice. Let me be tried fairly, not by a jury of the Association of
Goldsmiths Hall, nor by a jury of the Association of the Friends of
the People, but by men unconnected with either.' The prosecution
made no attempt to contradict Muir's assertion, but Blair, the Solicitor General, replied – quite inaccurately – that he was accused of
forming associations contrary to the Constitution, yet he objected to
gentlemen who formed associations in its defence. In despair Muir
implored the jury to be just: 'He believed them to be men of truth and
integrity, but he never could cease recalling to their attention the
peculiarity of their situation. They had already determined his fate.
They had already judged his cause; and, as they valued their reputation, their own internal peace, he entreated. . .'. Here Blair interrupted to say his conduct 'was exceedingly improper in taking up
their time'.

The *Morning Chronicle* commented that Braxfield spoke 'with
much strength of language'. Throughout the trial he treated Muir
with brutality and arrogance and bullied his witnesses, many of
whom were unsophisticated countrymen. When Muir apologized
for a slight mistake he was told, 'he was not in a place for making
apologies'. The printed reports of the trial given no idea of the
conduct of the Bench, which horrified spectators. Sir Samuel Romilly
wrote to a French friend M. Dumont: 'I am not surprised that you
have been shocked at the account you have read of Muir's trial; you
would have been much more shocked if you had been present at it, as
I was.'

The prosecution called thirteen witnesses. Muir objected to the
first, Johnston, because he had gone about saying he would do
everything in his power to hang him. The judges said this was no
objection as the witness might have said so to get himself disquali-
fied. In fact Johnston's evidence was totally innocuous. He described
a meeting, principally composed of young weavers, at which Muir
had recommended order and regularity and told them to beware of
admitting immoral characters as members. Muir had said that
Paine's works were 'foreign to their purpose'. Johnston added that
after the meeting, when they foregathered in a baker's shop, he

believed Muir had mentioned Flower's book on the Constitution. The Lord Advocate immediately asked whether Muir had recommended Flower's book. Muir rightly objected, as the book had not been alluded to in the indictment and he 'couldn't be expected to be prepared without warning on all the books in the world that might be called seditious'. Braxfield then ruled the question perfectly legitimate as it 'had a tendency to establish the charge of sedition', although the book could not be produced in court and could not be shown to be seditious. The trial bristled with such irregularities.

Johnston was followed by an extremely unpleasant character, the Revd. James Lapslie, Minister of Campsie. He was an old friend of the Muir family and often stayed at Huntershill. When Thomas was arrested he abandoned the Muirs and curried favour with the authorities by trying to collect evidence against him. He ferreted out prospective witnesses and voluntarily came to court to give evidence. Muir was able to call several witnesses who attested that Lapslie had been present when they were examined before the Lanarkshire Sheriff and had hinted that they would be given a helping hand if they gave evidence against Muir. The Crown therefore abandoned Lapslie as a witness, Muir's one success of the trial.

The next witness, Henry Freeland, a Kirkintilloch weaver, was one of those whom Lapslie had attempted to suborn. Freeland said he had asked Muir what he thought of Paine's book. Muir had replied, 'it had rather a tendency to mislead weak minds'. Freeland had taken it and found the leaves had not been cut. The Lord Advocate suggested – which may have been true – that this was a ploy to distribute the book surreptitiously. John Muir, a cousin, testified that, when he called at James Muir's house, Thomas asked him if he had seen Paine's book. He replied no, but that he would like to borrow it. Thomas said he had no copy, but sent out a maid to buy it with the witness's money at Brash and Reid's – a most respectable Glasgow bookshop. The witness, when asked if he would have purchased it, said, with sensible Scots thrift, that 'he would not, if he could have borrowed it.' Wilson, Muir's barber, testified that Muir had recommended it as 'good for casual readers' in his shop – a joking allusion to its great popularity. This was a typical example of the intolerable position in which the prosecution placed Muir by contriving that he should be judged by chance remarks taken out of context.

The next witness, one William Muir, caused turmoil in court. He refused to swear the oath as it was contrary to his religious principles, but promised to tell the truth. The judges were most indignant and said, if he would not swear, he would be committed to perpetual imprisonment and they had no idea how he could ever be let out. Thomas Muir said, 'he believed him to be a good and conscientious man and, though a prosecution witness, he would admit every word he uttered though not upon oath.' The court said this was impossible and he was committed to prison. A few hours later William Muir reappeared. The Revd. William Dunn had overcome his scruples and he was prepared to swear. He corroborated Freeland's evidence and said that Muir had loaned him eleven numbers of *The Patriot* at Huntershill to show to a reading party. Three other witnesses testified that meetings had been called not by Muir but by 'the lads of the place and people of the neighbourhood', that Muir's speeches and comments were uniformly loyal, and that he thought 'most books were too much in the spirit of party.' He particularly recommended Blackstone's *Commentaries*, Erskine's *Institutes*, and Locke – a rather stiff course of reading for some of his less well educated audiences.

The only witness who produced much evidence to substantiate the second charge was Annie Fisher, the former scullery maid in the Muir household, and a great deal of it was patently untrue and contradicted by other witnesses. Her evidence was startlingly erudite and remarkably detailed about events of a year before. She had clearly been bribed and coached – possibly by Lapslie who had been present at her examination just before the trial. Annie said that Muir often told country people coming to his father's shop that *The Rights of Man* was a very good book and that she had frequently bought it for his Uncle Alexander and others. She herself was curious to see what was in it and had read a copy belonging to Mr. Muir's servant. Later Muir asked the Lord Advocate why he had not called his uncle Alexander, cited as a prosecution witness. The Lord Advocate said his feelings would not permit him to examine an uncle against his nephew. Muir retorted that it was really because Alexander Muir would contradict Fisher's evidence.

According to Fisher, Muir frequently read French law books. She reeled off the correct titles of all the pamphlets Muir was accused of circulating. She made some suspiciously scholarly comments on Volney, and said Muir considered France the most flourishing nation in the world. She had also heard Muir say that the Court of Justiciary would need a thorough reform too, for it was nonsense to see the parade with which the circuit lords came into Glasgow; that they got their money for nothing but pronouncing sentence of death upon poor creatures. At this point Muir protested that he had not been charged with speaking disrespectfully of the Court of Justiciary. The judges, instead of rejecting Fisher's evidence on this point as they should have done, overruled his objection, saying that in a case of sedition any evidence bearing on the subject was valid, even though not specified in the indictment. But Muir had been accused of certain specific acts, not sedition generally; besides criticism of the Court of Justiciary was no proof of disaffection. Romilly wrote to Jeremy Bentham that he doubted

whether this would be a very safe country at this moment for you to be found in; for I heard the judges . . . declare with great solemnity, upon the trial of Mr. Muir, that to say the courts of Justice needed reform was seditious, highly criminal, and betrayed a most hostile disposition towards the constitution.

Fisher concluded her evidence by saying that Muir had sent her to ask an organist in the street to play *Ça ira*. The Lord Advocate declared this was used in France 'as a signal for blood and carnage'. Muir now made another cardinal mistake; he said that 'he disdained to put a question to a witness of this description'. Conceivably Muir was so disgusted by Fisher's betrayal of his family that he could not bring himself to question her, but he took notes of her evidence and commented on it in his final speech. Possibly what Fisher said was true and Muir did not dare cross-examine her, but her evidence was not corroborated by any other witnesses. It was so pat that Muir should have been able to trip her up with a few smart questions. As Fisher left the box, Captain Inglis, the reluctant juror, asked if she 'had any quarrel with Mr. Muir's family at parting.' She replied that, on the contrary, her mistress had given her 5s. and Miss Muir a petticoat and other presents.'

James Campbell, Robert Forsyth, and James Denholm were then called to give evidence about the United Irishmen's address. They disagreed as to precisely what had happened. Only Forsyth recollected that Muir had defended the address, but all testified that Muir had agreed to send it back for revision.

The question of Muir's return to Scotland was gone into and here Thomas found himself on awkward ground. He protested that a private letter should not be shown, but the Lord Advocate insisted on reading James Muir's letter which, as he pointed out, contradicted Muir's assertion that he had surrendered voluntarily. Now came Muir's objection: that the prosecution had not produced the declaration he made before the Stranraer magistrate and that Carmichael and Ross, listed as prosecution witnesses, had not been called. If Muir had known they were not to be present he would have called them for his defence. This was another point where a dispassionate defending counsel would have been more likely to succeed in finding out what had really happened, and putting Muir's actions in the best light.

The prosecution augmented their case by grossly distorting two minor points. At a meeting in Kirkintilloch on 3 November Muir had incautiously mentioned French military successes and favourably compared French economic progress (at first erroneously believed to be brilliant) with that of Britain.[2] The Lord Advocate said that by asserting France's economy was superior, Muir made his audience prefer France, diminished their attachment to Britain, and provoked revolution. Secondly, he twisted Skirving's evidence that Muir 'had been advised by friends that, if he went to France, he might influence leading people there to mitigate the sentence of the French King' into 'he was sent to France by the persons styling themselves the Friends of the People'. If Muir had been sent as an emissary from a British society to France, this would have been tantamount to high treason.

The prosecution case was remarkably flimsy. They failed to produce any evidence – for there was none – of the first charge. The third charge depended on the uncorroborated evidence of William Muir. The fourth was not proved. Muir admitted that he had read the United Irishmen's address; but, though its phraseology was rather wild, it was not seditious. The second charge was the only one on which any proof of Muir's guilt was adduced. Five witnesses gave evidence that Muir had recommended and circulated seditious books. Fisher was an extremely suspect witness and the others' evidence was not at all substantial. None of it corroborated the assertions of the indictment that by so doing Muir wished to 'produce a spirit of insurrection' and to stir the people to 'acts of outrage and opposition to the established government'.

Muir called 21 witnesses. The Lord Advocate complained that there was no need to call so many to testify to the same thing. Muir replied that he intended to bring witnesses from every part of the country where he had attended reform meetings. They were respectable, mostly from the 'middling classes'. The Lord Advocate implied that, being reformers, they were not reliable, but no one contradicted them.

The evidence for the defence was strong. All witnesses corroborated that Muir had impressed on audiences he harangued that reform must be sought by constitutional means alone. He encouraged the pursuit of knowledge and discouraged correspondence with Jacobin clubs. He thought 'Paine's system was impracticable; that a division of property was a chimera'; 'there were some things in Paine which would hardly do'. When William Reid, the Glasgow bookseller, had asked his opinion Muir had said, 'it was an improper book and there might be danger in selling it.'

The Lord Advocate sneered at Muir – 'a gentleman, a member of the Bar' – associating with one of his witnesses, Barclay – 'an ignorant old countryman' – who was an Elder of the Kirk at Cadder. Muir rose to his defence, using strong words which cannot have gone down well with the jury, but which indicate his point of view:

I tell the Lord Advocate, the aristocracy of Scotland, I glory more in the friendship of such an old, poor and virtuous man, than in the friendship of the highest titled peer, who derives the source of his guilty grandeur from the calamities of the people; who wrings out a splendid but miserable revenue from their sorrow and distress . . . which he squanders in dissipation. . . .

The Lord Advocate barely cross-examined Muir's witnesses. He conducted his share of the prosecution with moderation but, when addressing the jury, became abusive and grossly distorted the evidence. He began by stating that:

All those persons who have had the courage to come and stand trial at this bar, have met with the same fate – they have all been found guilty. I trust as the evidence has unfolded the diabolical and mischievous conduct of this person, he will receive a similar verdict. First he has circulated Paine's book with an obstinacy and pertinacity which plainly indicate that his . . . intention was to overturn our happy constitution. Secondly he was always making seditious harangues among knots of ignorant labourers and poor manufacturers who, had it not been for him, would have remained peaceable and contented and never thought of that incendiary Paine, nor of forming meetings, till he came, like the demon of sedition, recommending that club government which in another country has produced so much anarchy and confusion. . . .

He had lately returned,

the pest of Scotland . . . tainted from head to foot . . . weaving his filthy web to ensnare the unwary . . . unworthy to live under the protection of the law . . . . he had intended to revolutionise these countries in the manner of France.[3]

The Lord Advocate then most incorrectly mentioned that among the papers Muir had brought with him was a letter to Palmer 'a man whom most of you must know, who is indicted to stand trial at Perth in the course of a few days. You may in some degree judge of a man by the company he keeps.'

In reply Muir made a long, impassioned speech. It was a heroic political oration, a noble defence of reform, a contrast to the petty bigotry of the prosecution, but totally unsuitable as a legal defence. The prosecution had been doing their best to fill the jurors' minds with alarm and resentment; Muir's only chance lay in trying to conciliate them. He should have confined himself to the facts of the case which were overwhelmingly in his favour. He might have been able to make the prosecution case look so feeble that even the packed jury would not convict. When Muir refused to give Erskine *carte blanche* to handle his case, he may have decided that conviction was inevitable and he would make a final plea for reform, using the court as a forum for his views. Muir made several references to posterity. Although he greatly overestimated his importance, if Muir did wish to become a political martyr, he succeeded in his ambition, for it is largely due to his trial that his name is remembered today.

Gentlemen this is the moment for which I have long and anxiously looked. . . . The records of this trial will pass down to posterity. When our ashes shall be scattered by the winds of heaven, the impartial voice of future times will rejudge your verdict. . . . This trial is no trivial matter. It affects me, but it affects the country more. The noise of it will pass down to other times, and posterity may fancy their most valuable rights connected with its consequences.

He began speaking at ten in the evening and continued for three hours. The trial had been long, several times Muir referred both to his own and the jurors' exhaustion. At one point, when he was going into the legal argument against the doctrine of constructive sedition, the jury began fidgeting, impatient to get away.

Muir ably reviewed the evidence against him. He exposed the injustice of deducing a plan to create disaffection from the fact of his having, at most, encouraged the purchase of *The Rights of Man* twice during a long period. At the time he lent *The Rights of Man* there was no law against it. Muir would have done better to have cross-examined Fisher earlier on, but he carefully dissected the discrepancies in her evidence and commented that there were other servants who had better opportunities of hearing his conversation. The pamphlets he was accused of distributing were perfectly harmless. It was wrong to take passages from their context and claim they were seditious. The prosecution had mutilated the United Irishmens' address to insinuate that it showed they wanted a dissolution of the Union. Generously but tactlessly Muir praised the United Irishmen: 'In the last moments of my life to have been a member of that society shall be my honour and my pride.'

Muir's general defence consisted of quotations from Blackstone and Locke. He pointed out that the Lord Advocate had attended burgh reform meetings. He referred to speeches by Pitt and the Duke of Richmond in support of Parliamentary reform. All reformers when accused cited Pitt's previous championing of the cause, but this was fruitless; as the prosecution invariably pointed out, Pitt had long since abandoned such ideas. Muir went into the question of the freedom of the press, quoting Cromwell: 'My cause is too strong to be hurt by paper shot'. He cited Plato, Hume, and More's *Utopia* published even in Henry VIII's reign, but most of the jurors would happily have condemned them all. Thomas Erskine, Henry's lawyer brother, who had marshalled his arguments more effectively, had vainly attempted to show at Paine's trial that earlier speculative writers had similar ideas. Muir said that he had contended for a reform of the franchise

because I consider it to be a measure essentially necessary to the salvation of the State, and to the stability of our boasted Constitution. . . . The Constitution has suffered the ravages of time and of corruption. The representation of the people is not what it once was, and is not such as I trust in God one day it shall be.

Some of the jury at this point showed disapproval. Muir said that he felt himself nearly exhausted:

Gentlemen of the jury, this is perhaps the last time that I shall address my country . . . from my infancy to this moment, I have devoted myself to the cause of the people. It is a good cause – it shall ultimately prevail – it shall finally triumph. Say then, openly, in your verdict, if you do condemn me, which I presume you will not, that it is for my attachment to this cause alone, and not for those vain and wretched pretexts, stated in the indictment, intended only to colour and disguise the real motives of my accusation.

The time will come, when men must stand or fall by their actions; when all human pageantry shall cease; when the hearts of all shall be laid open. If you regard your most important interests – if you wish that your conscience should whisper to you words of consolation, or speak to you in the terrible language of remorse – weigh well the verdict you are to pronounce. As for me, I am careless and indifferent to my fate. I can look danger, and I can look death in the face, for I am shielded by the consciousness of my own rectitude. . . . Nothing can destroy my inward peace of mind, arising from the remembrance of having discharged my duty.

When Muir sat down there was a unanimous burst of applause from the audience, who cheered three times. The Lord Advocate and the judges shook their heads and clenched their fists with rage. When the din had subsided Braxfield summed up. He made no attempt to be impartial, or give the jury judicial guidance on points of law. He instructed them to take into account the prevalence of disorders and risk of anarchy. He took for granted several points which had not been proved. He voiced current conservative feeling, but it was an indefensible harangue for a judge to make.

Braxfield said that it was not necessary to prove the whole indictment to find the accused guilty. If any one part was proven, it established the accused's guilt.

. . . there was a spirit of sedition in this country last winter, which made every good man very uneasy . . . . Yet Mr. Muir had at that time gone about among ignorant country people and among the lower classes . . . making them leave off their work, and inducing them to believe that a Reform was absolutely necessary for preserving their liberty, which, had it not been for him, they never would have suspected was in danger. Judge whether this appears to you, as to me, sedition . . . . What could Muir do in France? . . . pretending to be an ambassador to a foreign country, without lawful authority, was rebellion. And he pretends to have had influence with those wretches, the leading men there. And what characters are these? I never was an admirer of the French; but I can now only consider them as monsters of human nature.

He then referred to Muir's witnesses:

. . . What right had they to representation? Parliament would never listen to their petition. Government ... in this country is made up of the landed interest, which alone has a right to be represented; as for the rabble, who have nothing but personal property, what hold has the nation of them? What security for the payment of their taxes? They may pack up all their property on their backs, and leave the country in the twinkling of an eye. ...

Braxfield discounted the overwhelming evidence Muir had produced that he counselled peaceable measures by suggesting that Muir discouraged revolt on the grounds that, until everything was ripe for a general insurrection, any tumult would only ruin his cause.

The court adjourned at 1.30 a.m. on 31 August. When it reassembled at noon Parliament Square was crowded. The statue of Charles II was covered with boys ready to fly off to report the verdict. The jury unanimously found Muir guilty. Braxfield then most improperly congratulated the jury on their verdict and invited the judges to give their opinion of what punishment should be inflicted. Scottish Common Law provided no precise penalty for sedition. The sentence was entirely at the judges' discretion.

There followed astonishing speeches from the Supreme Bench. Lord Henderland spoke first; the judges had a choice of punishment:

banishment, fine, whipping, imprisonment and transportation: banishment would be improper, as it would only be sending a dangerous man to another country. . . . a fine would only fall upon his parents who had already suffered too much by the forfeiture of his bail. Whipping was too severe and disgraceful for a man who had born his rank and character . . . . imprisonment would be but a temporary punishment.

He came to the remarkable conclusion that transportation was the most suitable punishment. Lord Swinton then took up the refrain.

There was scarcely a distinction between Muir's crime and high treason . . . it might be said to include every sort of crime, murder, robbery, rapine, fire-raising. . . . By Roman law, held to be Scots Common law where no statute existed, transportation was among the mildest punishments. Under Nero and Domitian people who excited the populace to sedition were either sent to the gallows or thrown to wild beasts.

Finally Braxfield spoke. The indecent applause of the previous night had convinced him 'that a spirit of discontent still lurked in the minds of the people', and it would be dangerous to allow Muir to remain in the country. Braxfield hinted that it was only due to the Lord Advocate's humanity that the prisoner had not been on trial for his life. He wondered whether Muir should not be banished for life, but settled on fourteen years transportation. Muir rose:

I shall not animadvert upon the severity or the leniency of my sentence . . . my mind tells me that I have engaged in a good, a just, and a glorious cause – a cause which sooner or later must and will prevail; and by a timely reform, save this country from destruction.

Muir has been criticized for not challenging the validity of a sentence of transportation. He said nothing till it was too late. Cockburn says that the judges were at fault in not informing Muir after the verdict that they contemplated such a sentence and inviting him to speak. Muir cannot have had much hope of acquittal, but he may well have been too stunned by the unexpectedly harsh sentence to produce coherent arguments against it on the spur of the moment – another disadvantage of defending himself. The clerk to the jury said that all were thunderstruck with the extreme severity of the sentence, none more than the jury. They met immediately after the court rose and unanimously agreed that it was far too severe. They thought Muir's guilt so trivial a few weeks imprisonment would be sufficient punishment, and resolved to prepare a petition to the court. When they met next day to sign it, Mr. Innes of Stow produced a letter he had received threatening to assassinate him for concurring in the verdict and this the jury considered made it impossible for them to interfere. Thirty-five years later Cockburn asked Mr. Balfour of Pilrigg, the clerk of the jury, how he could account for his conduct. He replied, 'We were all mad.'

Transportation was virtually a death sentence. Some ships sank before reaching Australia. Many convicts died of dysentery or typhoid, more in the harsh conditions of the new colony. Almost none survived to return on completion of their sentence. There was hardly any communication with home; 'a man transported was considered as a man never to be seen again'.

J.B. was moved to tell Dundas,

almost everybody, even the most loyal subjects, think Muir's sentence by far too severe. Two years imprisonment would have been thought lenient, if even a fine had been added few would have complained, but fourteen years to Botany Bay! You yourself I suppose will allow it is rather too much.[4]

Later lawyers and historians condemned the conduct of the Court.

The most exhaustive commentary on the trials is by the judge Henry Cockburn. His views have a Whig bias, but they are, in general, fair and sound. Cockburn believed Muir was completely innocent: the first charge against him could not possibly be substantiated, the second depended almost entirely on the dubious evidence of Annie Fisher. Concerning the third Cockburn remarked that Paine was widely and freely read. He remembered his father, a staunch Tory, listening while one of the Dundas family read *The Rights of Man* aloud. Copies of the book were still openly sold in Edinburgh at the end of 1792. As to the fourth charge, Muir had indeed publicly read the United Irishmen's letter, but it was not seditious.

The lawyer Sir James Gibson Craig later commented:

I would put into the hands of any man, be his principles what they may, the report of this trial, and defy him to point out any crime Muir had committed which could justify the punishment inflicted on him. One crime he committed against himself. He conducted his own defence instead of availing himself of the talents of Henry Erskine. . . . I know that one, at least, of the jury vindicated the verdict, not on the charge made against him, but on the speech he made in his defence.[5]

But it is extremely doubtful if Erskine could have got an acquittal before Braxfield and a packed jury.

Muir's was the first in a series of trials for sedition in Scotland. The others are described briefly later, but it is necessary to mention them now in commenting on Muir's. The borderline of freedom differs from age to age. In 1797 Professor David Hume (nephew of the philosopher) published a learned and able defence of the doctrines established at these trials by the Court of Justiciary. Thomas Palmer, who had no contact with the French or Irish and was defended by two counsel, fared little better a fortnight later at his trial than Muir had. Palmer was given seven years transportation for allegedly helping to write an address encouraging people to demand universal suffrage. His counsel, too, did not challenge the right to transport. It was too late when this right was ably challenged by counsel at Joseph Gerrald's trial the following year; with plenty of time to prepare their case the judges ruled it legitimate. Erskine conducted the defence of one other reformer, Charles Sinclair, whose case was postponed and subsequently abandoned.*

---

* Erskine claimed this was on account of his defence. Many, including Sinclair's

At Palmer's trial Lord Abercrombie declared that 'if the King's subjects were to enjoy the right of universal suffrage, they would not long enjoy either liberty or a free constitution.' However strongly the somewhat old-fashioned judges believed such ideas, and making every allowance for the hysterical temper of the time, they should have stuck to the facts. They accused Muir of actions with which he was not charged and which he had not committed. Without the faintest shred of evidence they accused him of plotting revolution. It was wrong to construe applause for Muir's speech as an argument against him personally. As an English lawyer wrote at the time: 'Justice called for a decision according to the quality of the act committed, not according to the opinions of others concerning it.'[7] There are, incidentally, several apocryphal anecdotes about Braxfield. One juryman, Horner, said that when he passed behind the bench Braxfield whispered: 'Come awa', Maister Horner, and help us to hang ane a' thae damned scoundrels.' Later, when Gerrald commented at his trial that Christ had been a reformer, Braxfield sardonically remarked: 'Muckle he made o' that; he was hanget.'

Although in some respects Scots law was more humane than English, the criminal law in Scotland was harsh and authoritarian, partly due to its basis in Roman law, where the safety of the state came before the rights of the individual. Another peculiarity of the High Court which had a very unfavourable effect on judicial character was that all its proceedings were final. There was no appeal to any other authority; no power of reserving a point of law for future consideration by the Court itself. The Lord Advocate had absolute power and the principle operated that under the 'native vigour' of the Court it could create new crimes and apply to them any punishment it chose short of death.

In violent times, when a minority are on trial for unpopular opinions, it is only too easy for prosecutions for seditious writings to be unfairly conducted. It is very difficult to find a satisfactory definition of seditious libel and, where guilt is doubtful, essential to acquit.

other counsel, Archibald Fletcher, said it was because he had turned spy. The truth of the matter lies probably in a contemporary newspaper account: 'As Sinclair is not to be tried a report has prevailed in Edinburgh that he acted as a spy; this has . . . almost driven him to madness. . . . It should be explained that Sir John Sinclair M.P., to whom he is nearly allied, has made interest with Government on his behalf.'[6] Sir John Sinclair, a Caithness landowner, was founder President of the Board of Agriculture, and compiled the statistical account of Scotland.

When people are expressing a right for which there is no precise form men can only be guided by custom and, in a free country, there are precedents for almost anything.

These trials were political prosecutions at a moment of intense excitement. The dangerous situation was cited as a reason, and later as an excuse, for their conduct and for the sentences imposed. It is to the discredit of the Scottish Judiciary that they were not conducted fairly and of the Government that, knowing the judges would assist them, they used the Scottish Courts, where decisions were final, to make an example of prominent reformers.

The contrast with later English trials is marked. There were differences in English law. The law of sedition was indefinite. The Attorney General was faced with the choice of the appalling indictment of high treason or the lesser charge of seditious libel. This was circumscribed by Fox's Libel Act, which had reached the statute book in the temperate early months of 1792. Formerly the judge had decided whether a pamphlet or article was libellous and the jury only decided whether the accused had actually published or uttered it. Now the jury were empowered to rule on both. Muir did not attempt to make use of this Act; it would have been of little help with a packed jury. It did make a difference in England, where juries had been encouraged – by Wilkes among others – to have independent minds, and attempts to pack juries roused an outcry far beyond the reformers' ranks. Shortly after Muir's trial a London jury refused to convict the proprietors of the *Morning Chronicle*, prosecuted for reprinting an allegedly seditious address. In 1794, when Thomas Hardy and other English reformers were tried for high treason, three hours were spent choosing the jury and fifty names were set aside on challenge. Certainly they had the brilliant Thomas Erskine to defend them, but in several minor assize cases of a similar nature, where no one of Erskine's calibre was employed, the accused were acquitted in the teeth of the judge's summing-up. Under English law Muir would at most have been guilty of a misdemeanour, and those accused later given sentences of a few weeks' or months' imprisonment. English reformers were partly saved by revulsion at the horrible fate of their Scottish colleagues.

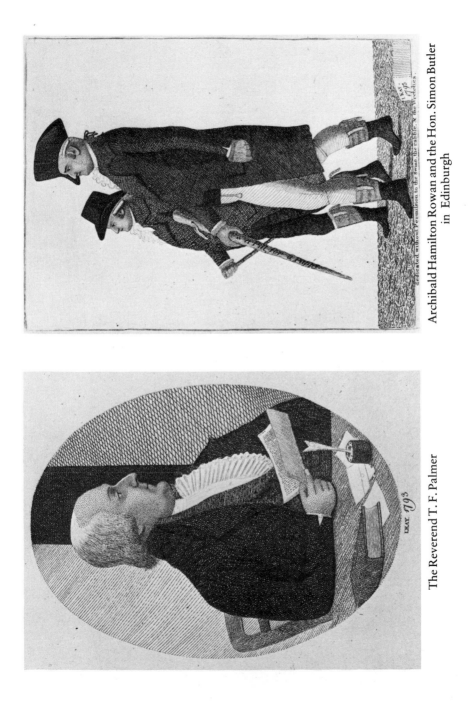

Archibald Hamilton Rowan and the Hon. Simon Butler
in Edinburgh

The Reverend T. F. Palmer

The Tolbooth in 1793

Lord Braxfield, painting by Raeburn

CHAPTER 7

The Hulks

So ended Muir's brief political career. Its climax, the trial, received enormous coverage in the newspapers and was universally condemned abroad. In France, naturally, there was great indignation. A German journalist wrote that the trial

must excite in the breast of every German an esteem for his native land. We here see a man sent to Botany Bay on account of an accusation to which a German court of justice would have been ashamed to listen.[1]

The trial is claimed to have inspired Burns to compose 'Scots, wha hae wi'Wallace bled'. The *Morning Chronicle* had a list of comparative punishments:

The authors of a pamphlet describing Parliament as 'fit for the gallows' a few weeks imprisonment.
Lindsey, who kidnapped a Counsellor to stop him voting, fined £50.
A forger seven years transportation commuted to serving in the Navy.
A murderer fourteen years transportation.

Three editions of the trial were printed, two of which were published in New York. By 3 October they were into second editions, selling at 3/– octavo and a cheap one at 1/3d. Muir's final speech was also printed as a pamphlet. One rather curious legacy was that this speech became popular as a piece for declamation in New England schools – though fifty years later the children did not know anything about Muir.[2]

Muir was held in the Tolbooth, a dark, smelly, unhealthy prison, crammed with debtors. Still, he had a room to himself and meals brought in. Sheriff Pringle asked Dundas to have Muir removed as soon as possible: 'His adherents intend to rescue him. . . . Handbills are pasted up instigating people to help.' He was not worried about this, but 'the minds of the lower class of people will be kept in a ferment while he remains here. His visitors have been very numerous and a list of their names kept.' Lord Daer and John Millar were the only ones Dundas might know. J.B. reported that Muir was keeping up his spirits amazingly. 'They say he is always so crowded with visitors (sometimes visitors of whom they are suspicious) that they cannot get a word of intelligence about France from him.' The severity of Muir's sentence seemed to have given the Friends of the People new life and vigour. There had been a much larger monthly meeting than for some time past, over 200 present. Strong disapproval was expressed of whoever had threatened the jury. On Muir's advice there were to be no more fortnightly meetings to debate political questions. Muir was to be presented with a silver box. J.B. went to see him 'as usual crowded with company, ladies and gentlemen'. Still upset by Muir's sentence J.B. reiterated that he did not like his present occupation but always 'adhered to Truth'.

Muir's parents came often. Their pockets were searched and they were much distressed by their visits. One of his greatest remaining friends, William Moffat, a Writer to the Signet (solicitor) saw him almost every day. His visitors were mostly reformers and people 'in the middle way of life'. The majority of Muir's former friends in a higher station and most of his 'brethren at the bar' stayed away,[3] because they either disapproved of his actions, or were frightened of incurring the authorities' suspicion.

Muir's sentence was intended as a warning to the Whig lawyers. Public opinion was hardening. Workers suspected of revolutionary opinions were dismissed, people removed their custom from reforming tradesmen. No one would give briefs to Whig advocates as the judges were sure to be biased against them. Mrs. Eliza Fletcher was rumoured to carry a dagger under her cloak and to train for the guillotine by decapitating hens in her backyard – though the fact that her husband Archibald continued to celebrate the anniversary of the French Revolution for many years cannot have helped their reputation. Cockburn, then a boy in Edinburgh, was taught, like other sons of the gentry, to regard even mention of the 'Friends of the People' with horror.

Muir sought consolation in martyrdom. At a United Irishmen's meeting Hamilton Rowan produced a letter from Muir who 'glories in the punishment inflicted on him and hopes the United Irishmen are ready individually to suffer the same or a severer punishment in so great a cause'.[4] Inspired by this letter a common chairman sent Muir his life savings, £300, to help support him in a foreign land.[5]

On 12 September Palmer was tried at Perth. He was charged with writing and publishing an address from the Dundee Friends of Liberty. Actually he had only amended the spelling and grammar and struck out the wilder passages. George Mealmaker, an artisan who admitted writing the address, was not charged. The carefully selected jury were nearly all Tory lairds. Once again several witnesses listed by the prosecution who would have produced evidence helpful to Palmer were not called. The trial was conducted by Lord Abercrombie. His summing up was fairer than Braxfield's but he came out strongly against the prisoner. The judges claimed Muir's offence had been aggravated because he agitated when the country was in a frenzy. Now they castigated Palmer for causing trouble when the country was tranquil. Cockburn considered Palmer technically guilty, but that he only deserved a minimal sentence.

By joining the Unitarians Palmer had made enemies in the Church; he had made no attempt to keep on terms with the establishment and, like Muir, had been marked down by the authorities as one of the most articulate, radical campaigners in Scotland. Unlike Muir, he had influential relations; but they were in the South and would not do much to protect him, as they considered him a tiresome crank and disapproved of his religious and political views. Later, various important friends of Palmer's wrote fruitlessly to Nepean and Dundas suggesting that he be allowed to choose his place of exile, and go to the United States. For the time being Palmer was kept in Perth gaol.[6]

Initially the authorities considered revoking the sentences. The Lord Advocate told his uncle it was absolutely vital that Muir and Palmer should petition for reprieve: otherwise, if their sentences were reduced, they would boast that it was because Dundas thought the verdicts were wrong, or the sentences too severe, and that he disapproved of the Court's conduct. Though Muir was reluctant to petition, his friends were pressing him to do so. There were rumours among the lower classes in Glasgow of an attempt to rescue Muir. Braxfield had received menacing letters. He enclosed one threatening his own assassination because of his treatment of 'that Saint Thomas Muir'.

I send it to you for the purpose of satisfying you that, if Palmer and Muir were even to apply for mitigation of their sentences, which I have no reason to believe will be the case, how inexpedient it would be at the present juncture to yield to their request.[7]

On 28 October he wrote again:

The bad consequences of Muir's remaining . . . here become every day more
apparent. Although it is still my opinion that, if possible, no distinction
should be made between him and any other convict, yet rather than allow
him to remain longer here, I consider his removal to London . . . to be
essential for the peace and quiet of this city.

The following day began the third and last Convention of the
Friends of the People, which Skirving had been largely instrumental
in organizing. Brave, kind, and devout, Skirving regarded the reform
movement as a religious crusade. He was well-meaning but tactless
and interlarded his speeches with too many biblical quotations. He
had far too high an opinion of his own and the other reformers'
importance and totally failed to appreciate the folly of continuing on
a course which was bound to alarm the authorities. For, now that the
moderate leaders had withdrawn, those left took the dangerous step
of inviting English Societies to send delegates. English reformers
welcomed the opportunity to demonstrate the reform movement's
solidarity, in spite of recent blows, and prevent its demoralization.
They knew the danger they were running, but wanted to challenge
the Scottish judiciary to treat Englishmen as they had Scots. It proved
difficult to collect funds in time for delegates to travel to Scotland
and in the end only three Societies sent representatives. The London
Corresponding Society elected Maurice Margarot and Joseph
Gerrald, who were to formulate a nationwide campaign. The Society
for Constitutional Information chose Charles Sinclair and Henry
Yorke. Yorke fell ill and did not attend. The Sheffield Society sent
Michael Campbell Brown, an actor turned attorney.

The English contingent had not arrived when the Convention of
about 160 delegates opened. For the first time the delegates declared
for universal suffrage and annual parliaments. Deputations were
appointed to call on prominent members who were absent to see if
they stood by their principles. Colonel Macleod assured them of his
steady adherence to the cause, but in his opinion the country was not
ripe for universal suffrage. The Committee of Secrecy of the House of
Commons respecting Seditious Practices later commented that: 'The
funds of the convention were extremely low – so low that at first
sight the assembly might appear an object of contempt, rather than
alarm.' It is extraordinary that the authorities did not appreciate
how small, impoverished, and uninfluential the Convention was.

The delegates promptly made contact with Muir, who 'suffered with a magnanimity that required their admiration'. A subscription was initiated for him and for Palmer. It was agreed that six members should dine with Muir every evening, but the magistrates decided that only two could be admitted. Several weeks previously, Muir's visitors had been limited to two at a time because he was receiving and generating too much attention. On the second evening trouble occurred. The inner jailor of the Tolbooth, Binny, 'as informal a Cerberus as ever kept the gate of Tartarus', attacked Muir's two visitors. Muir protested to the Lord Provost, who 'sympathised much with Mr. Muir', and said that six people should be allowed to dine with him. Sheriff Scott complained to the Lord Advocate that such fracas were one of the many inconveniences of Muir's remaining in Edinburgh. Another was that the Convention would extend its sitting to communicate and gossip with him – 'a circumstance which keeps them alive and present'.

A general monthly committee has been established. Under the influence of . . . Muir this committee will not be idle. Muir . . . is . . . up all night or the greatest part of it after his friends leave him at shutting of the prison in the evening. He is in bed all the forenoon. It is no stretch of conjecture to suppose he is employed in preparing matters for his friends and will be so employed as long as he remains here.

The English delegates finally arrived. Charles Sinclair was an inexperienced young man of twenty-two, a friend of Daer, very popular in Scottish society. Maurice Margarot was the son of a wine and general merchant of somewhat mysterious origin who operated in France and Portugal. He was born in 1745 in Devonshire. Most of his childhood was spent abroad and he studied classics at Geneva University. Nominally he was resident in London, where his home was a rendezvous for the radical faction in the days of Wilkes, but he was in France during the first years of the Revolution. He returned to England in 1792, joined the London Corresponding Society, and wrote many of its addresses. He was a lively, elegant, dark little man; in appearance and manner an Englishman's idea of a Frenchman. A strange, magnetic, forceful personality, charming but difficult, a tremendous egoist, plausible, unstable. Unlike the other leaders he was an agitator, perpetually dissatisfied and quarrelsome. Margarot was violently opposed to the rich and aristocratic. He had a deep, genuine passion for social justice and reform which he pursued obstinately, even when he knew it might lead to transportation. Margarot may have had secret dealings with the French – the one man the Home Office could have been right to suspect.[8]

Joseph Gerrald was liked and admired by all. He was born in the West Indies and inherited property there. He practised at the Pennsylvania bar for four years and in 1788 came to England to prosecute a lawsuit connected with his West Indian property. His wife died leaving him with a son and daughter. He was a man of brilliance and nobility, the most remarkable and inspiring of the reformers. He wrote a pamphlet on the practical problems of constitutional change which was widely read and frequently reprinted.[9] By the time he went to Edinburgh he was already far gone with tuberculosis.

Hamilton Rowan and the Hon. Simon Butler, Lord Mountgarret's brother, also arrived in Edinburgh on 4 November. Hamilton Rowan considered that the Lord Advocate's remarks about himself and the United Irishmen at Muir's trial had insulted his honour. He had referred to Rowan as a ferocious person and an infamous wretch. Hamilton Rowan had written two letters to the Lord Advocate challenging him to a duel. A warrant had been issued for Rowan on 28 October, charging him with sending via Muir a pamphlet of a dangerous and seditious tendency.

While Butler, as Rowan's second, confronted the Lord Advocate, Hamilton Rowan hurried off to see Muir in the Tolbooth. There, in a scene which must have delighted them both, a Sheriff's officer appeared with a warrant for Rowan's arrest. Macleod stood bail[10]. Rowan then called on the Lord Advocate, who said he did not consider himself accountable for any observations he might make in the course of official duty. The following evening Hamilton Rowan and Butler dined with Muir in the Tolbooth. Hamilton Rowan then visited Palmer in Perth; he had met Palmer when a student at Cambridge. There was a further exchange of letters with Robert Dundas, and Hamilton Rowan decided his honour was satisfied. Muir was cheered to see him again and introduced him to John Millar and other friends.

Hamilton Rowan and Butler left for Dublin on 8 November. *En route* they were entertained to a banquet in Belfast – a city notorious for setting up illuminations to celebrate King Louis's death. The toasts were: 'The swine of England, the rabble of Scotland and wretches of Ireland' and 'Mr. Muir, may his exalted sentiments penetrate the walls of British and Irish prisons and cheer the solitary tenants.'[11] A colossal sensation was caused by this futile expedition. The publicity it received was the final straw. Dundas at last acceded to his nephew's perpetual warnings about leaving Muir in Edinburgh as a focus of discontent and gave orders for his transference to London.

On 8 November William Scott told the Lord Advocate, 'Last night the innkeeper of the Tolbooth informed me that Muir had been in bed all day and in very low spirits from notice given of his departure, he had been seen to very few.' James Muir said Thomas was feverish for a week and coughed up blood. Impossible to tell now what was wrong with Muir. Perhaps he had incipient tuberculosis or an ulcer, and shock caused him to vomit blood. At any rate, overcome by the prospect of being taken away, Muir collapsed. On 10 November he wrote to Moffat:

... My dear and valued friend, in the remotest corner of the world your remembrance and that of Mrs. Moffat shall soothe me in my affliction, but my tears shall flow over the remembrance. I am really unwell. I cannot write much, nor have I time, but neither of you shall be wiped away from my heart. I am bidding you a long goodnight. Nevermore shall we meet again in this sublunary sphere. ... present my prayers to your wife and children for every blessing that the Almighty can bestow and, for the last time, unalterably yours. ...[12]

According to later reports Muir lay half forgotten in prison while the reformers clustered round the English delegates. It is far more likely that he felt unable to cope with visitors. Besides he only remained in prison until the morning of 14 November when, with four men convicted of robbery and forgery, he was taken to Leith in a coach and put on board the excise yacht the *Royal George*.[13] His parents, Margarot, and another reformer, Taylor, watched him taken on board. His parents gave him a small pocket bible inscribed 'To Thomas Muir from his Afflicted Parents' which he managed to retain throughout his later adventures. James and Margaret Muir were old, they knew they were unlikely to be alive when his sentence ended. To comfort them, as the jollyboat left the quay, Thomas pointed, like Anaxagoras, to the heavens where they would meet again.

Due to an administrative muddle, no order had been received for removing Palmer and other convicts from Perth, so poor Muir remained for a week on the cutter tantalizingly lying off shore in Leith Roads.[14] On 20 November the ship's mate seized a pair of very small pistols in Muir's possession. Muir, overwrought by his unhappy and humiliating situation, 'thought fit to take this amiss and wrote a very extraordinary card to the Sheriff'.

At the subsequent inquiry one of the convicts on the cutter, John Grant, gave evidence. He was a devious, evil man who was to cause Muir and Palmer endless trouble. Son of a highland farmer, he had studied law and, through Dundas, been appointed sheriff depute of Inverness-shire. He committed forgery and was condemned to transportation. Though penniless and supported by Muir in gaol, he tried to ingratiate himself with the authorities in the hope of a free pardon by giving evidence aganist his fellow prisoners. Grant said that 'Muir was certain the inner turnkey was hired by men in power to assassinate him for his aversion to the government. However he was upon his guard and had a pair of loaded pistols under his head every night.' These Muir had chosen from four pairs offered to him by Hamilton Rowan 'with which he had prepared himself to fight the Lord Advocate'.

Palmer arrived and the ship set sail on 22 November. During this week Muir's father suffered a stroke from which he never recovered.[15] The Captain of the cutter, Ogilvie, was later praised by Muir and Palmer for his 'attention and civility'.[16] He invited them and Grant to use the cabin and dine with him and the other officers. Grant continued his mischief-making by circulating a rumour that Palmer and Muir were going to murder the Captain and run away with the ship to France. Fortunately Ogilvie ignored this fabrication; though, to be on the safe side, the crew had orders to seize the prisoners if they went on deck at night to answer a call of nature.

When Ogilvie delivered his prisoners to the Superintendent of the Hulks at Woolwich he recommended him to treat them like gentlemen. 'He had done so and they had behaved like gentlemen.' But this was not to be. Palmer wrote: 'we were put in irons and slept in hammocks in a room with about a hundred cut-throats and thieves. Our company was a mutual solace.'[17] By order of the Under Secretary of State, however, Muir was removed to the *Prudentia* hulk two miles higher up river. According to the *Edinburgh Advertiser* they were set to hard labour in chains on the river bank. 'His heroic spirit rises under every difficulty.' An indication of the intense interest taken in the reformers is that newspapers gave detailed coverage of minutiae of their lives and published many of their letters.

Grant's stories may have encouraged Dundas to order such unparalleled harsh treatment. This time, however, he had gone too far and excited general indignation. The Lord Advocate wrote to Nepean:

> I understand from several quarters that the general opinion of the inhabitants here is that Muir and Palmer ought only to have been confined . . . and that their being handcuffed, or obliged to work like other felons, is made the handle of much glamour, and may have a bad effect. If you think it proper to show them any distinction from the case of other convicts, it appears to me your doing so would be of service. If the juries here take it into their heads that more is done to these gentry than is absolutely necessary, they may acquit where they would otherwise have convicted.

Nepean replied that there was a devil of a stir in London about Muir and Palmer. Palmer, robbed of his watch and money, deeply shocked by the convicts' horrible conversation, wrote to Moffat on 7 December:

> . . . Muir's health and sleep return. The doctor has pronounced him well. I snore so loud I disturb all the rogues. You have no doubt heard of their refinement in cruelty in separating me and Mr. Muir and delivering him with his then ill health and unguarded generous confidence into the hands of thieves and ruffians.[18]

Sheridan visited them, and Priestley, who was one of their most active and sympathetic friends; ostracized by fellow members of the Royal Society, he was about to emigrate to America.

A letter from Muir to Flower was published in the *Cambridge Chronicle*:

> . . . The great lesson we have to learn is submission . . . to the will of God . . . by the example of Him who was the object of all suffering. . . . Much need have I to be taught in his school. Hurled, as it were in a moment, from some of the most polished society in Edinburgh and London, into one of the hulks upon the Thames, where every mouth is open to blaspheme God, and every hand is stretched out to injure a neighbour. . . . I have been separated from Mr. Palmer . . . an act of unnecessary cruelty. My state of health is poorly; the seeds of a consumption, I apprehend, are planted in my breast. I suffer no acute pain, but daily experience a gradual decay. Of everything relating to my future destination I am utterly ignorant. . . .[19]

Meanwhile, because the English delegates had arrived, the Convention reopened on 19 November. Daer was present for a few days, but withdrew because of ill health. He was to die of tuberculosis on 5 November 1794. Proceedings were on the whole restrained and pious but, as the most forceful personalities present, the English took charge and foolishly encouraged the use of French terms. Delegates greeted each other as 'citizens' and called the meetings 'sittings'. While the Terror was raging in France, and the British had been defeated at Dunkirk, such behaviour was bound to create hostility. Uncontroversial subjects such as the dissemination of knowledge in the Highlands were discussed, but a secret committee of four was appointed to fix a Convention of Emergency if Habeas Corpus were to be suspended, or the country invaded. The Lord Advocate and the Solicitor General decided the proceedings were 'so strong' that they authorized the arrest of Margarot, Gerrald, Skirving, and others on 5 December. 'Behold the funeral torches of liberty' cried Gerrald as he saw the lights of the Sheriff and his men approaching.[20] Moffat was arrested but never charged. The editor of the *Edinburgh Gazetteer* fled to America. Dundas sent his nephew a note from the King praising his firm attack on the Convention.

On 16 November the Whig leaders Lauderdale, Grey, and Sheridan had called on Dundas to state their intention of bringing Muir and Palmer's sentences before Parliament. Dundas wrote to his nephew:

It is not my intention to gratify them in that respect, for if the judges' report expresses no doubt upon the subject, I will carry the sentences immediately into execution and meet their clamour in Parliament without . . . dismay.

Dundas asked the Scottish judges for their opinion.[21] They inevitably replied that the sentences were legal. Dundas then told Lauderdale: 'From what is stated in the report from the judges . . . I cannot consistently with my public duty take any steps for either preventing or retarding the regular course of justice.'

Lauderdale, Grey, and Sheridan called again on 10 December, saying they had been advised that the conviction of Muir and Palmer was illegal. They urged that there was sufficient reason to postpone sentence until after Parliament met. The judges had exceeded their legal powers by punishing verbal sedition with transportation. They emphasized the great difference between banishment and transportation. Dundas referred the matter to Braxfield.

Braxfield replied that Muir and Palmer had been convicted of sedition proper:

As I am perfectly clear that the Court have full powers to transport for the crime of sedition, so I am equally clear that in this case the punishment is not greater than their conduct merited, and that any mitigation, by the interposition of the royal mercy, would in the present conjunction be a most inexpedient measure.

Lauderdale, Grey, and Sheridan maintained that by an act of 1703 punishment for leasing making, i.e. verbal sedition, speaking ill of the Government – which was what Palmer and Muir had been charged with – was a fine, imprisonment, or banishment. Scotland could not transport, for she never had a colonial dominion.

Whig lawyers denied, Tory lawyers defended the legality of the sentences. Hume argued that, as men could no longer be sentenced to death for sedition, the next most severe punishment, transportation, was correct. Later legal authorities did not consider that transportation was warranted for such an offence by previous judicial judgements or statutes. Lord Colchester believed – probably correctly – that the punishment itself was illegal. The act authorizing the removal of offenders from Britain expired in 1788 and when it was renewed Scotland was omitted. No one cited this technicality at the time and undoubtedly it would have made no difference to the Government's determination to enforce the sentences. Public opinion forced Dundas to concede that Muir and Palmer should not be kept in irons nor compelled to work. They were allowed to spend evenings in the Captains' cabins and, though they slept with the convicts, their beds were partitioned off and a sentinel placed to prevent their being disturbed.

Friends continued to visit them. John Rutt* was warned by Palmer that the Captains spied on them. Rutt felt they so grossly overplayed their parts that they were bound to put anyone on their guard. When he dined with Palmer on the *Stanislaus* hulk that 'plausible gentleman' John Grant vied with the Captain in tempting them to indiscretion by proposing daringly democratic toasts. When Rutt called on Muir he met William Godwin, who had given Muir his *Enquiry concerning Political Justice*. The Captain told Godwin that his mate had become so passionately devoted to his work that he wouldn't let the volumes out of his possession. Godwin tiresomely told Muir that

* A radical journalist and wholesale chemist who befriended Muir and Palmer.

it was his duty to bear his lot with fortitude. Still he sent a long letter
to the *Morning Chronicle* complaining about the prisoners' treatment. Clothes sent to them were taken on board, but stores and
books returned. 'The principle which has been laid down by the
officers of government is that they are felons like the rest.'[22] He
compared the administration to Tiberius's and quoted Dundas's
comment to Sheridan that 'he saw no great hardship in a man's being
sent to Botany Bay'. Cobbett, on the other hand, at that time a
staunch Tory, wrote that the United Irishmen shed an abundance of
crocodile tears over the reformers, but the trials reflected eternal
honour on British jurisprudence.[23] The *Sun* commented that Muir
would have 'a good chance of being made Chancellor in Botany Bay'.

A purse was offered to them. Palmer declined but Muir thankfully
accepted. Palmer afterwards changed his mind and accepted too.
This purse came to about £600 and later was vested in the hands of a
committee of seven for the benefit of Palmer, Muir, Skirving, and
'even Margarot who, as a joint sufferer, was not to be overlooked
though his general character was not so high as the others'. On 8
January the King in Council signed an order for Muir and Palmer's
transportation.

There was no sanitation and little ventilation on the cold, damp
hulks. The death rate among the convicts was twenty per cent. As
severe winter weather set in, not surprisingly, Muir fell ill. Rumour
spread that he was dying or, with luck, at least too ill to be transported. The authorities became frightened of the odium they would
incur if Muir died. Dundas asked the Captain Surgeon of the hulks to
see if he were fit to be transported. He reported that Muir had been
very ill for some days with 'Acute Rheumatism' but his fever had
gone and he appeared to be recovering. Almost as soon as he arrived
on the *Prudentia* Muir had complained of chest pains, which seemed
to indicate 'the latent seeds of consumption'; he was also very
scrofulous. 'Mr Muir sleeps in the hospital of the *Prudentia* which he
prefers to any other part of the ship on account of the few kept there.
In the daytime he is permitted to walk the quarterdeck.' Eighteenth-
century medical terms were imprecise and used to cover many ail-
ments unknown at the time. Scofular, the King's evil, was tuberculosis
of the lymphatic glands. If Muir suffered from this disease it certainly
cleared up later on. On 10 January the weather turned foggy. The
Morning Post reported:

Mr. Muir is so extremely ill the physician who attends him has not the least hope of his recovery. In such a situation no unfortunate man can present stronger claims to the Royal Clemency.

The Superintendent of the Hulks offered to remove Muir from among the convicts, but Muir, 'who behaved with extreme decency and was thankful for what had been offered', did not want to change his berth for the short time left. Palmer, however, moved into a separate cabin. Grey meanwhile asked if Muir could move to New-gate as the river made his poor health worse. Two surgeons examined Muir again. They sent in a tart report. Muir had been given medicine which he had not taken regularly. However Dr. Hamilton of the London Infirmary had been sent by Muir's friends and had left a prescription which he was taking.

Muir's state of mind is tranquil and he is content to stay where he is. He is of a relaxed disposition, inclined to indulge himself in bed and this renders him susceptible to cold from every air that blows. Yesterday he got up at 1 o'clock, sat up longer than he has done for some days past, and is this morning better. He has no symptoms of immediate danger, but a change of weather would hasten his recovery.

The authorities decided that 'Muir's continuance on the hulks might endanger his life', so on 16 January he was moved to Newgate. Here, though a prisoner, he passed a stimulating month, for New-gate had almost become a radical club. Besides the usual collection of debtors there were political prisoners, mostly printers and book-sellers, none of whom, unlike Muir, had received more than a two year sentence. The jailers kept a list of Muir's visitors. Names of well-known men such as the M.P.s Smith and Maitland, and Godwin, were underlined. Besides the faithful Moffat who had followed him to London and called daily, Muir received at least two visitors a day.* The Barbaulds and Richard Shields came from Hampstead, friends travelled up from Cambridge. Muir was given an engraving of Dr. Price, which he hung over the mantlepiece in his room.[24] Muir did not receive so much attention merely because he was an object of interest and pity; with his talent for friendship he both renewed old acquaintance and made new friends. His parents did not travel south to visit him. His father may have been too ill to travel, or they could not face another harrowing parting.

* See Treasury Solicitor's files, 11/954. Contemporary prints of Newgate show prisoners and their friends walking in the courtyard.

On 29 January Hamilton Rowan was tried in Dublin for distributing a seditious pamphlet. Skirving and Margarot were tried in Edinburgh in an atmosphere of intense excitement during the first fortnight in January. The war was going badly; the Austrians and Prussians had been expelled from France and Toulon recaptured by Napoleon. Loss of European markets and continuing bad harvests caused discontent. As a result, radical ideas had become even more unpopular. Muir and Palmer had had no inkling of the harsh sentences they would be given. Those charged later could only expect the same, although none may have believed they would really be carried out. Skirving had the most to lose, a wife and eight children. He had a great sense of duty and stuck to the cause with the fanatical devotion of the Covenanters. Margarot is a more enigmatic personality. He could easily have gone to France where he had many connections. He enjoyed the limelight, was a convinced radical, and must deliberately have chosen martyrdom. Gerrald knew he had not long to live. His friends implored him to jump bail, but he felt it would be dishonourable not to stand by principles he had encouraged others to support.

Their trials were as unjust as the earlier ones, the juries packed, the judges determined to convict. Both Margarot and later Gerrald, accused Braxfield of prejudging them by remarking at a dinner party, 'The mob would be the better for the spilling of a little blood'. Skirving and Margarot were given fourteen years transportation. Dundas was making no more mistakes; they were taken straight to Newgate.

Skirving had not dared approach Henry Erskine. Erskine was, however, briefed by Sinclair's family and ably argued the case against transportation. Sinclair's trial began on 17 February. It was postponed several times and finally abandoned.* When Gerrald stood trial he said that he had applied to several lawyers but they refused to defend him. One Whig lawyer declined because he was not prepared to give a semblance of justice to such unfair proceedings, but Adam Gillies, a brilliant contemporary of Muir's, was appointed to defend Gerrald. Although he reasoned the case skilfully, it made no difference. Gerrald too received fourteen years' transportation. The *Scots Magazine* commented, 'The trials for sedition have to a considerable degree engaged the attention of the public on account

* See above, p. 82.

of their novelty in this country.' Cockburn considered the three men guilty of minor misdemeanours; that they were incorrectly tried and deserved, at most, a few months imprisonment. The Lord Advocate himself decided that Braxfield's behaviour was too much. When discussing further trials he told his uncle,

entre nous, I would prefer a commission were it only for this reason, that the President would . . . preside in place of the violent and intemperate gentleman who sits in the Justiciary, and whose present state of health and spirits is such as to afford no chance of his being more soberly inclined in his demeanour than he was last winter.

The small Whig rump led by Fox who remained in opposition took up Muir and Palmer's cause. The result was bound to be unsatisfactory as the matter was treated on party political lines. The trials were mere show, intended to serve the Tories regardless of justice. Also, as there was no appeal to Parliament in criminal cases, their being discussed in Parliament had little effect. The question was raised five times. On 31 January Lord Stanhope moved in the Lords that an address should be presented to the King entreating him to countermand sentence of transportation. He did not bring the motion forward correctly and no one supported him. On 4 February William Adam, a Scottish lawyer, argued that there should be an appeal from the Court of Justiciary to the House of Lords. Lord Loughborough, the Lord Chancellor, said the constitutional course was to petition the Throne for redress, and the motion was rejected by 49 votes to 1. On 24 February Sheridan petitioned the House of Commons that Palmer's sentence was illegal, unjust, and unconstitutional, again unsuccessfully. On this occasion a government supporter, the Marquis of Tichfield, thought the sentences should be suspended on humanitarian grounds, but Wilberforce, whose reforming zeal was remarkably selective, disagreed. He ridiculed the idea of humanity as applying to Mr. Palmer and said, 'Although he had not read Palmer's trial, upon his conscience he did not conceive the sentence ought to be suspended.'

On 10 March Adam moved an address to the Crown on behalf of Muir, seconded by Fox and opposed by the Lord Advocate and Pitt. Wyndham, Grey, Sheridan, and Whitbread also spoke. Pitt said the motion would create the impression that the House doubted the legality of the sentences. This might disturb the internal peace of the country. However he finally gave his consent. Adam was one of the few M.P.s who understood Scots law. He made an admirable two-and-a-half hour speech. He contended that there had been no instance of transportation in Scotland except in mitigation of punishment for capital crimes. Where banishment was mentioned in any Act of Parliament it precluded more severe punishment. He commented on the gross irregularities of the conduct of the trial, said there was not one case in Scottish criminal law to justify the proceedings; nor had the judges followed current practice in England. But the government backed the Scottish Judiciary. The Lord Advocate said there were only two classes of persons, those who wished to support the Constitution and those who wished to destroy it and introduce the anarchy of France. Transportation spared the English having such men among them as Skirving, Margarot, and Gerrald. One M.P. protested that Gerrald had not yet been tried.*

Sheridan made the point that even after the '15 and '45 no one had been transported. Fox said, 'So striking and disgustful are the whole features of this trial . . . I could not prevail upon myself to believe that such proceedings had actually taken place.' Pitt, in an unconvincing speech, said Muir and Palmer were 'men of liberal education and therefore should have guarded against the commission of crime which levelled them with the lowest and most ignorant part of mankind . . . the object of these gentlemen was to overthrow the constitution of the country.' Pitt, who was a lawyer, must have known this was untrue. His speech shows that he clearly appreciated the irregularities that disgraced the trial, but he spoke as a scaremonger, not an upholder of justice. He said that the judges would have been highly culpable if they had not punished such daring delinquents. Adam's motion was defeated by 171 votes to 32. Macleod was the only Scottish M.P. who voted for it. Parliament heartily endorsed the jury's verdict.

On 15 April Lauderdale introduced a motion in the House of Lords. He made a strong, clever speech. He pointed out that the publishers of Paine's book were fined £100; that, of the authors of the United Irishmen's letter, Drennan had not been charged and Rowan, who had been charged with seditious libel over another document, had received two years, whereas Muir, who had only read the letter and whose circulation of Paine had not been proved, was

* In fact Gerrald's trial had started that day.

sentenced to fourteen years transportation. Lauderdale also brought up a point raised by Adam, that the sentences contained an important error. They were pronounced with reference to an Act of 25 George III C.46 by which, if the convict were found at large in any part of the Kingdom of Great Britain or Ireland before the period of his transportation expired, he should incur death. The sentences omitted Ireland, but the statute included it and it was the statute, not the sentences, which constituted the law. This might have vitiated the sentences entirely. The point was quashed, but in the next equivalent case in 1798 the certification was corrected to include Ireland.[26]

The Whigs could not avoid bringing the matter up, but the result was unfortunate. It hardened the Government's attitude by making the execution of the sentences a point of party triumph. Pitt may have disliked the policy of repression, but believed it essential in wartime. The nation was so overwhelmingly loyal he could perfectly well have exercised clemency. The reformers had neither the desire nor the strength to fight. Many people feared a repetition of the Gordon Riots, but Dundas grossly overestimated the danger. Pitt, a far more intelligent man, should have had sufficient judgement to discount rumours and allegations. Ultimately he was responsible. Even if the Government wanted to make examples of these men they had no need to uphold such unjust sentences. Men who had committed crimes at that time punishable by death – murder and robbery – were reprieved, while Muir and Palmer were sent to Botany Bay. Ironically Lockie, whom Muir had defended for his part in the Birthday Riots, had his sentence of transportation remitted and was released in February.

A depressing aspect of the affair is that no one bar the small band of Whig parliamentarians objected. For a variety of reasons there was no organized protest in Scotland. Some people did not believe the sentences would be carried out. The majority of the upper class did not care, or disapproved of the reformers and, even if they thought the sentences too severe, would not object on their behalf. Still, whatever they thought of the reformers' conduct, they showed a sorry lack of courage in failing to protest at such a poor example of Scottish justice. The two Dundases lost all sense of proportion. In England the reform movement was quashed without such savage action. From Pitt's point of view two years' imprisonment would have been sufficient deterrent. Fox wrote to Lord Holland:

I do not think any of the French soi-disant judicial proceedings surpass in injustice and contempt of law those in Scotland; and yet I hear from good authority . . . that not only these proceedings are to be defended in Parliament, but that the sentences are to be executed and that sedition, the most vague and loose in its description of all misdemeanours, is to be . . . punished in Scotland as a felony. . . . I shall not acquiesce in this tyranny without an effort, but I am far from sanguine as to success. We live in times of violence and of extremes, and all those who are for creating or even for retaining checks upon power are considered as enemies to order. . . . Good God! that a man should be sent to Botany Bay for advising another to read Paine's book, or for reading the Irish address at a public meeting! for these are the charges against Muir, and the first of them as I think not satisfactorily proved.

CHAPTER 8

The Voyage

It had been intended that Muir and Palmer should sail in the transport *Canada*, but she was found to be unseaworthy and condemned. So they were to go with Skirving and Margarot on the *Surprize*, then lying at Woolwich. On 13 February at 4 o'clock in the morning Muir, Skirving, and Margarot were taken from their beds without any notice, handcuffed, and taken to the ship. The next night they were joined by Palmer and sixty female convicts. When the *Surprize* was delayed at Deal by contrary winds Muir wrote letters of melancholy resignation. One to an unknown acquaintance in London was published in the *Dublin Evening Post*:

. . . I am now upon the eve of leaving Europe and civilised life, perhaps for ever. But the memory of those whom I could call my friends, shall live in my recollection, and support and solace me in the remotest regions of this earth.

I believe I have completely recovered from that disorder, whose consequences excited some apprehension when I was on board the hulk. I am perfectly resigned to my situation. A man who dreads dishonour as the greatest of all possible dangers, should never use the term – suffering. The book of mankind is shut to me, but the volume of nature is widely opened. I am preparing my mind to those studies, whose object is the investigation of her animal and vegetable productions, for an innocent, if not useful amusement, – my imagination sometimes whispers to me, that I shall not be a spectator of inanimate nature merely, but that I may contemplate an infant empire, a new Europe in embryo.

If my years shall be protracted to the last term of my exile, I shall feel no desire to return to my native country. Alas I should be a stranger in the midst of a new generation. . . .[1]

In a letter to Flower, Muir, who had been ill in bed, apologized warmly and sincerely for his criticism of Flower's ideas:

. . . I am now perhaps for ever upon my departure from Europe and civilised life. The exchange is not perhaps so injurious as may be deemed. . . . Long before nature could have required it, my mind demanded repose . . . the repose, which by the exclusion of mean and trifling things, allows those energies to be directed where they cannot be spent in vain. . . . One circumstance afflicts me sensibly. To be for ever separated from the few friends whose friendship I prized, to be thrown into new societies, with which however worthy and amiable I can never associate with that ardour which is felt in early years, presents but a cheerless prospect. Even this upon reflection loses somewhat of its force. In the most remote region of the earth I shall doubtless, from time to time, hear of the exertions of my friends in the cause of mankind. Mixed with feelings of a more tender kind, I shall indulge the proud idea, that I too once associated with them and that I too once had a claim to their regard.[2]

The *Surprize* finally arrived at Portsmouth. Her hull proved faulty and she remained there for six weeks undergoing repairs. Until Muir and Palmer left London they and their friends had believed their punishment would be mitigated, especially as so many important people were working on their behalf. When they were put on the transport hope began to fade. Lindsey wrote, 'The sentence against Muir and Palmer is so unjust that I can hardly persuade myself still that it will be executed.'[3] Others, however, who believed government propaganda that they were dangerous republicans, approved of their punishment. When news arrived at Portsmouth of the failure of Adam's motion, some naval officers in a ship alongside the *Surprize* ordered their men on deck, gave them a bumper of brandy, and told them to give three cheers.

Palmer was taken ill with the flux. This was the name given to both typhus and typhoid, which were not differentiated at the time. Convicts who were transferred to transports after long confinement in the hulks often suffered from continual fever. Palmer was ill for weeks and never completely recovered. Muir had another bout of 'rheumatism'.

The authorities were bombarded with requests and complaints. Palmer had pulled strings through the sister of Lord Grenville, then Foreign Secretary, to be allowed to take all the luggage he wanted; also for his servant and protégé, James Ellis, an intelligent but poor young man whom he had educated, to be allowed to accompany him as a free settler. Permission was granted, but it was stipulated that Ellis was not to work as Palmer's servant in Australia. Palmer never married. The Captain of the *Surprize*, Campbell, accused him of sodomy. Whether they had a homosexual relationship or not, Palmer was greatly attached to Ellis, to whom he bequeathed all his property. Other friends of Palmer's, Mr. Boston, his pretty wife, and their three small children, had also decided to emigrate with him.

Among other articles Palmer took with him a gun, swords and
pistols, a bay tree, a case of tamarinds, and a lurcher given by his
nephew to help catch kangaroos – believed to be the only form of
meat available.

After his conviction Palmer lost his senior fellowhip at Queens'
which constituted half his income, but he was still comparatively
well off. Palmer and Muir had been allotted cabins on the *Canada*,
for which they had paid £50 each, and were going to travel 'in the
characters of gentlemen'. But the *Surprize* was more crowded. At
first they shared a room with soldiers. When a Sergeant Reddish
arrived with more soldiers, orders came from Dundas that Palmer
and Muir were to be moved in with the other convicts. They remonstrated. Reddish offered to go surety for their safe custody, so they
were given cabins on the same deck as the soldiers and were to mess
with the captain. Reddish's manners and education were far above
his position, and it is possible that he was, as he claimed, Canning's
illegitimate brother. He said he had joined the New South Wales
Corps as he was averse to the French war, made out that he had great
respect for Muir and Palmer, and in return shared their table at their
cost. Shortly before the *Surprize* sailed they began to suspect that he
was a spy.

Besides the crew, and Reddish's force, there was the guard of one
ensign and twenty-one privates of the New South Wales Corps. Six
of these were deserters from other regiments who had been recaptured and were brought on board ironed hand and foot. A high
proportion of the crew and soldiers were Scottish. Ensign Patullo, in
charge of the convicts, was a Dundee man; his wife came from
Edinburgh. The Patullos, who had known the reformers in Scotland,
were kind and friendly. There was a vast preponderance of female
convicts on board, sixty women, none over forty. The authorities
hoped they would marry and encourage the male convicts to be more
industrious. The convicts included seventeen Englishmen and sixteen Scots, one of them the unpleasant John Grant, who was once
more put to share quarters with Muir and Palmer. Another was
William Henderson of Glasgow. Muir had defended him two years
before against a charge of murdering his wife. Muir pleaded successfully and the jury brought in a verdict of culpable homicide instead of
murder. Now Henderson too was being transported for fourteen
years.

The ship was wet and cold in daytime. At 9 p.m. candles were extinguished and hatches closed. Then, with seventeen sleeping in a small room under close unperforated wooden hatches, it became uncomfortably hot. The ship was so crowded exercise was impossible. Palmer wrote:

My prison is damp and unwholesome with twenty-four people talking, swearing and blocking the light of our little hatchway. I am not yet murdered and I hope by the blessing of God to save my persecutors from the guilt. The officers say Botany Bay is splendid. All are willing to return as they make a good thing out of life there. Goods not money are needed. Half a gallon of rum buys twelve fowls.

Margarot, whose wife was going out as a free settler, wrote sharply to Dundas demanding that she should receive adequate treatment and ending:

with unfeigned thanks for all the severities I have experienced by your express order – bolts, padlocks, handcuffs, confinement in damp pestilential places with common felons, stinted ship allowance of provisions – all these, tho' highly prejudicial to my three fellow sufferers and likely to prove fatal to two of them, have had a very different effect on me . . . my mind preserves its independence.

The ship's officers objected to Margarot's sharing his wife's cabin close to government employees. They much disliked his political views. Campbell moved the Bostons' children and put Mrs. Margarot in their sleeping-place. This offended Superintendent William Baker, a civil servant going out to the colony, as he had to pass Margarot to reach his wife's cabin. Campbell, clearly having a difficult time, complained that 'the crowded state of the ship and so many different types of passengers makes it impossible to give everyone as good accommodation as they want.'

With his jealous disposition Margarot behaved very tiresomely. He wrote to the Norwich Societies to acknowledge £20 delivered by Thomas Hardy.

Hardy seemed to think the money was meant to be divided among the four of us, but I acquainted him that those gentlemen were infinitely better off than myself as they are continually receiving private presents and are moreover supported by many noblemen and rich M.P.s. So Hardy gave the money to me.

All four men sent off a flurry of letters, many in response to
addresses from various societies. A hundred copies of the United
Irishmen's address to Muir and his reply were published in March.
Several thousand people attended an open-air meeting at Sheffield
where it was decided to petition the King on the reformers' behalf.
Many poems were sent to the 'exiled patriots' including a song from
Southey, then an ardent radical*. The newspapers carried almost
daily reports about them as every particular was 'at the present
moment listened to with eagerness'.[4]

Many friends travelled to Portsmouth or sent money and com-
forts. For many years afterwards Rutt referred to his 'delightful talks
with Muir' and described dining with Captain Campbell, his officers, and the reformers, who faced their future 'with cheerful
fortitude'.

Hardy was visiting the *Surprize* when Thomas Bankes the sculptor
took a cast of Muir's face from which he afterwards made a bust. An
engraving was made of the bust with appropriate lines from Thompson's hymn beneath it chosen by Anne Barbauld:

> Should fate command me to the farthest verge
> Of this green earth, to distant barbarous climes,
> 'Tis nought to me; I cannot go
> Where universal love not smiles around,
> From seeming evil still educing good,
> And better thence again, and better still
> In infinite progression. . . .

Copies were distributed among Muir's friends; some were sent to
him in New South Wales. Hardy said it was a correct likeness. Muir's
appearance had altered; as Cobbett gleefully pointed out in one of
his diatribes against the radicals,[5] Muir had lost a lot of weight since
his imprisonment.

Muir worried about Moffat, 'whose attachment to me has led him
to spend in my company almost all the time I have been in England'.
Moffat would now have little chance of prospering as a solicitor in
Edinburgh. Muir had entreated him to move to London and he asked
reformers such as Jeremiah Joyce if they would be kind enough to
introduce Moffat to their friends. Muir gave Moffat his gold watch
and chain as a parting present, and wrote him a very amateurish

* See below, p. 186.

poem of ten verses later published in Kay's *Edinburgh Portraits*. It
began:

> This gift, this little gift, with heart sincere,
> An exile, wafted from his native land,
> To friendship tried, bequeaths with many a tear,
> Whilst the dire bark still lingers on the strand. . . .

and continued with gloomy forebodings of the future:

> I soon shall join the dim aerial band –
> This stream of life has little time to flow.
> Oh! if my dying eyes thy soothing hand
> Should close – enough – 'tis all I ask below.
>
> This little relic, Moffat, I bequeath
> While life remains, of friendship, just and pure, –
> This little pledge of love, surviving death,
> Friendship immortal, and re-union sure.

The *Surprize* finally sailed at the end of April. The trials and
parliamentary debates had received a very unfavourable press
abroad. The Committee of Public Safety announced that they would
give shelter to men persecuted in the cause of liberty. They ordered
the French Admiralty to take all necessary steps to rescue Muir,
Palmer, and Margarot.[6] Muir later told a friend that, according to
American newspapers, the frigates *Alcide* and *Fabius* searched for
the *Surprize*. But she set out for Rio in a strong convoy of East
Indiamen protected by the frigate *Suffolk* and corvette *Swift*. If the
French ships did sight them they never attacked.

Ships on the outward journey restocked with water and provisions
in Brazil. Sometimes they also called at the Cape and eventually
made a landfall at the west coast of Van Diemen's land. The voyage
of the *Surprize*, with its petty squabbles, its cruelty and conspiracies,
the incipient hysteria, is reminiscent of *Treasure Island*. The convicts
were crowded into the hold; some were drunk, some rowdy, some ill;
the stench, filth, and noise were appalling.[7] A few officers kicked and
beat the women. Many soldiers and sailors took female convicts into
their bunks. The ship also carried cows, goats, sheep, pigs, hens,
ducks, dogs, and cats.

It is impossible to disentangle the intricacies of the mutiny that was
alleged to have taken place a month out to sea. When the *Surprize*
arrived at Botany Bay an enquiry was held, but no official action

taken. Campbell submitted a report, Skirving and Muir wrote memorials, seen by Mackenzie in 1830 but subsequently lost. Palmer published *A Narrative of the Sufferings of Thomas Fyshe Palmer and William Skirving during a Voyage to Botany Bay in 1794.** Campbell's and Palmer's versions conflict with each other and the statements of other witnesses. Conditions on the ship and the tedious monotony of the voyage must have imposed an intolerable strain on everyone. The reformers had already endured many misfortunes. Palmer and Margarot had prickly personalities. Margarot resented the other three's comparative affluence and the fact that he had not been included in the Whig motions in Parliament. Mrs. Margarot's presence created jealousy. Palmer's entourage of Ellis and the Bostons caused friction. Campbell was paranoiacally suspicious, but he had reason to be on his guard. Convicts had revolted on other ships bound for New South Wales; sometimes the soldiers had mutinied with them. Mutineers had been shot or hanged from the yard-arm. In view of the squalid conditions, conducive to disease, in which convicts travelled, it was not surprising that they tried to seize control. Food was scanty and repellent; the guards severe. Still, on the *Surprize*, with so many young female convicts hobnobbing with the crew, mutiny seemed less likely.

Seeds of dissension were noticed at Portsmouth and multiplied at sea. Almost at once Muir left his companions' mess. The melancholy which had overcome him in the Tolbooth returned and he took to drink. He spent the voyage brooding alcoholically in his cabin, where he ate his meals alone. He may have associated with one of the women, which could be the reason why he separated from the others. At Portsmouth, Palmer and Muir had long amicable arguments about the Trinity; but now Palmer showed his disapproval of Muir's behaviour.

At first there were two messes for the cabin passengers, one for the officers and their wives and one for the reformers. Campbell wanted to save money by amalgamating them and invited Margarot, Palmer, and Skirving to dine with him in the great cabin. Only Palmer accepted, the others dined in the steerage which was cheaper. Trouble arose over Ellis's passage. According to Palmer, Ellis, as a free settler, should have travelled at government expense, but Campbell

* Jeremiah Joyce edited this and wrote a Preface from Lord Stanhope's house, Chevening.

said that if Palmer did not pay his fare Palmer was not to touch the tea stores during the voyage. Palmer paid up, 'as it was not wise to irritate such a man as Campbell', but as Ellis had to sleep in a hammock in 'the most flagitious brothel in the universe', Palmer and the Captain became on increasingly bad terms. Ten days out to sea Campbell ordered Palmer to leave the table at dinner-time and mess with Skirving below. Palmer was deeply shocked by the women's lewd, drunken behaviour. Their brawling and screaming echoed round the steerage, so he formed a private mess with Ellis and the Bostons in Boston's cabin.

John Grant caused trouble again. As he was destitute, Muir and Palmer had paid for his food at Portsmouth, but he was soon caught by the ship's steward taking a purse containing over two guineas from Muir's breeches pocket. He also ordered the ship's carpenter to break open a box of Palmer's, pretending it was at Palmer's request. On Friday 31 May Campbell called all hands onto the quarterdeck and announced that a dangerous plot had been discovered among the soldiers to mutiny and sail the ship to France or America. Grant was once more the inventor and fomenter of the conspiracy. He pointed out six soldiers he alleged were involved and Campbell had them clapped in irons. According to Palmer, Margarot, 'who had paid obsequious court to Campbell', now appeared as the captain's confidant, heavily armed to help protect the ship. Palmer's comment is certainly prejudiced, for at Portsmouth Margarot had had little to do with Campbell and it was totally out of character for him to kowtow to anyone. Earlier in the voyage Palmer, Margarot, and Skirving had spent many evenings together, but Palmer and Margarot had by now developed an intense dislike for each other and, like figures in a weather-box, as one fell out with the captain, the other took his place.

Campbell was on bad terms with MacPherson, his chief mate, and the following day took advantage of an opportunity to quarrel with him. MacPherson and Superintendent Baker had quarrelled over Baker's dog. MacPherson complained about it to Campbell. There were sounds of altercations in the round-house and Campbell ordered Macpherson's arrest. Campbell later declared that he had remonstrated with MacPherson for ill-treating the female convicts and being permanently drunk. The ship's doctor, Thompson, said that MacPherson had warned Campbell there was not enough food and drink on board and hinted that Campbell had pocketed the money given him to buy supplies. Baker had MacPherson's convict girl flogged to induce her to give evidence against MacPherson, but she stoutly held out. In the evening Muir and Mrs. Campbell drew up a conciliatory letter for MacPherson to sign, but he refused. Palmer and the ship's doctor, Thompson, then drew up a petition in his favour: 'Hoping that Captain Campbell was not forgetful of the frailties of human nature arising from liquor or passion. . .'. They also pointed out that if Campbell fell ill only Macpherson could guide the ship. The other officers and passengers offered to sign the petition, but it had no effect. Campell hailed an Indiaman by trumpet and announced that mutiny had broken out.

In the morning Campbell went on board the frigate *Suffolk* and repeated the story to the Commodore. MacPherson was sent over under guard; he did not return to the *Surprize*, but was later put in charge of signals on the *Suffolk*. Campbell came back in a state of great agitation. He distributed arms to the sailors and settlers and appointed armed watches. He had two blunderbusses mounted in the round-house on swivels. Palmer said that he rushed into the round-house, bolted the door, rushed out again, summoned one person after another, called for his dog, and 'would have done credit to any stage'.

The next day Lieutenant Page from the *Suffolk* came on board and all hands were once more called. Palmer described Campbell as accoutred like Robinson Crusoe, pistols in his belt, breast, waistcoat and breeches pocket, plus a sword and dagger. Draper, one of the arrested soldiers, was no longer in irons. Campbell walked up and down the deck 'in affected sorrow' and announced that Draper had accused Palmer and Skirving of giving him money, tea, rum, and clothes to obtain his help in murdering the principal officers and seizing the ship. Palmer denied giving Draper anything; on the contrary, he had frequently caught him stealing and denounced him. Draper then said the other soldiers held in irons had heard Palmer and Skirving plotting. They all denied it.

The officers retired into the round-house. When they reappeared Campbell announced that every second man was to be flogged immediately and the rest next day. They were to be pardoned if they confessed. After being flogged two of the soldiers, not surprisingly, said they wanted to give evidence. One offered to give evidence against Sergeant Reddish, but Campbell rejected that. As a result of their confessions several convicts were clapped in irons. The arrested men were put in the poop. A heavy chain was run through their hand and leg irons and fastened to a staple and chain whose other end was fixed to Campbell's bed below. They had to crouch doubled up all night; by day they had to sit in the hot sun with backs bleeding from flogging. Campbell said if they stirred he would fire through the ceiling of the round-house.

Campbell scented mutiny everywhere. Two soldiers were accused of stealing the contents of a cask of porter. They were put in irons and, when one protested, Campbell took this as proof of insurrection.

On Campbell's orders Palmer and Skirving were confined in a cabin less than six feet square in the steerage. The ship was now in the torrid zone and the heat there intolerable. They were both large men and had to share a two-feet-wide bed which, as the ship leaked, was soaked with sea water. When Palmer protested Campbell ominously retorted that he'd soon sleep in a narrower. He relented, however, gave Skirving permission to go up to his old cabin on the quarterdeck at night, and allowed them both up on deck for two hours a day. Palmer complained that his stock of pistols, guns, and swords was confiscated, they were deprived of papers, and money, and forbidden to wash at the pump. Further trouble occurred when Skirving gave the sentinel set to guard them two glasses of port on the King's birthday. Later when, like the rest of the crew, the sentinel got drunk on small beer, Skirving and Palmer were blamed and forbidden wines and spirits. Beer ran out, however, before the ship reached Rio, so many, including Palmer, got the 'flux', and Dr. Thompson said Palmer must be allowed to use his own wine and brandy for medicinal purposes.

Near Trinidada most of the convoy turned for the Cape of Good Hope. The *Swift*, with three East Indiamen and the *Surprize*, sailed on to Rio, arriving on 4 July. From Rio everyone sent home his version of events. Skirving's letter to Joyce adds a further mysterious variation not referred to anywhere else:

You must by now have heard of the deep plot against Mr. Palmer and me. It was laid against Mr. Muir not me, but the design of it was blown before the plot was ripe and he escaped. The odium I incurred by aiding his escape and openly showing my sentiments of such conduct provoked putting myself in his place. I thank God, being convinced this impolitic step was a principal hindrance to the execution of the infernal plot against the life of Mr. Palmer.[8]

According to Palmer, Margarot told Muir to leave 'the Old Man below' and Skirving to their fate, as they were sure to be hanged. Although this may be another of Palmer's exaggerations, Dr. Thompson later said that he had not believed the accusations against Palmer and Skirving until Margarot supported them. When Margarot wrote home from Rio he did not accuse Palmer of complicity in any plot. Apparently later, influenced by his violent hostility to Palmer, he threw in his lot with Campbell, declared Palmer guilty, and Skirving his unwitting tool. He remained well disposed towards Muir. Muir on the other hand firmly supported Palmer and Skirving.

On the whole Muir comes well out of the affair. Although he did not protest with the vigour he might have shown a year or two before, he worked to vindicate Palmer and Skirving. Mrs. Patullo, who seems to have been as confused as everyone else by events, said that she thanked Muir for discovering the horrid plot. Muir instantly said he had discovered no plot and 'disbelieved every word respecting it'. He asked Campbell to rectify Mrs. Patullo's mistake. Campbell then said; 'Yes, it was Grant who had discovered the conspiracy.' Palmer wrote:

Justice compels me to say that Mr. Muir's behaviour was the reverse of Margarot's. At the time of my imprisonment we were not on the best of terms. But the moment he discovered the measures taken by Campbell, his resentment was forgotten, he sent me word that he would join hand and heart with me in the vindication of my innocence and in bringing my oppressors to justice. He kept a watchful eye on Campbell and collected some curious facts.

Palmer wanted Muir to act as his legal adviser but Campbell said he could not. Muir then had an inconclusive interview with Campbell, at which Campbell said that Lieutenant Page had ordered Palmer's arrest and he was merely guarding him until they reached New South Wales.

Campbell later stated that

Mr. Muir does not appear to have had any hand in the plot. On every occasion Messrs. Muir and Margarot conducted themselves with . . . propriety and offered their assistance to protect the ship with readiness and willingness honourable to themselves and pleasing to me.

A rather different light is thrown on Muir's behaviour by Superintendent Baker's deposition. When they were at Rio,

> ... Muir being in conversation with Skirving who ... was under close confinement, and in the care of a sentinel with strict orders not to allow him to converse with any person ... when I told him in the mildest manner that in so doing he acted wrong ... he answered he had only been borrowing a book. ... He insisted on my inspecting the book. ... After many entreaties Muir parted with Skirving, and stood by the round house door, uttering a number of disrespectful words. At first I took no notice seeing he was drunk (which happens as often as he can get liquor) however, he changed his position from the round house door to the binnacle, and still continued to insult and abuse those in the employment of Government. ... I struck him in a slight manner when he fell down. He then declared he never would pay any attention to any orders or directions.

Reddish corroborated this. He had overheard loud words between Baker, who considered Muir 'in the same light as any other convict on board', and Muir, who replied, 'I am no convict, sir, and I wonder that Government should send such scoundrels on board to insult a gentleman,' and desired Baker to give up talking 'as he was infinitely beneath his notice'. This happened before eight in the morning and Muir was intoxicated.

The *Surprize* remained at Rio for five weeks, longer than usual because there were difficulties over filling the water casks, and the sick convicts needed time to recover. Muir was allowed on shore, and must have been sober much of the time as he often visited the Antonine monks and gave books to 'an excellent man' with whom he made friends.[9] The monks gave him pamphlets in Latin. He presented them with the engraving of Dr. Price which had hung in his room at Newgate, and the *Memoirs* of John Hollis, a sceptic and critic of Calvinism. In 1802 a naval officer, James Tuckey, was shown this book when his ship called at Rio. He copied out the inscription and poem which Muir had written on a blank leaf in passable Latin, ending with quotations from Virgil and Horace:[10]

> *Thomas Muir de Hunters hill*
> *Gente Scotus, Anima Orbis terrarum Civis Obtulit.*
>
> *O Scotia! O longum felix longumque superba*
> *Ante alias patria, Heroum sanctissima tellus*
> *Dives opum fecunda viris, laetissima campis*
> *Uberibus!*
> *Aerumnas memorare tuas summamque malorum*

Quis queat, et dictis, nostros aequare dolores
Et turpes ignominias et barbara iussa?

Nos patriae fines et dulcia linquimus arva.

Cras ingens iterabimus aequor. *

From now on, his opinions sharpened by harsh treatment, Muir invariably referred to Scotland as an oppressed nation. Some of his wilder statements were probably made for effect – to demonstrate that, though transported as a convict, he was really a Scottish patriot victimized by the English. How much of them he genuinely believed, or persuaded himself to believe, it is hard to judge. In the eighteenth century one's public *persona* was extremely important. Muir had been trying not merely to be a lawyer but to achieve the higher calling of Reformer. Now that this had failed, he turned to the role of Patriot and Martyr.

Fearing, correctly, that many English radicals would be charged by the authorities, Muir wrote to Rutt:

> . . . the remembrance of former happiness, the recollections of hours never to be recalled, and the uncertainty of the fate of the persons to whom I address myself, fill my mind with such mixed sensations as to render me unwilling and afraid to take a pen in my hand. . . . The storm may have passed over me, but you and they stand yet exposed in the midst of the conflict of the elements. . . . Painful and disagreeable circumstances have occurred in the course of the voyage. Soon enough you will be acquainted with them. To me they have been fruitful source of many melancholy days.

Stocked with meat, vegetables, and fruit, the *Surprize* set sail again. The reformers as well as the crew laid in tobacco for exchange. Both sides prepared for an official investigation in Port Jackson. The rest of the voyage passed uneasily. Baker and Palmer had bought

---

* Thomas Muir of Hunters Hill
  By Race a Scot, in Spirit a Citizen of the World, has made this gift.

  O Scotland! O my country for long blessed and proud above others, most holy land of heroes rich in resources, fertile in men, most fortune in its rich plains! Who could ever relate thy afflictions and the extent of thy troubles, and find words to match our sorrows and base disgrace and those barbarous laws!

  We leave behind the frontiers of our fatherland and its sweet fields.

  Tomorrow we shall journey again over the vast ocean.

  [The penultimate line is a quotation from Virgil, *Eclogues* I, 3. The last line is a quotation from Horace, *Odes I*, vii, 32.]

lime, lemon, and orange trees at Rio. Palmer was allowed to keep his in his cabin, though it is surprising, to judge by his description of his cramped quarters, that there was room for them. Palmer's flourished but Baker's suffered when they sailed into cold latitudes; they were also damaged by a cat and two goats. This infuriated Baker, who accused Palmer of damaging them, and a padlock was put on Palmer's door as an extra safeguard. Dogs also caused a great amount of trouble. Campbell's mastiff bit two sentries and Boston; Palmer's dog was rumoured to have nipped Mrs. Margarot; Campbell's and Palmer's dogs fought. Campbell got bitten while trying to separate them and had Palmer's lurcher thrown overboard. Margarot, Baker, and Campbell held nightly cabals in the round-house. The Patullos, the Thompsons, and Muir kept to their cabins and hardly ever appeared. Patullo said everyone was wretched with so much talk of conspiracy, terrified they would be falsely accused and arrested.

Near Amsterdam Island, half-way between the Cape and Australia, the *Surprize* left the East Indiamen, and reached Port Jackson on 25 October after a voyage of nearly six months – a swift one for those days. Campbell shot off to the Acting Governor, Grose, carrying 'a monstrous bag of papers'. The exiles were kept on board. They sent the Governor and other officials letters of introduction from friends in England. With Muir's assistance, Palmer and Skirving had drawn up a long formal petition demanding a fair trial to clear them of Campbell's accusations. 'As so few cases had so much engaged the attention of the nation as theirs, they wanted every circumstance investigated.' They tactlessly had this delivered to the Governor at the same time. Grose replied that their protest was a very inauspicious beginning to their term in the settlement.

Palmer asserted that Campbell and Margarot went round threatening witnesses, but once on shore officers and passengers gave evidence in Palmer's and Skirving's favour. Depositions were taken but the recorded evidence is hopelessly garbled. Much is hearsay or irrelevant, there are endless discrepancies. No one except Campbell and Baker appears to have really believed in the plot. Mrs. Patullo said that even Mrs. Campbell had thought it impossible that Palmer and Skirving were guilty, and that Draper had accused them to save himself. Palmer had gone around criticizing Campbell to all who would listen, but it seems surprising that Campbell should have

Woolwich: convicts at work

Port Jackson, near Botany Bay

turned so rapidly against Skirving, with whom he had been on excellent terms and whom he considered 'a most devout man'. Baker, who disapproved strongly of the reformers, egged Campbell on, but Campbell really had no plausible reason for causing so much additional misery to so many. Conversely, several witnesses, including Grant, reported that Boston had perpetually made violent republican speeches at Portsmouth. Why did no one suggest arresting him?

A damning report from Campbell about the supposed mutineers and a further salvo of letters were sent to England. On 13 December Muir wrote to Moffat: 'I have been constantly occupied in preparing . . . the defence of Messrs. Palmer and Skirving. That affair will make a noise in Europe.' Muir composed a letter which the three men sent to Joyce for publication, deeply regretting that their first letter of a public nature must be on such a painful subject, but Margarot, because of his behaviour, was expelled from their company. Grant, to his fury, received no reward and promptly admitted that the mutiny was a fabrication. Grose, about to return home, had no desire to get embroiled in the case, and the matter lapsed.

Muir and Palmer were right in claiming that the affair would cause a furore at home. But, being so closely involved, they did not appreciate that their quarrel with Margarot would cause great distress among the reformers and amusement to their enemies. When Palmer's account was published it further damaged Margarot's reputation. It is a lively piece of propaganda. Palmer was abominably and unjustly treated, but he does stretch the facts to make out a good case against Campbell and Margarot. Hardy, who had worked with Margarot at the London Corresponding Society, found it hard to believe that he had behaved so badly. Some years later, in an attempt to clear Margarot's name, he asked Francis Place, one of the most remarkable self-made men thrown up by the early reform movement, to sift the available evidence.

Place went into the matter with characteristic thoroughness. One volume of the Place MSS. in the British Library contains reports from various witnesses with his shrewd comments, but he comes to no clear-cut conclusion. He noted Muir's separation from the others at the start of the voyage, an indication that there had been dissension early on; that Skirving and Palmer had been unwise to give drink and money to the soldiers, and Margarot to become so friendly with Campbell, but that there was no evidence of malicious intent on anyone's part. Place could only base his findings on a retrospective study of surviving documents. He was 23 when the exiles went away and did not know them personally. Skirving was a kind, upright man. At the time of Palmer's arrest Muir was on better terms with Margarot than with Palmer. The fact that Skirving and Muir so completely dissociated themselves from Margarot does indicate that he had not behaved well. While in New South Wales Margarot kept a diary full of extraordinary malicious, false statements, product of a distorted mind. Exile undoubtedly exacerbated his unbalanced temperament, but to have sided with Campbell and abandoned his fellow reformers, through pathological jealousy of Palmer, was odd to say the least. As a result Margarot's life at Botany Bay was far more solitary and unpleasant than it need have been, and the rupture marred the reputation of all the reformers.

CHAPTER 9

Botany Bay

The four men were the first political prisoners in the colony. As they had never been accustomed to labour, they were not compelled to work like other convicts; but they were therefore not entitled to any provisions from the government stores. This meant that, if they did not receive enough private means from home, or could not grow enough to barter for essential goods, they would have to work for them. This was a great problem as provisions were very scarce and exorbitantly expensive. However, when the four first arrived, Grose said that, as they might need things which could not be bought for money, they were to send him a list and he would provide them himself.

They were allotted three brick huts side by side in one of the streets that straggled along the shore of Port Jackson nine miles north of Botany Bay (named after the many previously unknown flowers Joseph Banks discovered when he landed there with Captain Cook). The area, now covered by Sydney, was mostly wooded; but clearings had been made round the settlement, where only great red gum trees remained. In the centre of the township was an avenue leading past the chief officials' houses to the Governor's, the only two-storey building. It had a garden and was surrounded by a stockade. Convict encampments were scattered about the cove. There were two small jetties. The first settlers had landed in January 1788; in 1790 reinforcements arrived. Parramatta, reached by boat or a track from the coast through the gum forest, became the economic centre where crops were grown. In 1794 a new settlement was founded further north on the Hawkesbury river, but the colony occupied only about 900 square miles and almost nothing was known of the rest of the continent. By the end of 1794 the population had risen to about 3,000, of which half were round Sydney Cove. 2,000 were convicts, there were 67 free emigrants, and the rest were soldiers, administrators, and convicts whose term had ended. There were really only two classes of inhabitants, the convicts and their overseers.

The colony was administered by a Governor. He had a small civil establishment which consisted of magistrates, medical staff, superintendents of convicts, carpenters, among others. Nearly all his assistants were very young. He also controlled a small military force, the New South Wales Corps, formed in 1790. Members were recruited from regiments at home. Some joined as an alternative to hanging, others volunteered hoping to make their fortune. There were seventeen officers.

It was some time before land suitable for growing crops was found. There were no ploughs and few convicts had any farming experience, so at first almost all food was imported. Government ships came from Britain, trading vessels from the Cape and India. Cattle and sheep were introduced but many died or escaped into the bush. If ships were delayed by storms wheat had to be rationed and candles ran out. The chronic food shortage affected everyone's health; the convicts complained they were too poorly fed to work. Most convicts were improvident and lacked any incentive because they did not work for themselves. The majority were put to clearing the bush, building, and making roads. Cement was weak through lack of lime, so houses were only one storey high, made of brick or wattle with thatch or shingle roofs. They were often damaged by ants. Small boats were built but were poorly constructed.

There was also a great dearth of manufactured goods. A few ineffective attempts had been made to start industries. The Governor was hampered by the acute labour shortage and the fact that in London so many different government departments dealt with the colony. Every question and request for supplies took months to reach home and then might be passed from one official to another.

Life was primitive and squalid. There was almost no sanitation and the mortality rate from dysentery and the harsh conditions was very high. Many soldiers fell ill and had to be sent home. Although a few convicts were educated, decent men, the majority were illiterate and took refuge in drink. The women, who made the clothes and acted as servants, were more troublesome than the men. The Governors tried to encourage marriage, but most male convicts slept around indiscriminately and fought over the women. Those who became officers' and officials' mistresses were said to be at the bottom of all the most infamous transactions in the colony. There were hardly any books. One gentleman opened his sideboard and showed his guests 'my books' – bottles.

The aborigines had at first been extremely friendly, but ill-treatment by soldiers and convicts made them wary. Occasionally convicts tried to escape by boat, or walking north, some imagining China was not far away. They died or were brought back in poor condition. One group lived with the aborigines for some time because the natives thought they were the ghosts of their ancestors whom death had turned white. Some convicts escaped into the woods and became the scourge of outlying districts, living by theft and making constant raids on the houses and gardens. A few industrious settlers and ex-convicts prospered, but most convicts who had served their term became another problem for the authorities. They prowled round the settlements doing odd jobs, or joined the bands of escaped convicts in the bush. Still the country was beautiful and the climate, except for periods of great heat, magnificent.

There was no currency. The chief sources of money were bills on the storehouse and Treasury bills sent by the Home Government. The officers had access to these and also to regimental funds. As a result they were able to club together and charter cargoes or barter with the infrequent visiting ships. They could prevent sea captains charging exorbitant rates, but they acquired a near monopoly of imports. When Grose became Acting Governor late in 1792 he transferred authority from the civil magistrates to his officers, to whom he also made generous land grants and allotted ten field workers each, clothed and fed at government expense. The officers and a few civilians supervised the manufacture and sale of alcohol and imported rum. Because such huge profits could be made from alcohol they made no attempt to curb consumption. Rum became the currency. Still the convicts worked much harder when paid in rum than they did when employed by the Government.

The officers did contribute to the economic progress of the settlement. They soon became efficient farmers and grew most of the crops, which they sold to the Government. They were enterprising and ambitious and were largely responsible for the gradual but increasing prosperity. Also a class of vigorous middlemen began to emerge from the ranks of the convicts, free settlers, and petty officers.

Muir, Palmer, and Skirving were allotted two convicts each as servants. They bought farms near Sydney Cove. Palmer paid £84 for 100 acres. Skirving called his New Strathruddie after his home in

Scotland. Muir called his Huntershill – thirty acres in densely wooded country across the water from Port Jackson which Muir reached by boat.*

The reformers were separated by education and background from almost the entire community. As convicts they could not easily mix with the few cultivated men. At first they were regarded with deep suspicion and disapproval by the authorities. Garbled versions of their supposed crimes had reached Port Jackson, so remote from England that no one knew the true circumstances of their trials. Many officers believed they had helped carry out the French Revolution. But they soon gained respect. David Collins, Secretary to the colony, said that 'the gentlemen from Scotland were among the most orderly and exemplary individuals'. Bennett, who in 1841 interviewed people who had known them, said that 'they left behind them a most favourable impression of their characters and conduct and were regarded with the deepest sympathy'. The convicts admired them because they were not put to hard labour.

The exiles found that, though the benefits of civilization were lacking, the country itself was not so bleak and desolate as they had been led to expect. Palmer, whose eyes were inflamed by 'the disease of the country', wrote home praising the colony:

Mr. Muir, at whose house I write, and honest Mr. Skirving are both . . . I think, as easy and cheerful as myself. The reports you have had of this country are mostly false. The soil is capital; the climate delicious. . . . It wants only virtue and liberty to be another America. I never saw a place where a man could so soon make a fortune and that by agriculture. The officers have already done it. . . . An honest and active governor might soon make it a region of plenty. In spite of rapacity and robbery (on the part of the officials) I am clear it will thrive. . . . Transportation here will become a blessing. I heartily wish that all the paupers of Great Britain could make interest to be sent here. . . . It is a land of wonder and delight, the beasts, the fish, the birds, the reptiles, the plants, the trees, the flowers, are all . . . so beautiful and grotesque that no naturalist would believe the most faithful drawing.[1]

Palmer ended with a request for seed of the early York cabbage, onions, and everlasting pea.

Muir's only surviving letter from Botany Bay was written to

---

* Australian antiquarians disagree as to whether the Sydney suburb Hunters Hill is called after his farm, and precisely where it was. Probably it lay on the northern shore of what is now Sydney Harbour, at Milson Point.

Moffat, now living in London, on 13 December. Its tone is less invigorating than Palmer's, but he too came down to practicalities:

> ... I am perfectly well; ... pleased with my situation as much as a person can be who is for ever separated from all they loved and respected. ... I have a neat little house here, and another two miles distant, at a farm across the water. A servant of a friend who has a taste for drawing has etched the landscape you will see it.
>
> When any money is transmitted, cause a considerable part of it to be laid out at the Cape or Rio in rum, tobacco, sugar, which are invaluable, and the only medium of exchange. In a country like this, where money is really of no value, and rum everything you must perceive the necessity of my having a constant supply by every vessel. For a goat I should pay £10. For less than 8 gallons of spirits, at 18d the gallon, I can make the same purchase. Tobacco at Rio sells for 3d per pound, here at 3/6d. That too is an article to be considered. ... In closing a letter to you it is like taking a farewell for ever. Now my dearest friend I pray for every blessing of Heaven upon you and your family. No day passes without you living in my thoughts. ...[2]

The landscape Muir refers to was probably painted by Thomas Watling, a young professional artist from Dumfries who had been transported for forgery. When White, the Surgeon General who treated the reformers kindly, did not need his services to help build a hospital, he lent him out to paint for friends. Gregarious by nature, Muir faced the prospect of an extremely lonely life ahead. Margarot had his wife, with whom he carried on a running battle, Palmer had Ellis and the Bostons for company, Skirving had left his family behind, but he – like Palmer – was over fifty. Muir would now waste his best years in exile. Letters took months to arrive and it is not surprising that he wanted to impress his memory on those he had left behind.

Records of the colony in its initial years contain only a few brief references to the reformers. In 1797 a pamphlet was published in Paris, *Histoire de la Tyrannie Anglaise envers le Célèbre Thomas Muir, Ecossais*, based on interviews a M. Mazois had with Muir at Bordeaux. The Parisian editor who reworked Mazois's material exaggerated or invented many of Muir's later adventures, but he printed in roughly Muir's own words his enthusiastic description of the exotic, unknown land of New South Wales and an account of his life at Port Jackson: Muir spent his time cultivating his land with the aid of two servants, reading the books he had been able to bring with him, and fishing from a little boat he made. As a fisherman he was allowed to go out to the open sea. Fish were plentiful; the sandbanks filled with oysters, mussels, and cockles. There were fewer fish at Port Jackson than at Botany Bay, probably because its shores were devastated by enormous sharks. The natives were terrified of these monsters.

Muir said that the climate was superb, though in summer there was a scorching wind. The land was flat, stony in places, marshy in others, watered by an infinity of springs and streams. The main settlement was in an attractive position on a curving bay. There were avenues of mangroves, quantities of wild spinach. Many of the trees were covered with brilliant, deliciously scented flowers. Corn, maize, and other European grains and vegetables flourished. Cuttings had been taken from vines at the Cape and were doing extremely well. Several barrels of magnificent wine had been extracted from them. So far only about twenty-four cows and twelve mares had survived, but they were acclimatized and it was hoped they would breed. Pigs, sheep, dogs, cats, hens, turkeys, and ducks had multiplied. No one had yet dared penetrate far into the surrounding forests where there were wild dogs and tree frogs, birds with beautiful plumage and melodious plaintive song. There were snakes, some of which were dangerous, armadillos, scorpions, centipedes, lizards.

Muir described the kangaroo in detail. Only the garrison, or convicts who had been given permission, could hunt them. Their tender, tasty flesh resembled veal. They were chased by greyhounds, but the kangaroo often escaped, jumping twenty feet at a time and retreating into the thickest woods. The officers also hunted the cassowary, which tasted like beef and lived in the desert. It ran much faster than the hounds so it was very difficult to get within firing range. This, said Muir scathingly, made the hunt more attractive for those who only found pleasure in difficulties.

The government was despotic because the population was mostly composed of scoundrels and prostitutes, but they were well treated and helped in their enterprises when they behaved. There were about as many women as men, also children who had been born in the country. Fifty marines were always on guard to prevent men escaping to live among the natives. The Governor's power was very great. Punishments were whipping, imprisonment, exile on an isolated rock some distance from shore, or death. The indigenous inhabitants, who were numerous around Botany Bay, were dark-skinned with long straight black hair. They were very gentle and timorous, so apathetic that nothing the Europeans owned tempted them. As the climate was mild they were completely nude and those who had been given clothes made no use of them. They fished, ate wild yams, and travelled about in canoes. They had laws, a religion, and a form of government. They knew how to march in line and handled their lances, wooden swords, and huge clubs with great dexterity. They talked of a terrible gigantic animal with colossal footprints. It resembled a man, was covered with hair, had horns on its forehead, was twelve feet high, and carnivorous. Muir had seen its footprints, measured them, and this height did not appear proportionately exaggerated.

To judge from contemporary accounts Muir spent his time 'in ease and retirement living out of town'. The shy, quiet side of his disposition once more predominated – through force of circumstances as there was no one of his own age and inclinations with whom he could associate. He appears to have overcome the initial depression which drove him to drink. If he did drink too much on occasion no one noticed. Drinking to excess was a common eighteenth-century vice and, in such surroundings, it is unlikely that anyone would have commented. Judging from the fact that Muir remained on excellent terms with Palmer, who later emphasized his robust health, he must have kept any drinking under control. Also, perhaps due to the dry, sunny climate, whatever tubercular or bronchial trouble he suffered from disappeared. Muir wrote commentaries on the trials of Palmer, Skirving, and Gerrald, and began a treatise on the libel law of Scotland. He took these papers with him when he escaped, but they were subsequently lost.

The chaplain to the settlement was an evangelical who had been at Cambridge, the Revd. Richard Johnson. At first he had to preach in the fields as priority was given to building stores and houses. Finally Johnson built his own wattle and daub church, completed in 1793. This irritated Grose and, by the time an assistant chaplain, Samuel Marsden, arrived, Grose and Johnson were on very bad terms. Marsden was another Cambridge man, more robust, a protégé of Wilberforce. Johnson became depressed and exhausted by the authorities' indifference and the irreligion of most convicts. Matters improved when Governor Hunter, a devout man, arrived. Johnson and Marsden doubted their ability to reclaim the convicts and took refuge in farming, at which both were extremely successful. Though they worked among the convicts they made no attempt to have social contact with them. Johnson had no Christian compassion for the exiles. A year after they arrived he wrote to a fellow clergyman at home:

I have had many letters of recommendation of the seditious gentlemen . . . but the principles they have espoused and as strenuously propagated . . . are no good recommendation. I pity and respect Skirving the most . . . he has purchased a farm to which he has retired and is but little seen. Muir conducts himself as far as I have heard with propriety – Palmer is always upon the bustle, but I feel no partiality to my brother parson. Margarot has no communication with any of the above persons. I hear little of them, but can see in conversation they are yet warm in the cause in which they have embarked.

According to Mackenzie, Palmer, Skirving, and Muir held a service every Sunday behind their huts. Hunter, another Scotsman, would sometimes walk into his garden to listen to them singing psalms and hymns. Muir, who appears to have diverted his energy from politics to religion, tried to help the more amenable of the convicts. There were few bibles for those who could read and they found handwriting difficult, so Muir spent much time 'printing in large clear letters those passages from his bible concerning repentance and Christ's love for sinners which he thought were most likely to appeal to them'.[3] A printing press was sent out and, when two young convicts arrived who were printers by trade, Muir printed biblical extracts with their assistance.

Muir refrained from getting involved in local intrigues. In official reports Muir's and Skirving's conduct was described as exemplary, 'but the same could not be said of Palmer'.[4] Palmer wrote to Rutt on 13 June 1795: 'Mr. Muir, myself, Mr. and Mrs. Boston and Ellis live together and are well,'[5] the convicts paid to work on Palmer's farm had been removed, the soldiers forbidden to speak to him, and he had been threatened with the cells if he did not doff his cap to the officers. Though he was inclined to exaggerate, other sources corroborate his complaints. Palmer also said that when he arrived there had been good relations between the blacks and whites but they had deteriorated. As the colonists cultivated more land on the banks of the Hawkesbury, they destroyed the wild yams which the aborigines ate, so they were reduced to stealing Indian corn to stay alive. Troops were sent in to drive the natives away and many were killed.

Palmer and his fellow exiles found 'living enormously dear', especially as 1795 was a bad year. In January very heavy rains ruined the crops. The *Endeavour* brought arrack, tea, and muslin from India, but few provisions. Another ship arrived from the Cape with 30,000 gallons of brandy and the cells were soon full of drunks. In April meat rations were cut and by July all salted provisions had been used bar a few casks reserved for the soldiers. The convicts had to be issued with rice, which they detested, instead of flour. By August there was a salt shortage. According to Collins, Boston, 'who was supposed to possess skill in making salt from sea water, was allowed seven men to help him, but in four weeks only produced four bushells'. Due to the food shortage the convicts fought among themselves and there were almost daily robberies. The settlers were issued with arms for protection, but many got into convicts' hands. Muir's house was broken into and nearly all his property stolen. He got some of his clothing back, 'but still remained a considerable sufferer by the visit'.

Another store-ship, too heavily loaded, was forced to turn back just before the new Governor, Hunter, arrived on 7 September. His ship only brought a few barrels of salt meat, a town clock, and the principal parts of a windmill. A few days later two ships set off for India with fifty persons whose transportation had ended and many more convicts secreted themselves on board. This was particularly tiresome for the authorities, as the loss of even one man's labour made a difference. Still, by the end of the year the food shortage was over. The harvest was good, more shipments of food arrived, and men felt strong enough to work longer hours. By 1796 the fruit trees, oranges, limes, apricots, guavas, and figs, were providing good crops.

Hunter had been misled by Campbell's account of the mythical conspiracy, and spent part of the long voyage out planning how to deal with the exiles. However, he changed his mind when he met them. He wrote to a friend (in Leith):

The gentlemen whom the activity of the Magistrates of Edinburgh provided for our colony I have seen and conversed with separately. They seem all of them gifted in the power of conversation. Muir was the first I saw. I thought him a sensible young man, of a very retired turn, which certainly his situation in this country will give him an opportunity of indulging. He said nothing on the severity of his fate, but seemed to bear his circumstances with a proper degree of fortitude and resignation. Skirving appeared to be a sensible, well informed man. . . . He is fond of farming and has purchased a piece of ground and makes good use of it. . . . Palmer is said to be a turbulent, restless minded man . . . but I must do him the justice to say that I have seen nothing of that disposition in him. . . . Margarot seems to be a lively, facetious talkative man – complained heavily of the injustice of his sentence. . . . their general conduct is quiet, decent and orderly.[6]

Hunter was nearly sixty. Most of his active service had been spent in subordinate positions. He was pleasant and friendly, but easily deceived, petulant, self-pitying, and irascible. He did his best to improve conditions in the colony, but was not a forceful personality. One of his first actions was to restore authority to the civil magistrates. This made him very unpopular with the officers. Although Hunter attempted other reforms, he was unable to stem the general drunkenness and criminal behaviour of many convicts.

Palmer bought a stock of rum. This formed the basis for a lucrative trading business which he gradually built up and ran with great ability. Boston and Ellis were able to manufacture beer, vinegar, salt, and soap without interference and did extremely well because they were all very expensive commodities in the government stores. Under Hunter's regime Boston successfully sued Laycock, an officer of the Corps, the first case brought by a settler against the soldiers, Muir was not allowed to plead, but his skill and advice were largely responsible for Boston's success. A number of Boston's pigs frequently trespassed on land belonging to an army Captain. He did not mind, but Quartermaster Laycock, who had quarrelled with Boston about money, ordered Private Faithful to shoot one of the trespassing pigs. Either by accident or design the best pig was killed; blows ensued. Boston was struck on the head by a musket and summoned Faithful, Laycock and two other members of the Corps, claiming £500 damages. Collins, who, though he had no legal training, had been appointed Judge Advocate, presided over the case which took seven days and created a great stir. Boston was awarded damages against Faithful and Laycock.

On 14 October 1795 the exiles presented Hunter with a memorial drawn up by Muir. They claimed that the extent of their punishment was banishment, the means of carrying it into effect transportation.

The terms of the sentence had already been completed and they were now entitled to all the rights of free men, except that they could not return to Britain. They quoted Gerrald's trial at which counsel for the Crown had declared that, in his opinion, once landed in Botany Bay, the Scotch Court had no further jurisdiction over them. Hunter sent their memorial to the Duke of Portland, then Home Secretary. He said that he did not feel justified in forcibly detaining them. They had been

particularly cautious of not giving the public any claim on their labour, for they have not accepted any provision from the public store. . . . They have lived quiet, retired and as much at their ease as men in their circumstances can . . . yet they do not appear satisfied with their situation here considered as compulsory. They can have no other cause of dislike. Although they cannot return to Great Britain but at the risk of life, they might desire to go to Ireland.[7]

Long after Muir had escaped, Hunter received the Duke's reply: the Scotch judges condemned the memorial's thesis as completely erroneous. It was the Governor's duty to prevent the four men escaping; nor could they return with impunity to Ireland.

Gerrald arrived in November. After his trial he had spent a year in Newgate. He was suddenly whipped off to Portsmouth and sent away on the *Sovereign* transport. Margarot wrote to Hardy in his usual malicious manner: 'Gerrald is arrived . . . . he has fled my habitation, and the fraternal reception I gave him, to join others, who may, in return for those good things he has brought with him, encourage his failings and feed his vanity with insidious praise.' Gerrald spent two months with Palmer, then moved to a little house with a garden of his own.

Some of the convicts obtained permission to build a playhouse which opened on 16 January 1796. Gallery seats at the opening performance cost 1/–, but tickets could also be bought for flour, meat, or spirits. The first play performed was *The Revenge*, for which a celebrated prologue was written, attributed to George Barrington, a famous London pickpocket:[8]

From distant climes o'er widespread seas we come.
Though not with much éclat or beat of drum;
True patriots we, for be it understood,
We left our country for our country's good.
No private views disgraced our generous zeal,
What urged our travels was our country's weal;

And none will doubt but that our emigration
Has proved most useful to the British Nation.

During the performance less cultured convicts took the opportunity
to rob the audience's huts.

About six months after the exiles landed, a ship sailed into harbour which for a short while they believed was an American frigate
sent to rescue them. Their hopes were soon dashed as it turned out to
be an Indian trader. On 24 January 1796, however, a ship that was to
change the course of Muir's life appeared, the *Otter* from Boston.
Her captain Ebenezer Dorr's family owned a fleet of China tea
clippers. The day before the *Otter* docked, the store-ship *Ceres*
arrived bringing two Frenchmen and two Englishmen from Amsterdam Island where they had been marooned for three years. They had
landed as a sealing party from a French brig, which had shortly
afterwards been seized by a British man-o-war. The most enterprising and well educated of the four men, Captain François Peron, took
charge of the stranded party. They lived on seal meat and cured
several thousand sealskins, which they had to leave on the island.
Dorr had also called at Amsterdam and brought off as many of the
sealskins as he could. To his annoyance they were claimed by Peron
and his companions. After attempting to evade the issue, Dorr finally
handed the skins over and offered Peron the post of first officer on his
ship. Dorr needed more men for the next lap of his journey, when he
would be dealing with potentially hostile Indians.

The *Otter*, 168 tons with 3 masts and 10 guns, was bound for the
north-west coast of America, where furs and skins could be obtained
for barter from the Indians and sold in Chinese ports; from Canton
she would return to America via the Cape.[9] The *Otter* had put in for
wood, water, and minor repairs. She remained at Port Jackson for
three weeks. Peron was twenty-seven, four years younger than Muir.
He met and befriended Muir, who was delighted to meet an intelligent young man who did not treat him as an outcast, and with whom
he could once more talk French.

Mackenzie said that Muir's friends in America sent a ship to
rescue him. According to a letter of Margarot's printed in the *Edinburgh Advertiser*, 'It is reported that the Otter came in here for as
many of us as cared to go.' The Editor commented 'Hamilton Rowan
has been often heard to say he would send a ship from America for

them and it is conjectured that the Otter was hired by him for this purpose.' That incurable optimist Hamilton Rowan, after a dramatic escape from gaol in Dublin, had arrived via France at Wilmington, Delaware, where he was living in great poverty. He may have suggested to Dorr that he look out for the exiles, but there is no evidence of any contact. Although the exiles had hopes of being rescued by an American ship, the *Otter* appears to have been on a normal trading voyage. It was common practice for merchant ships that touched at the colony to take convicts away. The authorities had not sufficient manpower to prevent them.

In his subsequent account of his escape Muir said that it was agreed to give him and his servants passage to Boston, provided he could escape without compromising Dorr. Dorr would have taken Palmer and Skirving too, but they felt too ill and old for such a voyage; besides Palmer did not want to leave Ellis and the Bostons. Palmer and Gerrald urged Muir to go as he was young and strong.

. . . . Upon the evening of the 18th I pushed out . . . in a small boat, with two servants to whom I could not divulge my design before the moment of execution. About the middle of the next day we were received into the ship, which had left the harbour upon the morning of the 19th, at a considerable distance from land. . . . In an emergency so critical and to me, so momentous, I could not provide myself with any necessaries for the voyage . . . only the shirt and the coat upon my back.[10]

In fact Muir also took a few of his smallest and most precious possessions: his pocket bible, the engraving of his portrait, copies of his trial and other political pamphlets, the legal commentaries he had been working on. The French account of Muir's adventures adds a few romantic embellishments. Muir had been given a compass. He and his companions rowed far out to sea to the agreed meeting-point, but the *Otter* had been delayed. They passed the night dozing, shivering with cold. The next morning Muir tied his shirt to an oar and fixed it upright in the boat, which had drifted from the meeting-place, but the shirt was spotted by an American sailor.

Muir left a note bequeathing his books and papers to Palmer, and also a letter for Hunter thanking him for all his kindness. He said that he was only asserting his freedom and, if he arrived safely, proposed to practise at the American bar until he could return to his own country. Muir had only spent sixteen months in the colony when he made the courageous and apparently sensible decision to escape. The

voyage would be hazardous, long, and uncomfortable, but he would
be a free man again. Impossible to predict whether, if he had stayed
in New South Wales, he would have died, emerged a tiresome,
embittered wreck, or found a useful outlet for the energy and
enthusiasm he had once shown in the cause of reform.

On 16 March Gerrald died, aged 36. He was buried at his request
in his garden.[11] Three days later Skirving died of dysentery 'as the
labour of harvest was over'. He attributed his illness to the harsh year
of 1795, others to his pining for his family. Hunter, who showed no
anger at Muir's escape, wrote to inform Portland of the

> . . . changes among those people sent to this colony whose names had been
> much mentioned in public. . . so that no untrue reports may be circulated by
> their friends or connections [clearly a dig at Palmer]. Captain Dorr, . . .
> having been treated with much civility and assisted in his repairs as far as in
> our power, . . . contrary to a very pointed article in the Port Orders, carried
> from hence several people, amongst them Mr. Thomas Muir.

Hunter then mentioned the deaths of Gerrald and Skirving,

> . . . a very decent quiet and industrious man who was indefatigable in his
> attentions to his farm. . . . There therefore remain of the five persons . . .
> only two.
>   Those who are now gone have been often heard to complain of the want of
> that attention from their friends in England which they had been led to
> expect, but of which they had not since their arrival here received any proofs
> whatever.

Ships were slow and infrequent and local officials often defrauded
the convicts of boxes and parcels, unless they had been booked in the
log or mate's book. As Palmer complained, 'between the rogues on
ship and shore a convict is sure not to get them because he has no
redress.' In addition, reformers at home were having a difficult time
and had little money to spare. In Scotland there were only two
choices, to keep silent or to emigrate. Muir's former agent, Campbell, like Moffat, had moved to London. John Millar had left for
America with his wife because no one would give him work. Henry
Erskine, who took part in a public protest meeting at the Government's bills against seditious assemblies, was, as a result, dismissed
from his post as Dean of the Faculty of Advocates, an unprecedented
action. In England Hardy, Joyce and others had been arrested in May
1794, charged with High Treason. They were acquitted in October,

but the Government continued its policy of repression which lasted a generation. Coleridge described it:

There was not a city, no, not a town, in which a man suspected of holding democratic principles could move abroad without receiving some unpleasant proof of the hatred in which his supposed opinions were held by the great majority of the people.[12]

The rich, who could most easily have helped the exiles, had almost all abandoned reform. Besides, people at home had no real conception of the problems and shortages in New South Wales and, as the war progressed and conditions in Britain became harsher, the 'martyrs' slipped from the forefront of men's minds.*

On 6 March 1796 Margarot wrote to Hardy – briefly, because of a paper shortage. He wished Muir success in his escape, but would not be influenced by his example. He would remain at his post until 'my country recalls me or gives me up entirely'.[13]

On 23 April Palmer wrote that Muir was

... to visit the Friendly Isles, ... to stay some time at the Philipines, to proceed to China and then Boston, a voyage of two years. I told him I thought I should be at home before him [an ironic comment as neither would reach home again]. He went in excellent health and spirits as his constitution is of iron. With Margarot I have no intercourse, so I am left alone with none to associate with but my friends Boston and Ellis.

Eighteen months after Muir had escaped, Palmer wrote to a friend that he was keeping 'their spirits up in horrible circumstances'.[14] Muir's effects had been sold by the Provost Marshal to pay his creditors. A large deal box addressed to him had arrived aboard the *Ganges*. With great difficulty, Palmer obtained permission to open it in the Governor's presence. It contained brown paper parcels from various friends, newspapers, two counterpanes from the London Corresponding Society, and letters for Muir, which he burnt. Private property from Muir's father was taken to be sold.

---

* Though Muir was still a radical bogeyman. In 1796 a loyalist coin was issued with a picture of 'The Three Thomases' hanging on a gibbet – Paine, Muir, and Thomas Spence, Paine's publisher. On the reverse was inscribed 'A way to prevent knaves getting a trick.'

CHAPTER 10

Across the Pacific

The next lap of Muir's odyssey is recorded in Peron's diary.* Details of some of Muir's movements are missing, but the Diary does contain a vivid description of the *Otter*'s voyage across the Pacific. It was a remarkable journey. In 1796 the Pacific was largely unknown; few Europeans since Cook had been in these waters. The principal groups of islands were marked on the map. There were Spanish posts scattered on the western islands and a few whites were living in Tahiti and Hawaii. The sea was full of uncharted rocks, the islands of strange, potentially hostile peoples.

Muir was treated as a passenger and lodged in the after cabin, not with the other escaped convicts. Dorr was a harsh captain who did not treat his crew well. The convicts equally complained of his behaviour. Dorr's son said his father had trouble with the convicts on the voyage. They were a rough lot and both sides were probably equally to blame. In spite of the primitive conditions it must have been an exhilarating time for Muir. He had escaped successfully. Freed from the humiliating conditions of Botany Bay he was sailing with a congenial companion in calm, sunny weather, through pearly waters dotted with palm-covered atolls, to eventual reunion with friends in America. The Diary contains a tribute from Peron, a totally disinterested person, which indicates the good qualities Muir must have possessed:

Among the transported Mr. Dorr hid on board was one whose memory will always be dear to me. Mr. Muirr [Peron always spelt his name thus] was a man '*d'un grand talent*'; his unselfishness and his loyalty won my esteem and that of people who knew him in his adversity.

Sailing north of New Zealand, the *Otter* crossed the Tasman Sea. On 7 March she crossed the Tropic of Capricorn. 'The north wind

* Peron kept notes of his travels. When he retired to Piage in France he handed them to Bernard, a French Professor of Theology who became a *fermier* and tax-collector after the Revolution. Bernard edited the notes, and they were handed to a Parisian publisher, L. Brisset-Thivars, who deleted one-third and published the rest in 1824. The translations are mine. They are literal.

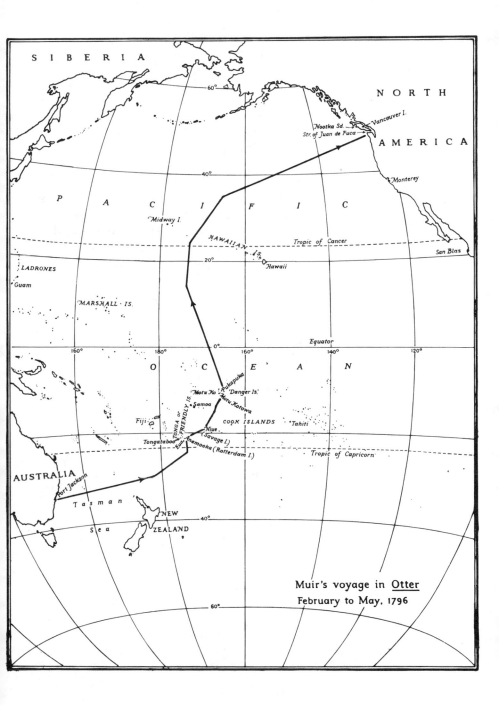

SIBERIA

NORTH

Nootka Sd.
Str. of Juan de Fuca

Vancouver I.

AMERICA

Monterey

P   A   C   I   F   I   C

Midway I.

HAWAIIAN   Tropic of Cancer

San Blas

LADRONES   I S.
Guam   Hawaii

MARSHALL · IS.

Equator

O   C   E   A   N

Pukapuka
Motu Ko   Danger Is.
Samoa   Motu Kotowa
TONGA or
FRIENDLY IS.   COOK ISLANDS   Tahiti
Fiji
Niue
(Savage I.)
Tongataboo
Eua   Annemooka (Rotterdam I.)   Tropic of Capricorn

AUSTRALIA
Port Jackson

Tasman

NEW

Sea   ZEALAND

Muir's voyage in Otter
February to May, 1796

blew gently. The air seemed embalmed with a delicious perfume of sweet-smelling flowers. . . . Birds and sea-plants floated on the water.' The next day they reached the scattered archipelago of the Tonga or Friendly Islands, surrounded by dangerous reefs, discovered by the Dutch in 1616 and visited by Cook in 1773–4. The *Otter* is thought to be the first merchant vessel to have visited them. She had now reached the area of the Pacific peopled by the handsome, gentle Polynesians.

On 8 March she approached Rotterdam Island, called Anamooka by the natives, where Bligh in the *Bounty* had called in 1789. A chief came out in a canoe offering cooked fish wrapped in leaves. He clapped his hands, laughed, and embraced them, then piloted the ship to a safe anchorage. Over 1,000 tall, strong natives climbed on board. They 'regarded everything with wonder and amazement'. The crew 'bartered with scissors and knives'. Soon 'the decks were covered with six kinds of bananas, water melons, yams, potatoes, oranges, pineapples, breadfruit, and sugar cane'. The islanders 'were reported to steal anything which took their fancy, and could easily have attacked us'. As a precautionary measure swords and guns were ranged on deck, 'our ten cannon charged and run out'. In fact the crew watched the natives carefully and never caught them taking anything. When night fell a cannon shot was fired. 'The islanders understood perfectly, climbed into their canoes, and returned home.' At sunrise, on the firing of another shot, 'the sea was covered with' 100 canoes racing to reach the ship. They brought 'material made from bark . . . mother of pearl fishhooks, clubs, spears, and bows and arrows all beautifully worked'.

The *Otter* cruised among the islands trying to find a way out to the north-east. There was continual contact with the islanders who kept fires burning at night to show their position among the coral reefs. One night there was a fierce storm. In the morning they found themselves broadside on to a great reef which had been off to the north-west the evening before, and just managed to get clear before another storm broke. Chiefs came out in huge double canoes, carrying eighty to a hundred people of both sexes. One chief offered six fat pigs. They gave him two axes, knives, scissors, a gimlet, and nails. One man deserted. Peron suggests this was

due to the attractions of the women. . . . the ones we saw, who may not be of a high class, did not appear to possess the slightest degree of modesty and gave themselves to the first person to pass by. . . . The climate of this archipelago is one of the most beautiful in the world . . . the fertile land covered with great palm trees . . . the people gay. . . .

A few days later, tempted by this paradise, another five convicts left secretly. They were the first Europeans to live in the Tonga islands. When missionaries arrived the ex-convicts proved very difficult. All the convicts met violent deaths.

On 16 March a way was finally found to the open sea (eastwards between the islands of Tongataboo and Eua). They sailed north-east and six days later sighted Savage Island (Niue), so called by Captain Cook – who discovered it – because of the inhospitable conduct of the inhabitants.

They passed Samoa and on 3 April came to a group of three small islands covered with cocoa palms. The *Otter* hugged the shore. Men appeared waving pieces of material, so, thinking this an invitation to land, they rowed into a bay. Peron and Muir embarked in a dinghy with four men:

We were suddenly stopped by a ridge of coral only 1½ feet below the water. By signs I invited the natives to walk towards us. They remained undecided for a long time. Finally six men came forward armed with lances and clubs. At a certain distance five stopped, the sixth, grasping a club in one hand and a branch of coconut palm in the other, came to the edge of the reef. There he made a speech of which I understood absolutely nothing, and threw us the branch. Thinking that the branch was a mark of goodwill I manoeuvred the dinghy close in and, accompanied by Mr. Muirr, got out onto the coral bank.

I walked towards the Indians holding in one hand the branch they had given us, and holding out my other hand as a sign of goodwill. . . . I showed them bananas, potatoes, and oranges, trying to explain that I wanted to obtain some in exchange for knives and iron. They looked at them and gestured that they did not want any. I cut a palm branch with a knife and gave them pieces. This performance surprised them. They approached, took the knife and some pieces of iron. I thought they were mollified by this present, and indicated my desire to go to the village. Directly they understood this request they shouted and yelled. They ranged themselves between us and their huts; waved their arms menacingly and, pointing to the dinghy, signalled that we should depart immediately.

Mr. Muirr, thinking that they had not understood our intentions, made overtures to them and, to prove that we had no weapons, stretched out his arms. At this gesture the islanders, believing we wanted to seize them, fled to their cabins, turning round from time to time to see if we were following. We made further friendly signs, but they only replied with furious cries and threatening gestures. Mr. Muirr and I decided to return to the dinghy. They

ran towards their canoes, but then changed their minds and did not launch
them.

Though Peron does not comment on the fact, he and Muir had
undertaken quite a hazardous expedition. Sailors had been seized
from long-boats and killed on previous voyages. It was only seven
years since Captain Cook had been eaten by the Sandwich Islanders.
Later three canoes approached the ship and, after much hesitation,
the natives exchanged coconuts and ropes for knives and invited
them to land.

> Almost certainly they had not seen strangers before. Their alarm at our
> appearance, their surprise at our white skins and our clothes, their ignorance
> of our utensils, everything convinced us that we were right to allot ourselves
> the honour of having discovered three new islands. . . . I called this group the
> Isles of the Otter.

To distinguish them the easternmost one was called 'Peron and
Muirr', the northern one 'Dorr', and the third 'Brown', after one of
the officers. In fact these were the Danger Islands, named when
Commodore Byron sighted them unexpectedly in 1765. He did not
sail close in and Peron and Muir were certainly the first Europeans to
land. The names were not adopted and the islands – Motu Ko,
Pukapuka, and Motu Kotowa – now form part of the Cook Islands.*

On 5 April the *Otter* set sail again. On 29 April she crossed the
Tropic of Cancer. On 20 May the crew sighted birds flying north-
west and trees floating on the water, signs that there was an island
concealed by mist. At last on 29 May the summits of the mountains
of America appeared on the horizon, a marvellous array of great
peaks, ridges, and plateaus, mostly covered in snow, rising in savage
grandeur, one row behind another. The weather was mild. As they
sailed closer they could see trees stretching from the sea up to the
mountains. The *Otter* approached land near the entrance to the
Straits of Juan de Fuca. She had been at sea three months and sailed
nearly 20,000 miles.

Both Spanish and English ships sailed north of California. Men
were still looking for the North-West Passage. The Spaniards, who
had pushed north founding settlements at Monterey in 1770 and San
Francisco in 1776, claimed sovereignty over all the north-west coast.

---

* These three islands, though a long way off, originally formed part of the manda-
tory territory of Cook Islands, administered by New Zealand. They are now part of
the self-governing territory of Cook Islands.

In 1788, with the approval of the British Government, an English-man, John Meares, made an agreement with local Indian chiefs, bought land at Friendly Cove, Nootka, and established a trading post. In October, the following year, a Spanish naval force demolished the trading post and erected a fort; they also seized four ships sent to Nootka by Meares.[1] The British Government protested. Spain was forced to withdraw her claim and, by the Nootka Convention of 1790, Britain and Spain were given equal rights to the land north of San Francisco. The Spanish fort was dismantled and no further attempt made for the time being to found a European settlement on Vancouver Island; but Spanish and British subjects were free to use the harbour and erect temporary buildings.

Trade on the coast was mostly in the hands of New England skippers; illegal in the eyes of the Spaniards as the United States had no comparable treaty with Spain. Ships spent up to two years collecting furs. They were small, well built, heavily manned in case of an Indian attack. Great navigational skill was required and vigilance in dealing with the Indians. Almost all early voyages involved a battle. The Indians were notorious for their treachery. As late as 1803 they killed all a ship's company bar two. One captain lost his son and was driven from his ship by an Indian Amazon and her braves. But equally some white men behaved with unnecessary savagery, attacking and killing Indians without provocation.

The *Otter* embarked on fur trading as soon as she arrived. She spent three weeks working off the complicated coastline of Vancouver Island. It was hazardous sailing in little-known waters. Sometimes they would enter a bay at high tide, only to find when the tide went out that they had narrowly avoided reefs. As she sailed westwards a clumsily constructed canoe appeared manned by fat, squat, swarthy Indians, wearing only a piece of cloth fastened round their necks with two leather thongs:

Their heads were covered with little pigtails. . . . In loud, sonorous voices they sang a war song, beating time with their paddles against the side of their canoes. A hundred yards from the ship they stopped singing, all stood up together and loosened the thongs of their cloaks which fell down around their waists. Completely naked they picked up their oars again and paddled silently and swiftly towards us. They inspected the ship's length and height carefully and lifted their oars simultaneously. One of them, about thirty, with a savage face and loud voice, spoke to us "Can-zi-ca-gan!" We took this for a polite greeting and replied "Can-zi-ca-gan!"

The officers held up blue cloth and indicated that they would exchange it for skins, but the Indians were not interested. They produced copper sheets and, as the *Otter* had none, paddled away.

The *Otter* was delayed by fog and blown south by contrary winds. On 3 June, needing wood and water, Dorr put into a cove (now Port San Juan). Peron and Muir, once more the first to investigate, went off in a dinghy to the nearest village. The Indians wore bear and deer skins. Their faces were blackened like chimney sweeps, their bodies smelled appallingly. An old man seated outside a hut pressed them to enter.

He rolled out pelts, put them on hollowed wooden stumps and invited us to sit. The dwelling was about 50 feet long, 20 feet wide and 7 feet high. Posts were stuck in the ground about 8 feet apart holding up joists over which were stretched poorly worked planks, leaving gaps between them large enough to put an arm through. The walls were made of planks placed one on the other and attached to the stakes by thongs of seaweed or dried animal's intestines. Three partitions divided the hut into four rooms. There was a big fire in the main room on which pieces of bear were roasting and on a hurdle above, supported by four wooden posts, were twelve split salmon.

Furniture consisted of baskets and rough bowls. The wooden stumps also served as beds, the pelts as mattresses and covers. The room contained mussel, oyster, and scallop shells, bad meat, rancid fat, and tainted fish. One corner was used as a lavatory. 'The clothes of these unfortunate people . . . were impregnated with an intolerable stench.' Not far away was a canoe being made from a tree, of hard, heavy wood about 4½ feet in circumference and 25 feet long. As tools the Indians used pieces of crooked wood to which flat pieces of iron were attached with gum and binding. 'We could not understand how they had been able to transport such a heavy load or how they moved the canoe to launch it.'

Muir and Peron made other exploratory expeditions. They found huge oaks and pines more than 100 feet high. Alas, no otter skins were to be had so on 8 June the *Otter* crossed to the southern side of the Straits of Juan de Fuca and anchored in Neah bay. Here the Indians had traded with Europeans before. 'Some wore bear, otter and beaver skins, but others had on old coats and bonnets. Some had top hats and their hair tied in queues on the nape of their necks.' Indians went all over the deck examining and touching everything. One seized a knife that a sailor put down. When his theft was noticed he showed neither shame nor regret, laughed, and gave it back. One watched the barber shave a sailor, then sat in the sailor's seat and signalled that he wanted to be shaved. 'So the barber lathered his face and shaved his beard which much amused his compatriots.' The Indians used 14-foot rods with pegs fixed like the teeth of a rake to catch herrings, and caught 50-lb. turbot with lines made of animal gut and wooden hooks. They had artistic talent, using lime to decorate their canoes with fish, birds, and animals.

On 12 June the *Otter* entered Berkeley Sound and anchored among a multitude of islands on which were several villages. The Indians were friendly. They came unarmed and asked politely to come on board. 'We were only obliged to keep a careful watch because of their penchant for stealing.'

. . . . The men were small, about 5 feet tall. They had very large heads and long black hair. . . . Some were naked. . . . The women wore bearskins, one hanging down the front, the other at the back. Their arms were bare, ornamented with leather bracelets; their ears pierced in several places from which hung glass bead necklaces. They were remarkably dirty. All the same their faces were attractive and cheerful. They responded to our sailors' expressive gestures, but refused to climb on board.

Three days later the chief of the largest village boarded the *Otter*. He was about fifty years old, squat with sharp eyes and a ferocious expression. He was called Out-Cha-Chel, the name of the district. Peron took advantage of his visit to land, and Muir, who was proving brave and adventurous in his new life, asked to accompany him. They agreed with Dorr that the chief should be held as hostage. More than three hundred people of all ages ran down to the shore and greeted Muir and Peron with loud shouts of joy, '*vacache*!' – 'good day'. 'We replied "vacache!" which increased everyone's good humour.' Accompanied by several Indians they climbed a hill with a superb view, returned to the village, were taken into several cabins, and finally to the chief's house, where a crowd of men and women squatted on their heels round a great fire, the only source of light. '"Vacache!" began again and we followed suit.' These signs of friendship were followed by 'gentle, naive advances from Out-Cha-Chel's women, who were in very playful mood'. Engrossed in mild flirtation the time fixed to return to the boat passed. Peron warned Muir that they must tear themselves away:

. . . the Indians would not let us go until they learnt that their Prince's return depended on our being allowed to leave. At the moment when we crossed the threshold of the apartment Out-Cha-Chel appeared. Mr. Muirr and I stood stupefied. The thought crossed our minds that Mr. Dorr wanted to sacrifice us, abandoning us to the mercy of these savages. Their antipathy towards strangers, the booty which plundering us promised, might induce them to commit a bloody deed.

How they must have cursed Dorr! Peron complimented Out-Cha-Chel on his good fortune in possessing such charming women and expressed regret at not understanding their language. Out-Cha-Chel interrupted brusquely, 'said that all these women were his, that the village Indians were his subjects, and that when he made war he always conquered'. Peron praised his riches and power, then made him understand that it was late and they must return to their ship. Out-Cha-Chel ominously shook his head, then led them towards great chests inlaid with human teeth, touching his own to explain clearly what they were. He opened a chest and pulled out human heads by their hair.

At the sight of these princely trophies, the Indians loudly praised his courage, assuring us it was really he who had killed these enemies. Mr. Muirr said to me that it could well be that he would put our heads beside them.

Their ordeal was not over. Out-Cha-Chel was determined to show them everything. He brought out his arms, long wooden bows, arrows tipped with iron, spears, daggers, and battered guns; his warrior's costume which consisted of helmet, mask, and a cuirass of thick buffalo hide. Out-Cha-Chel put on his armour, seized a lance and dagger, and made passes as if attacking an enemy. 'Satisfied with the grand impression he had given us of his power and warlike talent, he finally allowed us to leave.' They swiftly said farewell and regained the waiting canoe as quickly as possible. Annoyingly the abridged diary does not give Dorr's reason for letting Out-Cha-Chel go.

In spite of their hair-raising experience, the next day Muir and Peron landed on a neighbouring island. They found a corpse minus its head, which they thought might well have been one of the chief's enemies. Several Indians approached, but refused to bury the body and hurried away.

On 17 June when the *Otter* set sail, one officer remained behind with the dinghy to collect anchor lines, only rejoining the ship after another sinister episode. As soon as the *Otter* disappeared over the horizon Out-Cha-Chel and his braves surrounded the dinghy, seized several sailors, and attempted to drag them into his canoe. The attack did not appear to be premeditated as the Indians were unarmed, and the sailors were able to free themselves with knives and oars.

This event surprised us as until this moment the Indians' conduct had been friendly and even affectionate. Mr. Muirr and I congratulated each other on having emerged safe and sound from the hands of Prince Out-Cha-Chel.

On 21 June the *Otter* reached the island of San Miguel in Nootka Sound. At the anchorage was a two-masted ship, the *Sutil* from San Blas at the northern end of the Panama isthmus. Dorr hoped to obtain victuals at Nootka, but Tobar, the *Sutil*'s captain, who showed them 'every mark of kindness' had none to spare. An Indian chief, Makouina, insistently demanded to be allowed on board. On his second visit he brought a pretty six-year-old boy of whom he seemed very fond. Peron 'congratulated him on his son'. Makouina explained that he was not his son, but that he belonged to him and he was going to eat him for supper. They decided to rescue the child and, after long negotiations, Makouina sold him for three lengths of blue cloth.

At this point the editor cut a section from Peron's memoirs. Muir's movements, however, can be traced, thanks to the extraordinary bureaucratic methods of the Spanish colonial administration. One reason for the Spaniards' failure to contain the rising power of Britain and the United States on the north-west coast was their lack of delegation. Detailed reports on trivial events were sent back to Spain and are preserved in the Archives of the Indies in Seville. Officials asked the home government for approval of the minutest transactions. Orders were sent to them by the Prime Minister, Godoy, Prince of the Peace. He was a corrupt, stupid, ineffectual man, the Queen of Spain's lover, brother-in-law of the Marquis of Branciforte, who had been appointed Viceroy of New Spain in 1794. Branciforte was elegant and accomplished, but one of the most unpopular and unscrupulous viceroys. His main object was to enrich himself.

The *Sutil*, with a complement of fifteen, was the first of the patrol boats ordered by Branciforte to sail every six months from his Pacific naval station at San Blas to keep watch on foreign vessels, especially

fur traders, and warn intruders off. Tobar had reached Nootka on 16
June. Many of his crew were sick and he had hoped to find a
European ship with an officer who could treat them, but there were
none in the sound. He was about to leave when the *Otter* arrived.

Dorr, Muir, and a sailor went on board the *Sutil*. As the Americans
had not been included in the treaty between Britain and Spain, and it
was theoretically illegal for them to use Nootka harbour, Dorr
flourished a passport purporting to have been issued by the Spanish
Consul in Charleston. Tobar was unable to read it because it was in
English. Tobar told Dorr that Captain Broughton in H.M.S. *Providence*, accompanied by its supply sloop *Daedalus*, had arrived at
Nootka on 17 March. She had hovered along the coast surveying and
fishing, then left for Monterey on 21 May. Dorr appears to have been
far more astute than Tobar. According to Tobar, who may well have
misunderstood as his English was scrappy, Dorr produced alarming
stories of his men being attacked and killed by Indians, a totally
unfounded rumour that three English frigates had left Botany Bay for
Nootka, and another that two British frigates were to be used in the
fur trade. Dorr said he was sorry to find Tobar going about in such
dangerous waters in a small boat with a small crew. He offered to
give Tobar five sailors, stowaways from New Holland – a cunning
means of getting rid of extra hands he did not want on the voyage to
China. Six of Tobar's sailors were still sick so he accepted Dorr's
offer. The convicts were glad to go because, as Don Diego Borica, the
Governor of Alta California, reported, 'Dorr treats his crew badly
and pays them worse.'[2] Having thoroughly frightened Tobar, Dorr
suggested that the two ships should cruise north together. He did not
want to stay long at Nootka; there were none of the provisions he
needed so urgently and, as he harboured escaped convicts, he wished
to avoid Broughton.[3]

Muir now made a decision which seemed sensible on the face of
it, but was to have disastrous consequences. He left the *Otter* and
embarked on the *Sutil*. He set out his reasons in subsequent letters.[4] If
he transferred to the *Sutil*, he could disembark at San Blas, at the
northern end of the road along which the treasure trains travelled
from the Pacific to Mexico City. Muir hoped to cross to the east coast
and get a ship north. He would thus reach Philadelphia in about six
months. 'To me it is an object of the first importance to be nigh my
friends as soon as possible;' besides in China and in India he ran a

great risk of being intercepted by English ships. In addition, Muir was alarmed at the report of Broughton cruising in the area. H.M.S. *Providence* had been at Port Jackson for seven weeks the previous autumn, and he would probably be recognized by the crew. Muir was afraid that Broughton had been sent to look for him. Actually Broughton had been sent to impress the Spaniards with British strength[5] and it is doubtful if he even knew Muir had escaped. As Borica had not encouraged Broughton to stay at Monterey, he had left on 20 June to make a survey of the south-west coast of South America.

Muir was also unaware that the Spaniards, who had always been extremely suspicious of foreigners and wished to preserve New Spain from their contaminating influence, had recently passed a stringent edict forbidding their entry, especially protestants. This was largely because, in the eyes of the Viceroy, the United States was becoming a very dangerous neighbour.

Muir exerted all his charm and on the night of 22 June, as the ships were about to sail, persuaded Tobar to take him on board. His few belongings were transferred to the *Sutil* while the ships slowly worked their way out of harbour. The *Sutil* was soon separated from the *Otter* by northerly winds and blown south.

Peron went to China with Dorr. After a quarrel with him over the sale of his sealskins at Canton, Peron returned on another ship, arriving in Boston in December 1797. It would have been better for Muir if he had remained with Peron.

CHAPTER 11

◇◇

From New to Old Spain

Initially brief, but roughly correct, accounts of Muir's journey through Spanish territories appeared in American and English newspapers. The French pamphleteer gave a wildly inaccurate version; and later Mackenzie produced a fantastic tale that the *Otter* was wrecked and Muir travelled alone on foot 4,000 miles down the west coast of America, befriended by Indians, guiding his way by the stars. In fact Muir's voyage with Peron had been just as exciting and extraordinary as this apocryphal account of the next leg of his journey.

When Tobar was blamed for taking Muir on board, he told his commandant that 'Muir begged and pleaded to be accepted as a passenger. He wanted to go to New Spain and thence to the United States to join General Washington.' Tobar understood Muir was

a Scottish learned gentleman who, for defending his country and the Christian state of Ireland, had been persecuted by the British Government who had banished him; but that he was free to go where he would in other parts of the world.

During the voyage I caught him out in a few lies. He did not have any luggage, money, jewels, or clothes. His possessions in all were not worth more than nineteen pesos.[1]

Muir said he had given Dorr two hundred pesos for safe keeping and that Dorr could not give him the money because the ships separated.

This made me suspicious. The Captain is very well to do. . . . Secondly, having sent Muir the mattress and trunk when we were both under sail, he could have sent the money at the same time. I felt sincerely sorry for Muir. I am firmly convinced I was hoodwinked by him.

Muir almost certainly had to pay for his passage. As he was not now travelling to Canton, he may have tried to get Dorr to refund part of his passage money. If he did, Dorr, who was reputed to be mean and unscrupulous, probably refused to do so. Muir had been used to having money, but was learning how to manage without it.

After a storm that lasted for several days Tobar decided to put into Monterey which he reached on 5 July. He remained for over a fortnight to allow his sick crew to recover and repairs to be made to the *Sutil*. Monterey had a delicious climate and was surrounded by attractive, fertile country. It was the capital of Alta California, a province which stretched without clear-cut boundaries up the west coast. A chain of missions had been established from San Diego to San Francisco. The monks had introduced European crops and taught the indians how to rear cows, sheep, and pigs. Because of the gentle temperament of the local indians, California was at this time a peaceful, contented colony. The Spaniards had made no attempt to exploit this potentially rich and pleasant, but isolated, land; almost none had settled in the area. Behind the coast lay a vast, unexplored continent.[2]

Muir stayed with the Governor. He was treated as a gentleman and lived in greater comfort than he had experienced since his imprisonment three years before. Borica was an excellent Governor; a Basque, jovial, witty and a sympathetic character. After his appointment in 1794 he tried without success to persuade the Government to develop the province. His ideas and achievements were unappreciated and he was hampered by the Spanish authorities. He would have liked to return to Spain but, because of intrigues at the Spanish Court, was never allowed to do so. His wife was very popular; he had a pretty daughter of sixteen.

Borica treated Muir with caution but great kindness. Muir was touched and heartened by the welcome he received. A penniless fugitive would naturally put himself out to please, but it is clear that Muir's hosts were charmed by his warm, friendly personality. Also Borica was delighted by the arrival in such a remote place of a cultivated visitor who could give a first-hand description of the dramatic events in Europe. He was impressed with Muir's education and intellectual powers.

Borica reported to the Viceroy that

Muir was in Paris during the great revolution. . . . He gives very circumstantial accounts of all that occurred and a vivid, colourful description of the principal personages. . . . He appears to have a very clear knowledge of the political state of England.

At Borica's request he wrote out in French a summary of his career, taken from a printed copy of his trial. Muir gave Borica an engraving of his bust, and could not resist the temptation to claim that his friends were thinking of erecting a marble statue of him 'for the spirit and energy with which he had defended the rights of the Scottish people who had chosen him as their deputy'. Borica drily commented that this was Muir's version of affairs. He sent the Viceroy the copy of the trial and an exercise-book 'in which Muir seems to have written about his cause'. Borica rightly dismissed poor Muir's efforts: 'I did not have it translated because I thought it unimportant.' He also forwarded the engraving. Branciforte had a copy made which he sent to Godoy with a Spanish translation of Thompson's verses on the back.

Muir had always been a prolific correspondent. In this douce, hospitable atmosphere he wrote to his family and friends – the first chance he had had to do so since his escape. His letters were sent by Borica to Branciforte, who kept translations and forwarded the originals to Spain. None reached its destination; all are filed in the Archives at Seville.

Muir had been depressed and subdued in New South Wales, where many of the officers had not treated the reformers well. Understandably he was now triumphant, full of pride in his miraculous escape and adventures. His self-esteem had been greatly damaged. Muir had left Britain a convict, now he was a free man again and could vindicate himself in the eyes of Edinburgh society which had rejected him. Unfortunately his exploits had rather gone to his head and greatly increased his incipient vanity. His romanticism had developed into a *folie de grandeur*. He saw himself as a potential martyr who would now receive his just reward. Not that he considered his abilities outstanding, but rather that he was a potent symbol of liberty. Muir's letters illustrate salient aspects of his character, his good qualities, and his faults, which unfortunately were becoming more pronounced. Some allowance must be made for his bombastic tone, since he wanted to counter the poor impression afforded by his shabby, impecunious state; the high-flown compliments were a stock ingredient of eighteenth-century letters when young men were expected to develop a facility in writing letters to patrons. In writing to public personages Muir assumed a greater interest in himself than the recipients were now likely to have. Isolated at Botany Bay, he did not appreciate that the reformers'

Anamooka

Nootka Sound

Muir in France

James Napper Tandy

The Political Martyrs' Monument, Edinburgh

trials had been superseded as causes by the far more important events of the war.

Muir wanted to make contact with friends in America. He wrote to Washington and enclosed letters to Priestley and John Millar, asking Washington to forward them as he did not know their addresses. Muir was anxious to impress the Spaniards with his importance, so that they would help him reach the United States and it is probably partly for this reason that he wrote to Lords Lauderdale and Stanhope and to Fox. He also wrote a letter to his parents and another to two close friends in England, Lindsey and Shields. Surprisingly, there is no letter to Moffat. Perhaps he wrote a letter to him at another time which was not confiscated. In all eight letters Muir gave a brief account of his escape and voyage to California. He hoped to practise at the American bar and continue to fight for the principles for which he had been exiled until there should be a change in the ministry in England, when he confidently expected to be sent for because

I have the solemn pledge of those most likely to succeed Mr. Pitt that the first, the most just . . . step which they will take will be my recall, and those of my respectable colleagues, by a national ship dispatched for the purpose.

Muir counted far too optimistically on Washington's help and protection. He told Lauderdale: 'I will find in General Washington a friend, a protector and a father.' He wrote to Washington:

. . . I have claimed the protection of your name. I hasten to Philadelphia to solicit it in person. . . . I have likewise presumed to draw upon you for what necessary expenses may attend my journey. . . . these bills will be joyfully reimbursed in Europe. . . . If I cannot revisit my owen country, free and emancipated . . . I will consume the remainder of my days in the United States, happy if in the narrow range of my abilities I may be able to demonstrate . . . my devotion . . . to the land of my Asylum. . . . From my infancy I have considered myself your pupil and . . . in a land permitted almost to be visited by no one the name of General Washington presents me everywhere respects and attention. . . . Receive then from me not the vain profession of words, but the pure and unadulterated homage of the heart.

There is no evidence that Washington ever took any interest in Muir. There is evidence that he disliked contact with political refugees. When a member of the Senate brought Hamilton Rowan to his office, Washington was distinctly annoyed. He wanted to remain on

good terms with the British Government and would not have risked
annoying them for Muir's sake.

To Stanhope Muir wrote:

> . . . My exile, splendid in its cause, and proved in the applauding voice of my
> country, claims a new lustre from the toils and dangers by which it has been
> redeemed. It were vain to disguise that I feel a pride in the idea of the past, but
> that pride is meliorated and ennobled by the sentiment that all I have gone
> through, and suffered, and all that still I must go through and suffer, more
> firmly attaches me to the cause of Public virtue, that virtue for which your
> Lordship has been so eminently distinguished, and in comparison of the
> want of which Riches and pomp and titles, are low and poor indeed.

He asked Lauderdale, if his letter to his parents should miscarry
'From the fatality of the name upon the envelope' to give them a copy
of his letter. Optimistically he hoped to be in Philadelphia in five
months' time.

Although Muir's description of the Spaniards' kindness is somewhat effusive (he knew they would read his letters) his gratitude was
patently genuine. Muir always appreciated kindness and particularly
now after so many tribulations. To Fox he wrote:

> . . . I shall ever speak in terms of the highest esteem and affection of the
> treatment I have hitherto received from the Spanish nation. In Don Diego
> Borica, poor unknowen and exiled, I found a benefactor, whose unsolicited
> kindness will suffuse my eyes with tears until the last moments of life.

To his parents: 'The Governor of this part of the world, a Nobleman
of high rank, has shewen me such civilities as could not be believed.'
Borica's wife had even herself made soups for him to take on the rest
of his sea voyage. 'I never can be sufficiently grateful to heaven or to
these people. . . . The Captain [Tobar] with whom I have come has
treated me as a son.' Muir's letters to his friends reveal one of his
most likeable and consistent characteristics, genuine love, interest,
and concern. Muir may have been conceited, but he was not self-
centred. To Priestley:

> . . . The situation of my colleagues, in that forlorn, dismal, and inhospitable
> region, is mournful. . . . By them I was urged to this enterprise. . . . Palmer
> enjoys the best state of health, that of Skirving's is declining, and Gerrald,
> Alas, I left upon the bed of death – of Margarot, I can speak with little
> certainty, but I believe he is greatly to be pitied.

He told Millar of hearing that he and his family had been forced to
emigrate:

. . . May God grant you happyness according to your utmost wishes. My life since I left you has been a romance. . . . If I publish my voyages and travels, as I think I will, I smile, when I think that a man of the gowen must make his first Debut to the world, as a Navigator. . . . Do you know where Mr. Thompson Callender is? If you do, present him my remembrance, and tell him I hope to spend some attic evenings with him, once more – the idea of Reunion with those whom I love, whom I esteem, will animate my vigour, as I embark upon the immense way which yet remains before me.

James Thomson Callender was the Glasgow journalist who fled to escape prosecution in 1793. He became a successful journalist in Philadelphia and was befriended by Jefferson, but his malicious pen was to cause both Jefferson and Hamilton great discomfiture before he drowned, either when drunk, or by intentional suicide, in the River James at Richmond in 1803. Callender told Jefferson he was Muir and Palmer's intimate friend 'and quite as deep in the unlucky business as they were'.[3]

Muir told his 'Dearest friends for ever', Theophilus Lindsey and Richard Shields, that he had received a letter from Mrs. Shields in New Holland. He now hoped to be able to help his colleagues there. 'I know their wants.' He had 'circumnavigated the world destitute of everything. . . . Hitherto I have seen nothing but the hand of God exerted in my favour, and my mind is filled with profound gratitude.' He asked to be remembered to a long list of friends.

What scenes have I not witnessed. . . . My life is a romance, but a romance of mournful truth . . . . what do I not owe to the affectionate and motherly attention of the Lady Governess of this province. . . . What esteem have I not for those holy and venerable men, the Fathers on this mission. The true Ministers of God are everywhere the same . . . . gratefully I recognise the truth of the lines put by Mrs. Barbauld beneath my Bust. To that Lady and to Mr. Barbauld, present my most affectionate remembrance.

Muir rather spoilt the warm, enthusiastic tone of this letter by his high-handed last paragraph:

May God Grant my Dear friends that we may soon meet. . . . If I cannot revisit England, I will expect an interview with you in the Neutral Country of Switzerland. I have travelled over immense and unknowen oceans to visit you – You will not at least hesitate to cross a paltry stream to see me.

To everyone except his parents Muir commented to the effect that 'My health, after these tedious navigations, and after what I have suffered is infirm and shaking, but my mind is firm and erect.' But to his 'Dear Pappa and Mamma' he was reassuring:

You will be both surprised and happy to have a letter from me. . . . I sincerely hope you have enjoyed your health, and have kept up your spirits – For my part I am as well as ever and still the same. . . . By the time I get to Philadelphia I shall have compleated a voyage round the world. I will now be able to be useful to myself, to you, and to mankind. . . . Rejoyce . . . and bless God that I am again at liberty and in the midst of a good, a kind and humane people.

Thomas sent no message to his sister. Possibly he wrote to her separately, or relations may have been strained. Janet and her husband could well have disapproved of Thomas for disgracing the family and causing so much distress to his parents. Thomas may anyhow have had little in common with his sister. The few documents available reveal no affection for his sister comparable to that for his friends.

Muir asked the Viceroy for permission to cross his dominions and proceed to Philadelphia. He explained why he had incurred the hatred and vengeance of the English Government.

The people of Scotland have long groaned under the most hideous oppression. Their antiant Lawes have been insulted. Of their antiant Constitution they possess not even the shadow. This brave and high spirited people have made exertions to break their chains.

After this startling picture of life in Scotland Muir described the Edinburgh Convention and the part he had played in it. He sensibly emphasized his connection with the Irish and the fact that he had read their 'pathetic' address to the 'solemn and august assembly'.

. . . I have contended for the instant and immediate Emancipation of three millions of the Professors of the Catholic Religion. . . . I come into your country with no improper intentions. I wish to pass through it without delay to an Allied State.

While innumerable letters about Muir were exchanged between Borica, Branciforte, and Madrid, the *Sutil* sailed from Monterey on 21 July and reached San Blas on 12 August. This port was low-lying and mosquito-ridden, so kindhearted Tobar allowed Muir to leave the five other convicts and move up to Tepic, a small town 22 miles away, 1,000 feet above sea level, set in fertile land where limes, sugar cane, bananas, rice, vines, and tobacco grew. Here Muir remained for a month and, once more, acquired friends – a fellow-Scot, Robert Gibson, who was on his way to Manila, and a naval Captain, Don Juan Mattute, and his family.

Muir wrote to the Viceroy again. He was eager to resume his station 'in the scenes of the world'.

By long and tedious voyages and by sudden transitions into opposite climates my constitution has been affected and health impaired. It is to me a material object soon to breathe a more congenial air.... Delicacy and Propriety prevent me from applying to private individuals for resources.... They ... have no intercourse with those channels through which reimbursement to them must flow. I have deemed then most expedient, more suitable to my owen character, and more honourable to your Lordship to make to you a direct application. In the economical manner in which I propose to travel to the Havannah, my expenses cannot exceed seven or eight hundred dollars, and probably may be a great deal less.

After the concern for him shown by the French Republic, 'ally of his Most Catholic Majesty', Muir was confident the French Ambassador at Madrid would honour his bills, but it seemed more practicable to draw on General Washington. In 'the total shipwreck of my books and papers' he had lost all copies of his trial, but sent the Viceroy a pamphlet published soon afterwards, pointing out that one charge against him was that he had gone to Paris to save the life of the King.

Muir did not attempt to conceal his radical sympathies when in Spanish hands. He realized that the Spaniards would inevitably view him with suspicion. They knew he must have been sent to Botany Bay, 'the Siberia of the British' as the Viceroy called it, for some offence against the British Government. Muir did his best to make out a good case in awkward circumstances. Spain was allied with France and Muir hoped his connection with the Girondins would be an asset; the Spaniards, however, thought this meant that he had taken part in the French Revolution. Muir can have had little knowledge of Spanish American politics. Washington seemed the obvious man to invoke on his behalf.

Branciforte decided to send Muir and the five sailors to Vera Cruz and thence to Spain. He asked Godoy to obtain the King's approval for expenses. 'The cost of transporting foreigners is great. I am taking especial care of Muir who appears to have been the leader in parliamentary revolutions.' He was to be escorted 'economically yet with some distinction' by a naval officer, Don Salvador Fidalgo, and his lieutenant Don Andrés Salazar. Muir was accompanied by an Irishman from Philadelphia, Joseph Burling O'Cain, a young sailor who had been left at Santa Barbara by his English captain in 1795. Now, in accordance with the new law against foreigners, he was to be deported. He acted as Muir's interpreter.[4]

The old Spanish road along which they travelled still exists, the oldest road on the North American continent, built in the sixteenth century on the foundation of an Indian trail. Cortés had marched along it to the Pacific and built four boats at San Blas. The road was defended by forts or outposts at strategic points. Bordered by cactuses it was extremely dusty, but commanded superb views. It crossed green savanna, rolling hills with great ranches, deep valleys, and mountain ramparts. To carry bullion from the silver mines the Spaniards had metalled part of the Aztecs' road and broadened it for ox-carts which had wheels of solid ebony. Mules were hitched four abreast to drag stage-coaches over bad patches.

Muir was not overtly under arrest, but he was not allowed to wander about freely. The naval officers showed him round the cathedrals, baroque churches, piazzas, and arcades of Guadalajara and Mexico City, which they reached on 12 October. There he was questioned about his reasons for entering California, then sent on by coach to Vera Cruz, where he stayed with another Scotsman, Captain Abercromby, who 'instantly waited upon me with an openness and hospitality which spoke for the goodness of his heart', as he described in a further spate of letters.[5] Granted he had all the time in the world, the fact that he took the trouble to write sincere, charming letters of thanks to those who had been kind to him on the journey shows not only his good manners towards people he was highly unlikely to see again, but his capacity for making and appreciating friends.

Muir wrote in French to the naval officers who had accompanied him. He appears to have enjoyed himself on the way, for he spoke of the 'polite attentions' he had received and asked Don Fidalgo to present his respects to the friend in Guadalajara who had entertained them. Muir wrote affectionately to Juan Mattute, sending greetings to his wife and family, and to one Daniel Sullivan:

... I regret – I deeply regret – that I had not time to cultivate and improve your friendship – tantum vidi – Perhaps no circumstances in my exile have been so painful as those momentary connections with amiable and esteemed characters and those eternal separations. But ours, I flatter myself, will have a different fate, that once more we will meet in our common country, when that country purged and regenerated may present new claims to our affections. To me, however, it will long wear a sombrous aspect. Not yet arrived at the meridian of life, I have been a mournful witness, in the circle of those dear to me . . . of a wide range of proscription and of death.

It was not surprising that Muir was discouraged. Spain had been coerced by France into declaring war on Britain. Muir was a fugitive from the British Government but, ironically, he was now regarded by the Spaniards as an enemy alien. From his letters it is clear that, though he still hoped to go to the United States, he realized the Spaniards might insist on sending him to Spain. He hoped to be allowed to go from there to France. Muir wrote for the last time to the Viceroy, and thanked him for the hospitality he had received. War made a voyage to Europe more dangerous: 'it may be safer for me to embark in a ship of war to the Havannah where I may find some neutral bottom bound for the United States of America. But in this I submit myself entirely to your prudence.' Muir attempted to intercede on Tobar's behalf: 'If contrary to the lawes, he brought me a stranger to St. Blas, his ignorance, but not his intentions were to be accused. He erred from humanity. Permit me to supplicate that this error may be pardoned.'

Tobar had been imprisoned by the Naval Commander of San Blas for allowing Muir to stay at Tepic. Branciforte ordered a trial. Tobar was excused for accepting ex-convict seamen who were needed for the voyage, but dismissed for taking Muir on board. The Viceroy approved this punishment, though he thought Tobar was good at his job and it was only through ignorance and stupidity that he was taken in by Muir and Dorr's sharp cunning.

Once more Branciforte wrote to Godoy for royal approval. He had shipped Muir and Burling O'Cain on a naval frigate to La Havana, as it was unwise to keep Muir in the kingdom any longer. There was no proof except his word that he was who he claimed to be. The Captain General of Cuba could put him on the first ship sailing for Spain.

Muir reached Havana on 19 November, and was put in prison. 'Curious information concerning Muir' was printed in the American and British newspapers, largely based on a letter from Charleston.[6]

The Governor of Panama had told his colleague in Cuba that he was doubtful if a man of Muir's principles should be at large. So Muir had been imprisoned. 'His confinement is not rigorous and every indulgence is shown to him that is not incompatible with his situation.' The letter-writer had spoken to Muir 'who was much disappointed at not meeting an American agent there, as he had hoped through his intercession to be released, and be permitted to sail for that continent'.

Hamilton Rowan wrote to his wife from Wilmington 10 February, 1797:

This moment I received a letter [dated 3 December 1796] from Muir. He begs me to write to his parents – He got with danger extreme to New Spain, travelled . . . to the Havannah. . . . He is well and humanely treated, though at present a prisoner as an Englishman.

Because Muir's letter to Rowan was bound to be vetted by the Spanish authorities, he would not have dared criticize their attitude too severely, but later, when at liberty in Europe, he wrote to the Directory warmly praising the Spaniards except in Havana. There the scene changed. The Governor, without explaining his reasons, treated him as a prisoner. 'I remained four months in the castle during which time I endured every kind of illtreatment.' Mackenzie, never a very reliable source, says that Muir caught yellow fever at Vera Cruz. In Cuba, due to sleeping in a damp, dirty bed, he suffered from acute rheumatic pains; a humane Spaniard, however, sent him in clean linen, the first he had had for a long time.

The Captain General, the Count of Santa Clara, reported that:

While investigations were made about Muir he was put in a cell destined for distinguished persons; but this was only for a few days in which his addiction to alcohol was observed, which was excessive to the point of committing acts of indecency. Later I ordered that he be put in a fortress where he had such liberty and space as his cell permitted. As he was slightly ill, he was moved to the military hospital where he was taken good care of and . . . paid half a peso daily . . . . the fear that he might spread his political maxims which might upset the laws of New Spain was more than sufficient reason for . . . not treating him in another manner.

Clearly Muir was not treated with the kindness and courtesy others had shown him, and, his hopes of joining his friends in America gone, once more, under stress, he took refuge in drink.

Not long after Muir had sailed for Cadiz on the frigate *Ninfa* the

Captain General received a furious letter from Victor Hugues, the French Directory's agent in the Windward Islands, protesting at the Viceroy's cruel and barbarous conduct in imprisoning Muir in a dungeon. Indignant letters then passed between the Spanish grandees. Branciforte blamed that 'Infamous, ungrateful, perfidious, turbulent man who had made unjust, clamorous and false complaints to the French.'

On 25 March Muir embarked on the last lap of his voyage, which would carry him back to Europe. He had been away for three years. According to Mackenzie he was treated as a common sailor on the *Ninfa*, carrying treasure and silver specie. She was accompanied by another 36-gun warship, the *Santa Elena*. They took four weeks to reach Spain. Cadiz was blockaded by a squadron under Sir John Jarvis. Two British ships, the *Irresistible*, 74 guns, and the *Emerald*, 36 guns, sighted the Spaniards as they approached the port but, in the darkness, mistook them for two Venetian ships that had left Cadiz the previous evening. The Spaniards hove to in Conil Bay, near Cape Trafalgar, unloaded their treasure into fishing boats, and sent it ashore. Muir asked to be allowed to go on shore, but his request was refused.[7]

The following day, 26 April, the British attacked and, after a battle lasting one and a half hours, compelled the Spaniards to surrender. The Spanish lost eighteen killed, thirty wounded, the British one killed, one wounded. After he had endured so much, the fates that hounded Muir dealt him their cruellest blow. Just before the *Ninfa* surrendered he was hit in the face by a splinter from a ball. According to Fonnegra, the commander of the *Ninfa*, Muir fought bravely by his side.

When the action was over some officers and crew of the *Irresistible* boarded the *Ninfa* to take possession. Muir later described the scene:

... I lost my left eye and my face was severely disfigured. I remained six days in the hands of the English. They knew that I had left Havana in tha *Ninfa* and so searched for me. They were told that I had been killed in the battle. Disfigured, covered in blood and almost in the throes of death, they did not recognise me. They sent me on shore with the rest of the prisoners and I was taken to a hospital.

Scottish newspapers printed a letter from an officer on the *Irresistible*, to his father in Glasgow: 'Muir who made so wonderful an escape from Botany Bay was one of five killed on board the *Nymph* by the last shot fired by us. The officer at whose side he fell is at my hand and says he behaved with courage to the last.'⁸ On 5 May another officer reported: 'By a vessel just come out of Cadiz we understand Mr. Muir is not dead, but badly wounded. . . . He says he made his escape after we boarded the frigate where he saw some of his townsmen and countrymen.'⁹ Long afterwards Moffat described the poignant coincidence by which a surgeon from Glasgow, a school-friend of Muir's, found him and dressed his wounds.¹⁰ *

The French consul, Roquesante, learnt of Muir's arrival in the Royal Hospital on the Isle de Leonin in Cadiz harbour. Roquesante was extremely kind. He visited Muir every day, arranged for him to have special nursing, and tried to persuade the Spanish authorities to let him take Muir to his house. He claimed that Muir had been granted honorary French citizenship under a decree of the National Assembly. Roquesante informed Delacroix, the French Foreign Secretary, that he had contacted Muir, 'famous throughout Europe for his principles and his opposition to the English Parliament'.¹² The Governor of Cadiz, however, regarded Muir as a prisoner of war, a dangerous man of forceful personality backed by many friends. The authorities in Madrid ordered Muir to be questioned when he was fit enough, and five sentries were put to guard him.

On 30 May Muir sent the Directory a letter, dictated in French, with his feeble, scrawled signature. After a brief résumé of his adventures, he expressed his deep gratitude for Roquesante's kindness and showered effusive praise on the Republic, the sole support of liberty, now his only country and protector, where he wanted to return as soon as he was strong enough. Delacroix ordered Perignon, the French Ambassador in Madrid, to arrange for Muir to travel to France, and told Roquesante to give Muir financial assistance, though economy was necessary due to the parlous state of France's finances.

* Cobbett wrote a virulent piece delighting in Muir's misfortune. This was set into verse by an American, Matthew Carey:

> . . . Of liberty, the haughty spark,
> And equality has got th' mark –
> An empty purse, lean meagre sides,
> And mutilated face besides.
> A thousand blessings on the ball
> That caus'd his wounds. Such fate befall
> All Jacobin traitors, great and small.¹¹

In August, feeling better, Muir had another burst of letter-writing. He told Delacroix that he was now nearly recovered but held prisoner because he was Scotch. He asked the French Government to intercede on his behalf. The Ambassador and Consul had already done all they could, but with no result. He reiterated his sincere desire to work for the prosperity of the Republic in that limited sphere which accorded with his talents. He would sacrifice the last drop of his blood to defend her.

A letter to Paine was published in the *Edinburgh Advertiser* with an account of Muir's escape and his retention in hospital for a long time between life and death:

... Since the memorable evening on which I took leave of you ... my melancholy and agitated life has been a continued series of extraordinary events. I hope to meet you again in a few months.

Contrary to every expectation I am at last cured of my numerous wounds. The Directory have shewn me great kindness, their solicitude for an unfortunate being, who has been so cruelly oppressed, is a balm of consolation which revives my dropping spirits. . . . Remember me, most affectionately, to all my friends who are the friends of Liberty and Mankind.[13]

Perignon sent Godoy a series of increasingly peremptory notes demanding Muir's release. The French were keenly interested in a man who had suffered at the hands of the English for his attachment to the Republic. Both Muir and the French now placed marked emphasis on Muir's initial enthusiasm for the French Revolution. Talleyrand succeeded Delacroix as Foreign Minister and energetically took up Muir's cause, assuring Muir of his particular affection.

The Spaniards finally admitted that Muir was not a prisoner of war, but Godoy was reluctant to release 'this person who had behaved badly in America'. He wrote a note on Muir's file: 'See if it is known what this devil was doing.' Muir was finally released on 16 September, provided he never returned to the King of Spain's dominions. Perignon, who informed Talleyrand that Muir would leave for Bayonne as soon as he was well enough, thought the Spaniards' conditions 'could certainly have been expressed in more obliging terms'.

With Muir's now usual ill-luck, two days after he had sufficiently recovered to leave for Madrid, on 17 October, Captain Charles Stewart sailed into Cadiz. His sister, Mrs. Meliss, was a great friend of Mrs. Eliza Fletcher. Stewart wrote to tell Muir that he had heard in

New York that Muir was in Cadiz 'in a situation which his known conduct and patriotism did not deserve'. Encouraged by 'injunctions from your absent friends' Stewart had chartered a vessel to take him to America which would 'give infinite pleasure to' himself and Muir's friends. Stewart implored Muir to return to Cadiz. He added that, when he left New York on 3 September, Muir's relations in Scotland were well.

If Muir could have survived the journey to America in his precarious state of health, he would have found old friends and greater financial help than he was to receive in France; he would have been in a neutral country, not one at war with his own. But would the Spaniards have released him into the care of Captain Stewart? Muir wrote from Madrid thanking Stewart, but, alas, it was too late to return. He was now in the hands of the French, who had done so much on his behalf.

There was wide coverage[14] of Muir's triumphal arrival in Bordeaux at the end of November, where he was entertained for several days. The building of the Société de la Grande Quille, in the Grande Place, was illuminated, and a band played in the hall, decorated with the national colours and emblems of liberty. A deputation of female citizens presented Muir with flowers, myrtle, and laurels. A huge crowd gathered outside; Muir appeared on the balcony and was welcomed with cries of 'Long live the defenders and martyrs of liberty!' About five hundred people attended a civic banquet on 4 December. There were patriotic toasts to the French Republic; the philosophers and free men of all countries; the brave young Scottish advocate emancipated from his trials, his perils, and his toils, now the adopted citizen of France. After various speeches Muir spoke:

> Citizens I am not accustomed to speak the French language in public; but were I endowed with all the facility of speech and eloquence it is possible to possess, I should not be able to express the sensations I now feel. I am transported with joy to find myself at this moment among you: but when I compare my present situation with my brethen and countrymen, who sigh in dungeons or languish in exile, I experience sentiments of the most profound melancholy. . . . The Liberty of the Universe is not yet lost. The patriots of England, Scotland and Ireland will soon break their chains. . . . The same spirit which animates you, animates them also. . . .[15]

Muir then fainted into the arms of the American Consul at his left hand.

A few days later an engraving, touched up with water-colours, from a portrait of '*le célèbre Thomas Muir*', was on view everywhere. In this Muir's hair was powdered, he wore a black patch over his eye socket, part of his cheekbone had been blown away, and the left side of his face had dropped. Under the picture was printed a short résumé of his life and a poem in his honour.

Muir's adventures were described in French newspapers as he continued his triumphant progress to Paris by slow, easy stages. His arrival was heralded in *Le Moniteur*, the government newspaper, in a long front-page article by Pierre David* on 2 December: 'Let this apostle of philanthropy come among us, let him find in his new fatherland friends and brothers, and may our victorious cohorts call him back to the country which gave him birth there to establish liberty.' David ended with a warning that 'It would be impolitic as well as inhuman to leave in oblivion and expose to penury those illustrious strangers to whom we offer a refuge.'†

In Paris a government deputation waited on Muir to offer their congratulations and a further banquet was given in his honour. Muir called on Talleyrand, who received him most cordially. Muir wrote to the Directory:

> . . . Your energetic conduct has saved the liberty, not only of France, but also of my country, and of every other nation in the world at present groaning under oppression. . . . To my last breath I will remain faithful to my adopted country. I shall esteem, Citizen Directors, the day on which I shall have the honour to be admitted to your presence, the most precious of my life; and, if I have passed through dangers and misfortunes, that moment will for ever efface their remembrance and amply compensate them.[17]

A useful piece of propaganda which was promptly circulated to the press.

---

* This was Pierre David, diplomat, poet, and authority on the Middle East (see *Nouvelle Biographie Générale*), not David the painter – as various authors say.

† The *Dictionary of National Biography*, basing its information on Alger's *The English in the French Revolution*, says that Muir arrived in Paris on 4 February, 1798. From documents in the French Foreign Office files this is clearly incorrect. Muir must have been in Paris in mid-December.[16]

CHAPTER 12

France

Muir returned to a country markedly different from that he had left four-and-a-half years before. One or two of his old acquaintance were still in power, but many were dead. The corrupt Directory, tottering from one financial crisis to another, had taken the place of the Girondist enthusiasts and Jacobin fanatics of 1793. The regime depended on the Army of Italy under Buonaparte, a popular hero who had just been enthusiastically received on his return to Paris. Although there was a Jacobin majority, the Directory consisted mostly of moderate republicans who were as afraid of anarchists as of royalists. The Directory needed money for the army and was hard put to find it. There were many scandals and frequent denunciations of speculators and the Minister of War. Paris reflected the general impoverishment; it was very dirty, and houses had fallen into decay. In spite of a nominal prohibition the Palais Royal shops were full of English goods, but '*Guerre aux Anglais*' was placarded in streets, cafés, and churches. Spy mania flourished. There was a constant to and fro between France and England of spies and refugees. During the first years of the Republic, financiers and the *nouveaux riches* had fared best. People of vastly different origins now rubbed shoulders in the Directory's entourage. There was no principle of social hierarchy save power or money, neither of which Muir possessed.

Once again information about Muir's life is extremely scanty. His letters and memoranda preserved in the French archives are written in quite creditable French, but contain much republican jargon. Misfortune and harsh treatment had impaired Muir's judgement, never his strong point. His exhilarating reception in France went to his head. He, who had been out of Britain for nearly four years, set himself up as an authority on British affairs; a representative and mouthpiece not only for Scottish and Irish exiles, but for the discontented at home. His professed opinions had become distinctly more extreme. He talked wildly of tyranny and dungeons. Basking at first in the temporary adulation accorded a new hero, half blind, increasingly ill and exhausted, Muir's year in France marks a sad decline. Like so many other political refugees, the brave and promising young advocate, the popular and admired young man, exaggerated his own importance to maintain his position in society, and deteriorated into a tiresome egotistical propagandist, forced to plead with the authorities for funds, spouting political claptrap, involved in futile intrigues.

For some years the French had been planning to invade the British Isles. Several abortive attempts had been made. In the autumn of 1797 Admiral Duncan defeated the Dutch fleet at Camperdown and so foiled a scheme to send 15,000 men to Scotland. However, Napoleon's brilliantly successful campaign against the Austrians forced them to sign the Treaty of Campo Formio in October. Britain was now France's sole opponent. The *Armée d'Angleterre* was formed and Buonaparte put in command. At first he was keen to invade both Scotland and Ireland, and ordered boats to be built.

France, a traditional refuge for Scots and Irish, had welcomed radicals as she formerly welcomed Jacobites. Paris contained a colony of expatriates and now there was an influx of Irishmen dependent on French charity; for government pressure had forced the flight of many of the more extreme members of the United Irishmen.

Muir was soon introduced into Irish circles. As happens so often with exiles, the Irish had split into two groups. Lacking the influence they had possessed at home, they became increasingly bad-tempered and hostile to each other. The most remarkable of them and leader of one faction was Theobald Wolfe Tone. Son of a bankrupt coachmaker, he was the same age as Muir. He had won a scholarship to study at Trinity College, Dublin, but, embittered by lack of immediate success at the bar because he had no influential connections to help him, he turned to politics. Tone was a typical revolutionary: courageous, lively, a brilliant conversationalist, poor, impatient, intolerant, conceited, with a streak of genius and heroism. He was efficient and energetic. Buonaparte and Murat thought well of him. He had been appointed a general in the French army.

The leader of the other faction was a ludicrous, extremely ugly little man, Napper Tandy; immortalized in the song:

I met wid Napper Tandy, and he took me by the hand,
And he said, 'How's poor ould Ireland, and how does she stand?
She's the most disthressful country that iver yet was seen,
For they're hangin' men an' women there for the wearin' o' the Green.

Tandy was also a Protestant, a rather unsuccessful ironmonger, who
had become very popular in Dublin as leader of a campaign to curb
municipal corruption. He was co-founder with Tone of the Dublin
United Irishmen. In 1795 he fled to America but, when the prospect
of invading Ireland arose, sailed for France. Although without
experience, he believed himself to be the only competent soldier
among the United Irishmen. His pride was wounded when Tone
received more respect and attention from the French than he did.
Tone complained that Tandy pestered the Government with applica-
tions and memorials. He was infuriated when Tandy told the French
he was a former officer and man of property in Ireland to whose
standard 30,000 Irishmen would rally. Tone had thought little of
Hamilton Rowan, but appreciated that his name and position would
be useful. Equally Drennan, Muir's Belfast friend, had considered
Tone unreliable, his views too violent, and resented Tone's determination to take command of the United Irish government. So it was
not surprising that Muir gravitated to Tandy's faction rather than
Tone's. Besides Muir could dominate Tandy, whereas he would have
had to subordinate himself to Tone.

  Muir also made contact with two elusive Irishmen involved in
many cross-Channel intrigues. One, William Duckett, was born in
Killarney in 1768, and had been educated at the Irish College in
Paris. After writing inflammatory articles he fled to France in 1796.
He was a very active man who wrote excellent reports on Irish
affairs. Tone, who viewed many men with suspicion and let them
know it, mistakenly suspected Duckett, who pursued him from one
government bureau to another. According to a British spy, Duckett,
who was often to be found in Muir's lodgings, was not well thought
of by Talleyrand, but worked under instructions from Delacroix,
now Minister of War.

  The other Irishman was Nicholas Madgett, aged 58. He too had
been a student at the Irish College in Paris and was employed by the
French Foreign Office. By the time Muir met him he was in charge of
their translation bureau. The British kept a wary eye on him. Madgett
also drew up reports on Britain, despatched secret agents, and helped

to foment an Irish rebellion. He was sent to Orleans to persuade Irish prisoners held there to join the proposed Irish expedition.[1]

In spring 1798 a spy reported that Madgett was 'one of the most active instruments of the Directory in everything respecting Ireland. He lives in the rue du Bac, near Muir, with whom he is in the strictest intimacy.'* Tone thought Madgett honest but weak and debilitated by age – he suffered from gout. Madgett was a perennial optimist 'always full of good news'. His slowness irritated Tone: 'Madgett hunts for maps and then thinks he is making revolutions.' Tone also complained that Madgett wanted to do everything himself and kept him in the background. Muir, on the other hand, appears to have remained on good terms with Madgett.

Shortly after his arrival, a letter from Muir to the Minister of Police was published in the journal *Ami des Lois*:

. . . I am a United Irishman. I am a Scotsman. I can speak in the name of these two nations. . . . it is not with the English people that La Grande Nation has to fight, it is only with a hundred or so scoundrels. When they fall the peace of the universe will be established.[2]

Muir also wrote articles about the United Irishmen for *Le Bien Informé*, an influential daily paper edited by Nicolas de Bonneville. Tone considered them 'very foolish'. So he led a deputation of United Irishmen, who called on 'the famous Thomas Muir' to ask him not to write any more such pieces. Tone described the meeting in his autobiography:

Of all the vain, obstinate blockheads that ever I met, I never saw his equal. Muir told us roundly that he knew as much of our country as we did . . . that he had seldom acted without due reflection, and when he had once taken his party, it was impossible to change him; and that he had the sanction of the most respectable individual of the United Irishmen [Tandy] whose authority he considered as justifying every syllable he had advanced.

After a three hour discussion they parted acrimoniously: 'The fact is Muir and Tandy are puffing one another here for their private advantage . . . issuing accommodation bills of reputation.'

Alas there was clearly much truth in Tone's comments. On the other hand Tone, who found most Irish refugees 'vulgar wretches',

* The spy was Turner, see below page 178. He pointed out that the crown lawyers had taken Madgett for a fictitious name when it appeared in correspondence quoted at a treason trial – 'but I assure you it is as real as your or mine, as I have frequently been in conversation with him at Muir's lodgings'.

often made mistaken snap judgements. Jealousy and vanity, the besetting sins of revolutionaries, were only too prevalent among the Irish. Tone and his supporters had an additional reason to be irritated by Muir's throwing his weight about . They were doing their best to dissuade the French from invading Scotland as they wanted all men and arms concentrated on Ireland.

At first Paine and Tone had made friends, but the two strong personalities soon clashed. Tone described Paine as 'intolerably conceited and vain beyond all belief. He drinks like a fish, a misfortune which I have known to befall other celebrated patriots. He plumes himself more on his theology than his politics.' Paine gloomily supported the Directory because another Terror or the Bourbons seemed worse alternatives. He frequented the Irish Coffee House in the rue de Condé where Irish, English, and Americans met to discuss politics. He lived in his friend de Bonneville's house – a wretched little place – and contributed articles to his newspaper. Paine argued that it was easier to land 10,000 men in England than to send them to India and urged the Directory to attack. He gave £100 to the cause, saying there could be 'no lasting peace for the world until the tyranny and corruption of the English government was abolished'. Napoleon consulted Paine, and invited him to accompany an expedition of 1,000 gunboats and 100,000 men as political adviser.

Muir's temperament was in many ways similar to Paine's. Paine was a far more remarkable person – an original thinker and a journalist of genius. Paine's manners, however, were rather boorish, he had little education and no aptitude for languages. Though Paine had been married he appears, like Muir, to have had far more interest in politics than sex. Both men were kind and thoughtful to their friends, both were fluent conversationalists and had developed exceedingly good opinions of themselves. They were sincere in their radical convictions, but their characters had deteriorated in adversity and they drank too much, to bolster their self-deception.

On 29 December Muir wrote to Talleyrand's secretary: he did not lack money in his own country, but a law had been passed in England forbidding the remission of money to France under pain of high treason, and he could not correspond with his parents for fear of compromising them. 'I can tell you without conceit that I am perhaps the man the English government fears the most.' He would have to accept money from the French Republic, but he would not receive it as charity or even as a loan, only in the name of the Scots nation, and, 'if the government is sincere, as I believe it, intending to carry out an invasion, all will be paid by Scotland with interest and enthusiasm'. Talleyrand had asked him what sum he needed. Muir suggested 8,000 livres.

I will describe my way of life. 1. My wounds, the feeble state of my health, the loss of an eye and poor vision in the remaining one, oblige me to have a carriage. 2. For the same reasons I need a secretary to take down my dictation. My secretary is the amiable young man Molet whom you have met, who has fought for four years in the republican armies. Molet should be treated honourably, not because he quitted his post with the consent of his superior at the French consulate in Cadiz to help me on the journey, but because he is always at the Republic's service. 3. My food is nothing much, only soup and a plate of meat with one or two friends to share it. I do not spend anything on myself as all those who know me can witness; but in my present position I need lodgings which will not give wretches a pretext to say that patriots are despised in France.*

His heart was entirely French. He had suffered in the sacred cause of the Republic. 'Little blood rests in my veins, but that little which remains will flow another time.'

At first Muir's life must have been moderately comfortable, to judge from an encounter with two friends from college days, John and Benjamin Sword, rich Glasgow merchants who shared Muir's political views.† The brothers sailed to Hamburg in August 1797 and eventually reached Paris, where they spent a month.[3] Paine told them that Muir was expected and, after his arrival, they called on him. Muir was in the first flush of his enthusiastic welcome. 'Mr. Muir appeared to live in style and kept his carriage.' The brothers dined with Paine and Muir. During the evening they 'differed in the point of religion which Paine reprobated while Muir endeavoured to defend it'. After remaining together till pretty late they parted. According to John he and Muir called upon Helen Maria Williams but she was not at home. According to Benjamin, Muir became

---

* This letter sounds rather stilted as I have translated more or less literally from the French.

† Although the brothers later returned to Scotland, John planned to move to France 'the glorious land of liberty, justly the admiration of Europe and of the whole world'. He arranged to travel with a Glaswegian friend of his and Muir's. He asked Muir to use his influence with his 'friends in power' to rescue his belongings, seized by a French privateer.

intoxicated and so failed to keep his promise to introduce the brothers to Miss Williams.

Most Scottish Whigs were at this time very pessimistic about the country's future. The brothers were more extreme in expecting, honestly but erroneously, that revolution was imminent. They encouraged Muir and his colleagues to believe that many Scots were disaffected.

Besides his other pretensions, Muir had apparently also set himself up as an authority on Spanish America. In her *Tour of Switzerland*, published in 1798, Miss Williams retracted her previous high opinion of her friend the Peruvian general Miranda as a result of 'evidence lately confirmed by Mr. Muir and other gentlemen whose testimony, relying on facts collected during their residence in the Spanish dominions, leaves me no alternative'.

In January 1798 a spy reported that the Directory intended to establish separate republics in England, Scotland, and Ireland. The 'Scotch Directory' was to consist of Muir, Sinclair, Cameron, Simple (Sempill), and Lauderdale; Macleod was to be Minister of War. In England Paine, Horne Tooke, and Thelwall were to be members, in Ireland Napper Tandy, Lord Edward Fitzgerald, and Hamilton Rowan.[4] Though this may all have been the spy's fabrication, it does give an impression of the gossip being bandied about Parisian coffee houses, and Muir's currently high standing.

Muir showed considerable panache as a refugee. Besides helping plan a Scottish invasion he acted as mediator for other émigrés. He was better educated than some of them, his command of French was good, and he gained and retained Talleyrand's confidence. On 12 February the *Moniteur* reported that Muir had interceded on behalf of various Irishmen who had been captured on English ships and imprisoned at Bordeaux. They were to receive better treatment and not be part of an exchange of prisoners, which could have had unpleasant consequences as some of these Irishmen were 'fleeing from the despotism of the British Government'.

Muir was reunited with another Glaswegian, James Smith, whom he had met in Paris in 1793. Smith had since arranged for his son to join him and had married a Frenchwoman. He was now having difficulties over the renewal of his passport and in June Muir wrote a rather illegible letter of recommendation for him to the Minister of Police.[5] Talleyrand added a note – Muir assured him that Smith merited the protection of the French Government. A spy informed Castlereagh that Muir had 'got some 1,000 livres [said to be 10,000] that's almost gone. He has with him a young man of the name of Smyth, a gunmaker from the same place in Scotland. Fled about five years ago. Smyth expects to be sent over to Scotland in about three weeks on a mission by the French Government.'

There are many memorials from exiles in the French archives, all intended to bolster the impression that the three kingdoms were on the brink of revolt. The French gave at least some credence to these fanciful assessments, possibly because they derived comfort from them. Submitting his own and others' reports was one of the few means by which Muir could make himself useful and repay the French for rescuing him.

An English radical, John Ashley, arrived in Paris in March. A dark, imposing man, he had at one time been secretary to the London Corresponding Society.[6] But his reasons for leaving England were not really political. Ashley had a wife twelve years older than himself. He fell in love with a younger woman; ructions ensued. Eventually he decided to go to France alone.

Ashley submitted a memorial to Talleyrand with a covering note from Muir. His description of life in England was quite false. Shortages caused by the war had reduced London to a fearful state, many soldiers were disaffected, people were ready to act from the 'virtue of their beliefs and motives of despair'. Ashley greatly exaggerated the importance of the Corresponding Society, saying disingenuously that its numbers had never exceeded 15,000, and declared there were 30,000 men in London ready to move against the Government when the opportunity should arise. In a postcript to another memorandum Ashley said that he had not foreseen a long stay in France and needed financial assistance until he could 'speedily return to England with an army of liberty'.[7] As Ashley was an intelligent, sober man he can only have written such accounts to please the French and encourage them to give him financial support.

Robert Watson, an astute Scottish adventurer with extreme radical and anti-clerical views, more than 20 years older than Muir, joined him in May at the Hôtel de la Marine near the Palais Royal.[8] He was also a former member of the Corresponding Society, who had been held without trial for two years in Newgate before fleeing to France. He sent Talleyrand another wildly exaggerated account of the strength and potentialities of popular organizations in Britain. He led Muir to believe that Kennedy* and Cameron, members of a small extremist group, the United Scotsmen, would be useful agents.[9] From the scanty information available one cannot judge whether Watson and Ashley privately gave Muir more accurate information than they did the French or, if they exaggerated as grossly as in their public declarations, how far Muir believed them. As they had associated entirely with sympathizers they may genuinely have believed the extent of radical support to be much greater than it was.

Muir submitted various advisory memorials. In one, written in February 1798 while staying at Passy, he described Britain at the end of 1792 and beginning of 1793 – the climax of his career and the last period of which he had first-hand knowledge. As Talleyrand was a witness of much that had happened, Muir asked him to correct his ideas – a necessary warning as the memorandum was biased and contained no information which Talleyrand could not have obtained elsewhere.

Muir made a sound comparison between French émigrés and British radicals. Émigrés travelled round European courts proclaiming that the French people would rise to support them. Now, as in 1793, Muir had run across his compatriots in Parisian cafés who claimed that the English would welcome the French and help establish a republic. Both groups were mistaken. Then, in a violently chauvinistic attack, Muir declared that the English would do nothing because their Government bought them with meat and beer. They were the most ignorant and barbarous people in Europe; illiterate, characterless weathercocks. The King was cleverer than men thought, 'a greater hypocrite than Tiberius'. Pitt and Dundas had talent, but were perpetually drunk, even in the Commons. They and their cronies controlled the Bank, the East India Office, and government contracts.

Pitt had found additional support in the Anglican Church. Anglican clergy were either very rich reactionaries who lived in scandalous luxury or poverty-stricken wretches. The Presbyterians and dissen-

* Kennedy had been assistant secretary to the last British Convention in Edinburgh. He was said to have issued arms and organized resistance to the Militia Act of 1797. Little is known about the minute short-lived groups the United Scotsmen and United Englishmen, who intrigued with the United Irishmen. In 1799 they were suppressed by law, but they were finished already.

ters were quite different, far more intelligent and feared by the Government. Many men who supported the initial stages of the Republic became frightened by its excesses. The Government had cunningly raised the cry, always a means of rallying the nation, that the Church was in danger. By employing spies to spread fear of atheism and loss of property, they persuaded even Presbyterian businessmen to turn against liberty and France.

The Opposition was feeble and did not command the people's confidence. English republicans were divided into two types – Men of the People and Men of Letters, some of whom Muir knew intimately. They believed people must wait tranquilly until the spirit of liberty destroyed despotism. Ordinary people were divided by religion. Members of the Established Church were patriots through discontent, hatred, and personal interest, not to be trusted. Those who belonged to the disestablished Church were true patriots and far better educated. French politicians should not neglect any of the opposition, but should principally treat with the dissenters who were energetic and persevering.

Muir (who still had a sense of proportion in some things) said he would end his already overlong letter with notes on the popular societies. The Friends of the People, who included members of both chambers, wanted to extend the franchise, but were adamantly opposed to republican principles. The Constitutional Society contained distinguished men of letters and dissenters. They were republicans, but unable to decide on the time or manner to effect change. Most members of the Corresponding Society would declare for France at the first opportunity. Though ardent, they lacked talent and knowledge. The Society was exposed to wild intrigues, and there was a danger that the majority would become pawns of new Robespierres and Marats. These agitators spread the doctrine of bloodshed and division of property. Still, most of the Society were honest and the Republic must direct its energy into channels worthy of its noble intentions.

Muir concluded by apologizing for the imperfections of his report, he was still convalescing. Although there was a germ of truth in many of Muir's comments, he allowed his prejudices to outweigh any attempt at objectivity. Talleyrand thanked Muir for his memorandum and rashly said he looked forward to the next.

In May Muir sent him a portentous document covering nineteen folio sides on the political and military state of Scotland, divided into seven sections: The political constitution of Scotland; the injustices this constitution caused; the Scots moral character; the manner in which this character was expressed; their physical strength; the means of effecting a revolution and sustaining it from abroad. Muir's exposition was muddled and diffuse, his history resembled that of French pamphleteers. He described the Scots as almost uniformly intelligent and virtuous, waiting for the signal to revolt. Some sections bear a strong resemblance to Watson's pronouncements. The two men probably had many joint discussions about their plans and ideas.

Muir claimed that from the accession of James I and VI the English Government had done everything in its power to bind Scotland with chains and suppress the Presbyterian Church, which had always championed the people's rights. The English parliament had controlled the Scottish parliament by bribery (which was true). A century of blood and tears had followed. The Court paid historians devoted to its interest to interpret Scottish aspirations for national independence as fanaticism. Thousands of republicans were massacred. Finally liberty triumphed; the Stuart tyrant fled to Saint Germain (Muir's presbyterian dislike of the Stuarts was reinforced by his belief in the Norman Yoke theory, according to which the Stuart kings had tried to deprive the British of liberty). The Scots were told Union was the only means of saving their religion, which was menaced by the Catholics, but they did not want to unite with the English whose customs, spirit, and mode of life were totally different.

Though the people tried to rise everywhere they had no leaders. England bought Scotland's freedom. Since Union, Scottish nobles had gone to England; they were bribed with English money and corrupted their compatriots. As a result the English controlled Scotland's M.P.s, universities, and Church. Venal teachers had been appointed to subvert education; new customs and excise laws had stifled commerce. In 1745 the country was disarmed (Muir skimmed smartly over the fact that the rising and disarmament had been caused by supporters of the hated Stuarts).

The Scots were a moral people. Unlike the worthless English mob, sunk in total ignorance, they had been educated since the seventeenth century. They could never be taken in by political impostors – give them the means to gain their freedom and they would not succumb to anarchy or royal dictatorship.

Before the French Revolution the Scots had paid little attention to demands for parliamentary reform. After 1789, however, they declared they cared nothing for Whigs or Tories, but would gain liberty for themselves. In England popular assemblies were full of *agents provocateurs*. He himself had warned his colleagues of the danger from informers, but in Scotland only one reformer became a government spy. Muir was unaware of J.B.'s activities, but he must have known this claim was untrue.

Muir then gave an account of the 1792 Convention, greatly exaggerating its scope and influence. It was not at all like the later Convention, 'a miserable plaything of the English Government'. The authorities were so alarmed they fortified the Tower, sent the militia to the border, and drew up the fleet. The deliberations of the 360 Scottish representatives were worthy of the occasion, calm, wise, imperturbable. Alas they lacked arms, money, or means of defence. They turned their eyes to France, but she was in difficulties. Still the Convention had revived the national spirit. Since then liberty had marched across the soil of Scotland with giant strides. The country was a volcano on the verge of eruption.

Muir said it was not for him to advise the French Government on what measures to take, but he would attempt to describe the present state of affairs. The Scots were divided into lowlanders and highlanders. The highlanders, though devoted to their country, were forced to emigrate. They were magnificent soldiers. They had much in common with the Irish, and, according to English newspaper reports, highland soldiers had recently refused to fire on the United Irishmen. The lowlanders consisted of republicans and aristocrats. The ancient aristocracy, who had lost most of their wealth and power, had been superseded by lawyers, petty lairds, and businessmen. They possessed the vices of the aristocrats without their virtues, and were far more dangerous. There would be no difficulty in rousing the Scots to fight the English Government and establish an independent republic. 100,000 patriots would rise – a conservative estimate, in Muir's view, as probably 200,000 would fight, and if they were successful more would join in.

The Scots would not make the same mistake as the Irish in embarking on a scattered, ineffectual uprising. The French should send them soldiers, arms, and money. He had heard the Irish in Paris say they did not want a French army to land in their country, but the Scots did. They needed help. Their soldiers had been sent abroad, their young men were untrained. English soldiers were billeted everywhere, the lairds a bunch of spies. The French would be greeted with greater enthusiasm than in England or even Ireland.

A proclamation should be issued, allowing freedom of worship and the right for Scots to choose their own ministers. Muir reminded Talleyrand that they were sober people, and French generals should make sure that their troops did not offend northern susceptibilities. Inviolability of property should also be proclaimed. This would help dispel fears propagated by the English Government, and the rich would not resist when they saw their possessions respected. A provisional government must be appointed at once. The dangerous point in revolutions was between the removal of one government and the creation of another. This was the reason the American and French Revolutions had been so much more successful than the Irish.*

Muir did produce a few shrewd comments on the Scots, and his hints for conduct after invasion were sensible – though the French would have got a shock to find how sparse the Scottish support would be. Otherwise his report is a sorry piece of clumsy propaganda and childish diatribe, giving a totally misleading picture. It is difficult to tell how much of his farrago Muir believed, how much of his revolutionary enthusiasm was an attempt to ensure French goodwill and increase his influence, how much was based on misinformation or his own wishful thinking. The Irish, in an effort to get French help, grossly exaggerated the amount of support they would receive on landing. Muir may have done the same, Did he really think an invasion of Scotland could possibly succeed? Paine, who had been out of England since 1792, believed invasion was feasible, for 'the mass of the people are friends of liberty. Tyranny and taxation oppress them. . . .' A French invasion would 'give the people an opportunity of forming a government for themselves and thereby bring about peace'. Muir had been away for four years. His conception of the current situation came from the censored press or unreliable refugees; his only up-to-date information about Scotland from such ardent critics as the Swords and Watson.

A distressing aspect of Muir's memorials is his disregard for

* See pp. 177–9 below.

historical fact and his petulant scorn for the English – undoubtedly fostered by his treatment at the hands of a largely English Government. Muir had almost no first-hand knowledge of the people he condemned. He was, of course, anxious to emphasize the Scots' superiority and dislike of France's true enemy, the English. Although Muir was intensely patriotic and, like most Scots, believed Union had been a mixed blessing, before he was transported even spies never suggested that he wanted the Union to be dissolved. His private views were probably more extreme than those he expressed publicly, but he had been content to strive to improve Scottish representation in the British Parliament. Circumstances had intensified his youthful radical inclinations; imprisonment and illness had warped his judgement and damaged his critical faculties. His genuine devotion and gratitude to the French, the atmosphere in which he lived in Paris, his companions' revolutionary views, the United Irishmen's struggle for freedom, all worked to reinforce his detestation of the English Government and his desire for Scotland to be freed from alien domination. Also, whether consciously or not, Muir may have exaggerated English iniquities and Scottish national aspirations to excuse what even his parents might consider treasonable activities on his part.

On 1 May Muir had written, this time from the Maison d'Espagne, rue Colombière, to a cousin William Muir, a merchant at Hamburg:

... I wrote you from Cadiz. I have long expected to hear from you. I am impatient to know the state of my father's family, which, as all communication is closed between England and the Republick, is extremely difficult to be procured. I am almost entirely recovered from my wounds.

I may probably soon pay you a visit. I have after an exile of five years much to ask and much to learn. If it is possible, inform my parents that, if the prevention of almost every wish and the sincerest proofs of general esteem can render a man happy, I may ... lay claim to that happiness. But my mind is greatly agitated when I reflect upon the affliction which I have so long occasioned to them, not, however, from folly or extravagance, but from my attachment to liberty and the general cause of humanity.[10]

As well as meeting his cousin, Muir may have hoped to contact agents from the United Scotsmen. Hamburg was the centre for spies. Dubious characters arrived from London or boarded ships to be smuggled into Yarmouth. Irishmen with false names ordered arms. Whether correctly, or merely because he was Thomas's cousin, the

British authorities suspected William Muir of holding 'revolutionary principles'. Sir James Crawford, British Ambassador in Hamburg, sent Lord Grenville 'the names of Jacobins written on a picture hanging in citizen Muir's room'. Nothing came of Thomas's scheme to visit Hamburg. William may have been irritated by his rather boastful tone, or moved by his pathetic reference to his parents; at any rate he preserved this letter.

Mackenzie says that Muir wrote affectionate letters to his parents who were 'greatly agitated by fresh hopes and fears on his account'. In 1837 William Tait appealed in his Edinburgh magazine to Muir's relations 'who owe his memory and the world the debt of making public as much of his correspondence with his family as concerns the abiding interests of the human race'. There was no response. The letters may have been destroyed, contained too much unacceptable revolutionary jargon, or intimate details his family preferred not to be published. It is a great pity that there are no first-hand descriptions, except Tone's, of Muir at this time, especially from those who had known him before he was transported and could have commented on any changes in character and mental abilities.

The refugees were running out of funds – Tandy was starving and reduced to selling his shoe buckles. Muir wrote letters from different addresses, perhaps because he was periodically forced to move to cheaper lodgings. On 20 May he sent a petition to the Directory, transcribed by his secretary Molet in French emphatic rhetorical style:

. . . You have brought me back to life and liberty. . . . I will only forget your kindness with my last breath. Nevertheless I am very unhappy. I eat your bread without being of any use to the Republic. If my physical strength had matched my inclinations I would have asked for the honour of fighting your enemies, but alas that is impossible.

Only one means remains by which I will no longer be a charge on the Republic. My property in Scotland is small, but sufficient for me to live anywhere I wish in honourable independence. As much as possible of that must be obtained quickly for, in the event of the death of my father and mother, who are already advanced in years, and who weep for me night and day, it will be taken from me, not perhaps by the British Government, but by heartless, avaricious relations who, to achieve this end, pretend to be its devoted partisans. So I must provide my father with the means to send me as much of his fortune as he can without embarrassing himself.

Still, even if I do not receive a sou, I can make myself independent. I have notes of my exile and travels which only need editing. They will form a two volume quarto work. This is awaited with the greatest eagerness in England. I should get at least £3,000 from the London booksellers. All that needs to be done is to send the MSS to any agent you chose at Hamburg and the booksellers' agents will lay up at once.

The object of this petition, citizen Directors, is to beg you to give me permission to buy a domaine nationale for 150,000 francs which I hope to be able to repay in two years. Please put me in possession at once so that I do not have to abuse your kindness any more. I have given the Foreign Minister details of my family. It is impossible to express my gratitude for all his kindness. . . .

This letter hung about in French government files until the following year an official added the chilling comment, '*depuis Muir est mort*'. There is no evidence to show whether Muir's suspicions of his relations – presumably his sister and brother-in-law – were well founded or just another figment of his clouded brain. Years later one of Muir's nephews, James Blair, helped organize the erection of a monument to him. He may have been brought up to revere his uncle, or his attitude may have been a reaction against his father's disapproval.

In 1821 a Mr. Witherspoon of Cheapside told Thomas Hardy that he had a box of manuscripts, letters, and papers of Muir's. It would only have been feasible to publish Muir's memoirs, if they merited it, when the climate of opinion swung back towards liberalism in the 1820s. No campaigners for the Reform Bill made use of them. Either they proved unpublishable, no one was sufficiently interested to edit them, or they were mislaid or destroyed soon after 1821. Mackenzie, whose biography was published in 1831, made unsuccessful enquiries about Muir's papers. Nor does Witherspoon appear to have contacted Muir's relations, for James Blair went to Paris in 1837 to look for his papers – and found none. Judging from his reports, Muir would not have been in a fit state physically or mentally to produce a satisfactory book.

In his second report, Muir had referred to the abortive rebellion taking place in Ireland. Although there were only a handful of Scots or English in Paris or at home who might support an insurrection, there were many Irishmen working to that end. In December 1797 the Directory had planned to invade Ireland the following April. But when Napoleon inspected the French fleet at the end of February he realized that the navy was in no state to launch an invasion. Also

Dumouriez feared that, even with the help of the inhabitants, an invader could hardly hold out more than three months. Napoleon persuaded the Directory to back an expedition to the East instead. This was kept secret and, as cover, a pretence made that invasion would take place. The Directory had little money, and now only intended to make small raids, hoping to stir up civil war. Muir could play a small, unwitting part in helping divert British attention from Napoleon's true plans. On 20 May 1798 Napoleon set out for Egypt. Four days later an uncoordinated Irish rebellion broke out. Encouraged by its initial success in Wexford the Irish in Paris approached the Directory for assistance. They received vague promises, much goodwill. Although some detachments from the Army of England had been sent to Switzerland and the Rhine, the Directory could have sent others still mustered on the coast, but they were deterred by previous failures. The Ministry of Marine's incompetence caused further delay. By the end of June, before any French help arrived, the Irish rebellion had been crushed.

Too late the Directory, hard pressed to find the money, half-heartedly agreed to another Irish expedition. This was to consist of 8,000 men. A force of about 1,000 under General Humbert was to sail from La Rochelle; another small group from Dunkirk; 3,000 men under General Hardy would start from Brest to be followed later by 4,000 more. Tone was sent off to co-ordinate the forces. Muir, meanwhile, was bustling about in Paris. None of the refugees realized that one Irishman was a spy who sent reports to Castlereagh. Samuel Turner, educated at Trinity College, Dublin, then called to the bar, had been a member of the executive committee of the United Irishmen. He escaped to the Continent in 1797. He was known under various aliases to the English Government and awarded a secret pension of £300 a year. Turner had quarrelled with Tone and his associates, so sided with Tandy's faction, though he thought little of Tandy who 'has a few laced coats which he is eternally overhauling and gazing on. He is too insignificant for the British Government to take any notice of him.'

According to Turner, Tandy called a meeting of the United Irishmen in conjunction with Muir, Madgett, and John Hurford Stone. Muir then waited on Talleyrand with a petition which Talleyrand took instantly to the Directory. As a consequence Tandy was appointed General, his supporters composed his staff (and Tandy must have been thankful to have a salary at last). Tandy was given command of the *Anacreon*, a swift corvette, and, with his entourage, set off for Dunkirk on 11 July. Three days later a party of French officers plus Tone and other Irishmen left for Brest. Turner said a friend of Muir's from Glasgow had arrived in Paris and Muir had arranged for a Scottish banker in Paris to go to England.

Turner completely hoodwinked Muir and Madgett, who swore him into the Secret Committee for managing the affairs of Ireland and Scotland in Tandy's place. Turner then went to Hamburg, leaving Muir and Madgett as the only remaining members of the committee. If Turner's reports have any truth in them, Muir had some influence with Talleyrand.

The Irish invasion was a disastrous failure. The Directory had voted the inadequate sum of 200,000 francs and the Treasury only paid out part of this. As a result there was trouble among troops who had not been paid, and bickerings among the generals. Humbert landed with his small force at Killala Bay on August 23. He had a remarkable initial success but was obliged to surrender to vastly superior forces. Hardy's men, who were supposed to sail at the same time, were delayed for a fortnight till money for stores and wages was produced. Then for three weeks the wind blew from the west and they were unable to leave Brest. When the wind changed they were effectively blockaded by British ships.

On 16 September Tandy plus 270 Frenchmen, a number of Irish refugees, and a large supply of arms, slipped through the blockade and landed on the coast of Donegal. Only a few peasants came out to greet him. Tandy raised the standard, made a fatuous speech, and was carried back drunk to his ship. He fled north drinking brandy. The *Anacreon* reached Bergen. Tandy travelled on to Hamburg where he was arrested on 22 November. The following year the Germans yielded to English pressure and he was taken to Dublin for trial. Napoleon interceded on his behalf. He was exchanged for English prisoners of war at Bordeaux and lived to a ripe old age as a general in Napoleon's army, more fortunate than his cleverer and nobler associates. Tone finally left with Hardy's flotilla of nine ships which reached Lough Swilly, only to be cut up by a British squadron on 12 October. Tone was captured and committed suicide in prison to avoid the ignominy of hanging.

· · ·

The last trace of Muir in the French archives is a memorial sent to Talleyrand on 18 October.* In the covering letter Muir said he was transcribing the memorial himself as it was so important. This time he wrote in English – presumably to keep its contents more secret. Despite his poor eyesight Muir's handwriting is firm and legible. His outline of future strategy is more concisely and clearly written than his earlier résumé of Scottish history.

He explained that the report concerned insurrection in Scotland, London, and the fleet. All these objectives could be achieved with little danger if a confidential messenger could be sent to England to invite 'one or two persons from Britain to meet me not in Paris but in some other less suspicious place'. He could 'give instructions and arrange the plan of operation'. The British fleet had recently mutinied and the ringleaders been hanged. Muir emphasized that British sailors would only be utilized now while they were brooding over their wrongs and meditating revenge. 'Sailors should be told they could keep the full value of any ships they sailed into French ports.

The memorial began with an assurance that few Scots would be so foolish as to emulate the premature Irish rebellion. A confidential agent must be sent to Scotland to assess the patriots' strength and prepare for a rising.

...I must confess that I know not one of my countrymen in Paris whom I could propose. I know the purity of their principles. I have scrutinised their conduct with a watchful eye. They have not that prudence, that secrecy and that fortitude indispensably requisite for so delicate and so dangerous a trust. The superior wisdom and information of the Government no doubt will discover a person properly qualified. . . .

It would be less hazardous to send money to purchase arms locally than to send arms. Powder would have to be sent; it could easily be smuggled in as contraband liquor. Patriots could obtain artillery by seizing the Carron works. There was a subterranean passage by which Edinburgh Castle could be seized. About £30,000 would be

* It is dated '27 Vendémiaire an 9' (1800). This is almost certainly a mistake and should be 'an 7'. Meikle says this memorandum is by an unknown Scotsman, but it is far more likely to be Muir's. Some of the information was probably supplied by others, but it is signed by Muir, written in his style, and the author says that, having previously stated his reasons for believing that the political situation of Scotland demands the French Government's attention, he will now point out the means of effecting a revolution. Muir had promised to do this in his long memorial on Scotland.

sufficient to produce an insurrection of the miserable, debauched London populace. The real difficulty was the choice of agents. Most members of the London Corresponding Society were unreliable, idle, vain, or dissipated men who took to politics as an easy means of advancement. At first ordinary men of courage and moral honesty would be needed. It would be very difficult to find a sufficient number in England where there was virtually no middle class, but Hardy and the printer Ross, themselves Scots, would be able to give a French agent reliable information. In Scotland, however, there were many more. Muir gave six names, including John Clark the Whig advocate and George Meliss, the banker whose brother-in-law, Stewart, had tried to rescue him. Muir said he would not suggest Lords Lauderdale, Stanhope, Orford, and Semple (Sempill) because they were closely watched and had done all they could. Talleyrand himself would have to decide if Fox should be approached.

Muir very much wanted to see James Kennedy and Neil Cameron in Paris. Cameron had been outlawed and was hiding in London, Kennedy he hoped was on his way to Paris with important information. To recapitulate – Scotland was organized and ready to revolt. An insurrection must be organized in London at the same moment. The fleet must be secured. This scheme could be accomplished with little bloodshed or expense. Many discontented people who would oppose foreign invasion would welcome a revolution originating among their own countrymen. The English attention was at present fixed on Ireland. The Government should order French journals to ignore Scottish and English affairs to lull the English Government into security.

Although Muir starts with the apparently confident assumption that rebellion would succeed, there is an air of uncertainty and a lack of conviction; the assurance of his own and others' earlier reports with their optimistic quotation of the thousands who would revolt, is missing.

Nothing is known about the last months of Muir's life. Mackenzie says he died at Chantilly on 27 September 1798, four months before his death occurred. This date was accepted by later historians. There seems no obvious reason for Mackenzie's mistake. Among obituaries of remarkable personages, the *Gentleman's Magazine* for February 1799 includes, 'At Paris Thomas Muir the celebrated

Scotch Advocate . . . . the wound he received on board the Spanish frigate in which he returned to Europe, it is said never was cured, and to that his death is ascribed.'

27 September could be the date on which Muir decided to leave Paris for the quiet little town of Chantilly twenty-five miles away. Paine had lived there at one time and might have recommended it. Why did Muir leave Paris? He may have planned to conceal himself from Pitt's spies before meeting James Kennedy. Watson had encouraged Muir to believe Kennedy was on his way.[11]

Watson was still trying to rouse non-existent revolutionaries. In November he issued an 'Address to the people of Great Britain'[12] advocating a general rising to welcome the French as saviours. Watson warned the 'patriots of Scotland' that the same fetters were being forged for them as for the Irish. 'Did Wallace fight and Ossian sing in vain? Scotsmen have sworn to recover liberty or perish in the attempt amid the smoking ruins of their country.' Scotland would regain its pristine glory and be free. Conceivably Watson and Muir genuinely persuaded themselves that many of their fellow countrymen would revolt, and believed that they were working to preserve Scotland as a nation. Muir wrote: 'We have achieved a great duty in these critical times. After the destruction of so many years we have been the first to revive the spirit of our country, and give it a national existence.'[13] Muir would have been a happier man for believing this. It was not true.

Political intrigues may have been only one factor in Muir's decision to leave Paris. In May he had wanted to retire to a *domaine national*. He was poor and ill. Many of his Irish acquaintance had gone; still, Madgett, Stone, Smith, and Watson among others remained. Friendship had always meant much to Muir. Possibly his remaining friends neglected him. He could not see clearly out of his one eye, eating was difficult, his appearance no longer attractive. It was not a cheering time. The high hopes of the revolution had crumbled. The government disapproved of de Bonneville and Paine's idealistic radicalism. Muir's expatriate friends had lost heart, many were in financial straits. As news of Tandy's fiasco and the Battle of the Nile arrived, Muir must have realized that the tottering Directory was now unlikely to order an invasion of Scotland and what little use he had for them was finished. He may have sensed that his strength was ebbing and, as on the voyage to New South Wales, preferred to cut himself off, to creep away to die. Perhaps his wounds affected his mind and he did not realize he was failing, or he drank to forget.

His death was registered by the Mayor of Chantilly on 26 January 1799 at the Mairie of Chantilly in clumsy, misspelt French. In the morning a little boy of 12 told the postman of Muir's death. When the postman had finished his round he consulted the clerk to the Justice of the Peace and another friend. They told the Mayor that they knew nothing about Muir except his name, neither the place nor country of his birth nor his age. The postman said he used to deliver newspapers addressed to Thomas Muir. The Mayor went back with them to Muir's lodgings to make sure he was dead. The cemetery where Muir was buried has been built over and there is no record of his grave. Although the officials at Chantilly appeared to know so little about Muir, others must have been in touch with him, for on 30 January the *Moniteur* carried a eulogistic obituary: 'Thomas Muir the Scotsman so celebrated for his love of liberty, for his misfortunes . . . has just died from the wounds which he received about two years ago. . . .' He was 33.

Mackenzie says that on his deathbed Muir sealed up the bible his parents had given him and asked that it should be forwarded to them. Whether true or not, it did reach them. Muir's father died in 1801. A year later Huntershill was sold.[14] His mother, who died in 1803, asked that a portrait of Muir should be kept in the house, but the house subsequently changed hands and the portrait was removed. Under it was an inscription:

> Doomed from this mansion to a foreign land
> To waste his days of gay and sprightly youth,
> And all for sowing with a liberal hand,
> The seeds of that seditious libel truth.[15]

A sad, lonely end for a brave man. Only a few heroic people have the strength to withstand adversity and remain unchanged. One tragic aspect of Muir's life is the deterioration in mind and character through sickness and misfortune, through entanglement in the twilight world of refugees, of a young man who, though vain and impetuous, had been liked by many, had helped many, a man of principle, generosity, and warmth.

◇◇◇

CHAPTER 13

The Monument

Of the five reformers who were transported, only Margarot returned home. In 1801 Palmer, whose term of transportation was ended, joined Ellis and Boston, whose children had died, and sailed north in a Spanish ship which had been captured and taken into Port Jackson. They had bought the ship intending to trade in the Pacific and then return to England. She was very leaky, so they were forced to put into the port on Guam, a Spanish island, where she was registered. Naturally she was seized with her cargo and they were arrested. They lived with the Governor of the Ladrones Islands for a year and a half. Palmer had a recurrence of the dysentery he had contracted on the hulks, from which he had never really recovered. He died in 1802. Because of his religious beliefs Catholic friars refused him Christian burial and he was buried by the sea-shore. Two years later an American sea captain exhumed his body and took it to Massachusetts. Boston was murdered by natives at Tonga in 1804. Palmer, Boston, and Ellis had made a considerable amount of money in New South Wales. Palmer left his fortune to Ellis, but when he too died Ellis's sisters in Dundee inherited.

Margarot, who remained a trouble-maker throughout his stay in New South Wales, landed at Liverpool in 1810 with only three guineas in his pocket. He had spent £450 on the passage home for himself and his wife. He tried vainly to revive his business in France and was reduced to writing begging letters to old friends. Hamilton Rowan sent him £50. Margarot was dissuaded with difficulty from suing Joyce for publishing Palmer's narrative without checking the facts. He gave useful evidence before a committee of the House of Commons on transportation. He died penniless in 1815 aged seventy.

When reform agitation started again in the late 1820s the five transportees – suitable propanganda symbols – were recalled as some of the first champions of reform. Pamphlets were issued containing reports of Muir's trial, long quotations from his speech, and praise of the 'martyrs'. Mackenzie published his biography, appropriately dedicated to the Whig Lord Advocate Jeffrey, in 1831.

Either he was ignorant of, or suppressed, Muir's dealings with the Directory. In March 1799 the Committee of Secrecy of the House of Commons had reviewed Muir's career, ending with the comment: 'It is well known that he afterwards escaped from the place of his transportation, and has recently resided in France, pursuing a conduct marked by the most inveterate hostility to his country.' This had been forgotten, or was not generally known, by 1830. There was no mention of it when plans for erecting a memorial to Muir were criticized.

When the passing of the Reform Bill was celebrated in March 1831, a transparency of Muir was among the Glasgow illuminations.[1] There were celebrations all over the country for several weeks after the final passing of the Act – the English section on 7 June, the Scottish on 17 July, 1832. Ageing reformers at Sheffield sang:

> Oh could the wise, the brave, the just,
> Who suffered – died – to break our chains,
> Could Muir, could Palmer from the dust,
> Could murdered Gerrald hear our strains. . . .[2]

In Edinburgh a Jubilee was organized by the Trades Union Council on 10 August. Vast crowds assembled on Bruntsfield Links. 15,000 men, marshalled according to their trades, carrying banners and symbols of their various crafts, marched into the city under an arch bearing the motto 'A United People makes Tyrants Tremble'. An empty chair was draped with black in memory of Muir. One banner bore a motto of which he would have approved, 'for a nation to be free it is sufficient that it wills it.' The Cabinet and Chair Makers carried a black placard inscribed 'Tribute to the Memory of Muir, Gerrald and Others who suffered in the Cause. Individuals may perish but Truth is eternal;' the United Hosemakers one 'To the memory of Muir, Palmer, Skirving, Gerrald and all other Patriots who have suffered in the Cause of Reform.'[3]

In 1837 Joseph Hume, radical M.P. for Montrose Burghs, who was Francis Place's spokesman in Parliament, initiated a plan for a memorial to the exiles. Hume wanted 'a public and national demonstration of the deep gratitude and respect the people of the United Kingdom feel for the martyrs'. He grossly exaggerated this feeling, but, spurred on by Place, a section of liberal London and the provincial English press took up the project with enthusiasm. A meeting was held in London in February at which about a dozen M.P.s, and Feargus O'Connor, the Chartist, were present – Irish M.P.s, were particularly enthusiastic. On 23 March a meeting was called in Edinburgh. There were speeches deriding the judges and Tories and praising the five reformers. Hume, who attempted to turn them into folk heroes, used phrases such as 'blood of martyrs . . . blackest date in the annals of the criminal court of Scotland'. He also remarked, with only too much truth, that 'The whole of Mr. Muir's history was such a catalogue of misfortunes as perhaps no man had ever equalled in so short a time.' Southey's poem, 'To the Exiled Patriots', written when they were transported, was quoted, beginning:

> Martyrs of freedom, O ye who, firmly good,
> Stept forth the champions in her glorious cause:
> Ye who against corruption nobly stood
> For justice, liberty and equal laws.*

The Edinburgh Town Council agreed to give a site in the old burial-ground on Calton Hill. A committee was formed, including Francis Place, John Rutt, now 77, Thomas Muir Moffat, son of Muir's faithful friend, William Muir, whom Thomas had failed to meet in Hamburg so many years ago, and James Blair. Muir's sister and her husband were dead. His only surviving close relatives were two nephews, James, a lawyer, and Captain Thomas Blair of the East India Company, and their sister, now married to the Revd. Laurence Lockhart. Both nephews endorsed their uncle's political views.

Fund-raising dinners were held. Meetings took place all over the Lowlands. The liberal papers gave wide coverage to the proposed monument to the 'Scotch Political Martyrs'. One or two English newspapers commented that they might more properly be called 'the British martyrs'. Only two were Scotch, one English, one an English/Irish mongrel, one English with a dash of French – still it was Scotch law which had condemned them. Muir's poem to Moffat was

---

* Southey was no longer an ardent liberal. In his Dedication to *Don Juan* Byron comments on this change of heart:
>   Bob Southey! You're a poet – Poet-Laureate,
>   And representative of all the race;
>   Although 'tis true that you turned out a Tory at
>   Last, – lately yours has been a common case.

reprinted. *Tait's Magazine* published a pamphlet, *The Political Martyrs of Scotland*, to tell younger reformers 'who were the men whose
memories Mr. Hume wishes them to vindicate and honour and what
they did and suffered more than forty years ago'.

The Monument, like their trials, was the pretext for a political
battle: a Whig counterblast to the statues of Pitt and Dundas
stationed in prominent positions in Edinburgh. Originally there was
a scheme for two memorials, but the one in London was scrapped. As
a gambit to encourage reform it would have been much more effective in England, but the Scots naturally insisted that, if there were to
be only one memorial, it must be in Edinburgh. Many distinguished
men subscribed, including Lord Brougham, the Earl of Essex, the
Dukes of Bedford and Norfolk, Lord Holland, and about twenty
M.P.s including Grote and Daniel O'Connell.

Inevitably there was friction. There were many still who remembered the trials and had approved of their outcome – though some
had by now changed their opinion. Some said Margarot should not
be included, but were persuaded to relent. When Sir William Drys-
dale pointed out that Muir had fought with Spaniards against his
fellow countrymen, Moffat wrote indignant repudiations in the
press. The Tories, who strongly opposed the scheme, contrived to
delay its acceptance for some time. An attempt was made to bring in
a bill of interdiction on the grounds that a cemetery could not be used
for the erection of monuments in honour of men convicted of crime
and not even buried there. But, after long battles in the courts, the
argument failed – a son of Lord Henderland, who had been one of
the trial judges, refusing an application for an interdict.

On 21 August, 1844 Hume laid the foundation stone. About four
hundred members of the Complete Suffrage Association, dressed in
black, walked in procession four abreast past Parliament Square and
the Court where the sentence of transportation had been passed. A
platform had been erected on Calton Hill, because the burial-ground
was far too small to accommodate the procession and the crowd of
spectators who accompanied it through the streets. Three thousand
people collected round the platform. Among those present, much
moved by the occasion, was William Moffat, now an old man.

There were rousing speeches, punctuated with cheers. One
speaker, who was greeted 'with thrilling cheers', was a son of Skirving, a young boy when his father had been convicted fifty years

before. Hume placed under the stone a glass jar containing copies of current newspapers, Oliver and Boyd's Almanac, a report of the trials, a list of the Scottish subscribers to the monument, and a few current coins. The audience then took off their hats while Hume read the prayer Gerrald had spoken when he was arrested. The committee of management and the subscribers entertained Hume to a dinner followed by a soirée. The Lord Provost, other dignitaries, publishers, and lawyers were present. Macaulay, then M.P. for Edinburgh, avoided being present in the city at the time. 'Though I by no means approve of the severity with which these people were treated, I do not admire their proceedings.'4 Toasts were drunk to Fox, Lord John Russell, Grey, the martyrs, the Irish M.P.s, and 'the present judges of our supreme courts'. There were fierce references to the nobility, 'who always looked to their personal interests in preference to those of the nation'.

The chairman, Sir John Gibson Craig, Bt., made some interesting comments published in the *Scotsman*:

... No one who was not personally engaged in the occurrences which gave rise to the trials of Muir and the other martyrs, can form the most distant conception of the state of the country at that fearful crisis. The French Revolution had convulsed the civilised world, and had excited the most lively interest throughout Great Britain. On the one hand the most enthusiastic hopes were entertained that it would be productive of the greatest blessings, and secure the greatest possible liberty to mankind, and on the other hand, there was the utmost alarm that it would be productive of the most dreadful consequences.

The whole kingdom was distracted into parties, who acted with the most determined opposition to each other. Society was in a great degree dissolved – the dearest friendships severed – the nearest relations separated – the most bitter hostility prevailed – and everyone acted as if those who entertained opposite opinions were his deadliest enemies. ...

At the end of September 1845 the monument, which cost about £900, was completed. A flag was hoisted in honour of the event and several men climbed the structure to watch the laying of the cope-stone. Ninety feet high, it was designed in the style of Cleopatra's Needle and set at the highest point of the cemetery. It can be seen from many points in Edinburgh and forms an interesting feature of the skyline, though it is doubtful if many people today know or care whom the monument commemorates.

There was more trouble over the inscription, for close relatives of the judges and jurymen were still alive. Finally a simple statement was chosen. On one side, 'To the memory of Thomas Muir, Thomas Fyshe Palmer, William Skirving, Maurice Margarot and Joseph Gerrald. Erected by the friends of Parliamentry Reform in England and Scotland 1844.' On another side a quotation from Muir, 'I have devoted myself to the cause of the People; it is a good cause; it shall finally triumph.' and a quotation from Skirving's speech in the Court of Justiciary, 'I know that what has been done these two days will be rejudged!'

'A sparing inscription,' commented Cockburn. 'How the judges' names are omitted I cannot understand, for it is, in truth, their monument.' Cockburn disapproved of the memorial. He considered only Muir guiltless; if they had been properly tried, the idea of raising a monument would never have occurred, as some of the five men might still have been alive. But Cockburn, though a Whig, was Dundas's son-in-law and disliked radical enthusiasm. The monument would have given great pleasure to Thomas Muir.

Thomas Muir's background must have affected not only his character but his career. His education and upbringing are to some extent responsible for the defects as well as the virtues of his personality. If Muir had not become Millar's pupil, he might have entered the Church and joined Haldane's evangelical movement. Muir was not obsessed with theoretical ideas of Utopian government. His political campaign concentrated on one practical object – parliamentary reform; it had much of the fervour, the passionate belief, the persistence against odds, of the Covenanters.

William Tait described Muir as 'successful and honourably distinguished in his profession. . .'.

His talents and eloquence, the affability of his manners . . . the general estimate in which he was held in the west of Scotland, but above all, the contagious influence of his enthusiasm for liberty, rendered him a particularly dangerous character [to the government]. It was he who gave life and energy to the entire movement.

Others considered him too self-confident, headstrong, obstinate.

His naivety in failing to appreciate the increasing antagonism to his views was partly due to his family's lack of sophistication or of contacts who might have given a helpful warning. Repression was

only a small cloud on the horizon when the Friends of the People was
formed. Muir did not grasp the fact that, while men of property such
as Major Cartwright were tolerated as tiresome cranks, the same
latitude would not be extended to insignificant members of the
middle classes.*

   In the hierarchical society of the time Muir and his family must
have suffered slights and rebuffs as they moved up the social scale.
Muir may have resented the exclusive arrogance of Scottish aristocrats and Edinburgh society. Like many insecure men he took refuge
in vanity. But he was not self-centred. You cannot move others
unless you are interested in their opinions and their grievances. Muir
had a strong desire to help the poor and inarticulate, a passion for
social justice. He had genuine affection and concern for his friends, a
characteristic of a warm and sociable century which cultivated the
art of friendship – when men tried to live up to a higher calling of
whatever kind, and acted out on the public stage the role they had
chosen as liberator, missionary, man about town, with an abandon
which involved their whole personality, and sometimes distorted
their judgement.

   Whether consciously or not Muir's espousal of reform must have
been partly motivated by ambition. It brought him fame and influence. Under the electoral system at that time, though he would have
made a useful M.P., his chances of election were nil as he had neither
great wealth nor powerful relations. But a more consistently ambitious man, keen to protect his legal career, would have moderated his
campaign when it was opposed by the government and no longer
backed by senior Whig lawyers. With a little more caution Muir
could have remained in the band of young Whig advocates, who
came into their own after the turn of the century. Like so many
ardent supporters of the Revolution – Wordsworth and Coleridge
among others – he might have turned Tory in middle age. It is more
probable that, if still alive, he would have taken part in the liberal
revival of the 1820s. It is, incidentally, an interesting facet of
eighteenth-century attitudes that men believed the ranks of society
were fixed and rigidly defined, whereas in fact there was a great deal
of social mobility. Braxfield and Archibald Fletcher are typical

* Through his wife's connections with the establishment Hamilton Rowan was
finally pardoned, though he had been involved in treasonable activities. Muir's father
lacked the power to obtain such a reprieve for his son.

examples of Scotsmen of humble origin who rose to positions of importance.

For the short time he was active Muir gave promise of considerable political and organizational talent, but his life was too brief and disastrous to reveal its true quality. If he had been born a few years later, or lain low till better times, he might well have succeeded, like Place in England, in building up a successful radical organization in Scotland. Muir was only an active reformer for about six months, but he helped to organize the first political associations of ordinary men in Scotland, and encouraged them to play a part in governing their country.

In general the early reformers were politically immature. They produced grandiose plans without solid backing or realistic calculations of what they could achieve. They naïvely believed that their cause was bound to succeed as it was morally right. Their ideas were not widely popular. The dissenters, in particular, were disliked. The reformers of the 1790s were men of integrity, but none had the calibre of a great leader; nor had they Wilkes's panache or Wyvill's influence. Their campaign was carried out in the teeth of the authorities' opposition. The burgh reformers who refused to join the Convention had warned Macleod and Muir that their persistence was foolish. They might be proved right later, meanwhile to continue would defeat their object.

The Societies the exiles helped found had a different complexion from that of earlier groups whose members were nearly all gentlemen, most of whom had the vote. Members of the Scottish Friends of the People and the London Corresponding Society came almost entirely from families who had never had any share, direct or indirect, in government. They wanted a far wider extension of the franchise which would lead to a fairer distribution of power. It was the fact that the plebs were beginning to demand the vote which so alarmed the Government. The reformers overestimated their chances of success because on various previous occasions sections of the ruling class had taken up the cause of reform. The only M.P.s who helped them were failed politicians such as Sheridan. The few members of the upper class who gave support fell away after the outbreak of war. Indirectly the exiles were casualties of the French Revolution, which brought latent antagonisms into violent reaction. As Lord Cockburn wrote,

Everything, not this or that thing, but literally everything, was soaked in this one event. Everything rung and was connected with the French Revolution; which for above twenty years was, or was made, the all in all.

The liberal spirit did not revive till peace came in 1815.

Muir was intensely patriotic, proud of his country and her achievements, but he was too much of an internationalist to be contained within the narrow confines of the modern term Scottish Nationalist. He had the vision to look beyond the boundaries of his own country; he appreciated that combination with the Irish and English Societies would give them all more influence, but he failed to grasp how greatly this would alarm the authorities. To many liberals religious toleration and international fraternity were more important than mere patriotism. It was comparatively easy to slip over the borderline into what most men would consider treachery.

Palmer's obituary in the *Monthly Magazine*[5] claimed that the martyrs would 'gain an honourable place among those who have sacrificed at the shrine of their country's happiness, their wordly interest, their personal freedom and their lives'. To some extent Muir and Palmer's sacrifice was unintentional. They had no reason to fear transportation. Gerrald knew he was dying. Only Skirving and Margarot deliberately chose martyrdom. It was the extreme severity of their sentences that made the exiles so famous at the time; a disgraceful episode in the history of Scottish justice. 'God help the people who have such judges,' said Fox. The immense disproportion between punishment and offence made a great impression. These trials were one reason for changes made later in the Scottish legal system.

Muir had a touch of the arrogance common among consciously progressive thinkers. To mention only two of his contemporaries. Place was incredibly self-satisfied, Cobbett a great egoist. Such men are in some ways tiresome personalities; but less committed men would be ineffective. Reformers have to believe implicitly in themselves and their cause if they are to sway others. Their inability to gauge how far public opinion would follow them, and control their actions accordingly, led to the exiles' transportation.

Much of Muir's Paris memorials must be discounted. He was a sick man who had suffered great hardship and was struggling for official support. He only became an implacable enemy of the British Government through the harsh and unjust treatment he had received. Force of circumstances arrested and distorted his political development, sharpening his radical and chauvinistic opinions. Stone chose to intrigue with the French for ideological reasons. Paine chose to exchange British nationality for that of more democratic America. If Muir had reached the United States he would probably have led a satisfactory life there far removed from British politics.

The reformers' ineffectualness was partly caused by inadequate communications and lack of opportunities to spread their views. Most people were too poor and scattered to agitate. The reformers' lasting achievement was that they initiated means to combat these difficulties. The agitation only lasted five years, but was extraordinarily intensive. Although they only had very limited resources and knew nothing of political organization, by readings, discussions, and debate they introduced humble members of their societies to the problems and potentialities of self-government in miniature. They made the Government aware of their grievances. Helped by the ferment which swept the country in the wake of the Revolution, they peacefully disseminated their ideas. Later campaigners inherited the system they originated: the propaganda of pamphlets and political lectures, the clubs, the workmen's meetings, the idea that every committee member must play a part, the axiom that delegates were responsible to their electors, the belief that all men were capable of reasoning and could, by mutual self-help, learn how to govern. Although the early Societies disappeared, they created a precedent for future ones.

The pioneer advocates of parliamentary reform were unsuccessful and therefore soon forgotten. They have little direct connection with the piecemeal legislation of 1832, 1867, and 1874. Their movement belongs mainly in spirit as well as time to the eighteenth century. They had been influenced by the Glorious Revolution and the change from Whig supremacy to Tory domination. They were heirs of the Levellers, but divided from them by the Age of Reason; forerunners of the Chartists, but separated by the growth of industrialization and the French wars. Like the Levellers they demanded universal suffrage and extolled a mythological past when all men had been equal before God. Like the Chartists they were concerned with the effects of the great economic changes taking place, although they did not fully understand them. For many years their doctrines were included in radical programmes, but their emphasis on justice and on self-improvement through education were dropped in favour of fairer distribution of wealth.

Most political movements benefit from a few preliminary martyrs to inspire those who succeed later, profiting from their mistakes. At the time of the Reform Bill there were a significant number of publications celebrating the earlier reformers' struggle. By the time of the later bills men with different modes of expression and ways of life had taken up the cause. The Act of 1832 only enfranchised a few, but it was a beginning. It was in one sense a tribute to the men who failed before and it was right to commemorate them. The Reform Act did not so much change the Constitution as make men politically conscious, and this Muir and his companions had tried to do. That their time was inauspicious does not detract from their work. Though Muir among others did not see it clearly, alterations in the franchise were being sought as a means of changing the social structure. The Societies he helped found were a small step towards modern forms of democratic government.

Notes

◇-◇

CHAPTER 1

General Note: Principal sources: books listed in the Scottish section of the Bibliography.

1. *Caledonian Mercury*, 18 October 1781; 25 October.

2. Advertisement in *Glasgow Herald*, 21 February 1782.

3. This account of Anderson and the fracas is based on 'Senex' [R. Reid], *Glasgow Past and Present*, vol. III; J. Coutts, *History of the University of Glasgow*; A. Millar, article on Thomas Muir in *Aberdeen People's Journal*, 24 July 1886. Not everything Coutts says about the Anderson affair is corroborated in the minutes of Glasgow College, but these minutes are not now complete.

4. High Court of Justiciary, Edinburgh, 30 May 1792, Scottish Public Record Office.

5. Barclay noted in the minutes of the Kirk, 23 March 1791, that Muir wished to resign.

CHAPTER 2

General Note: Principal sources: Veitch's *The Genesis of Parliamentary Reform* and other books in the General section of the Bibliography.

1. *Caledonian Mercury*, 31 July and 8 August 1782.

2. Alger, *Englishmen in the French Revolution*, p. 52.

3. *Edinburgh Herald*, 18 July.

4. *Caledonian Mercury*, 24 March 1792.

5. Letter to C. Grey. E. Hughes (ed.), *Durham Historical Review* vol. xxv, No. 119, p. 31. Grey Papers lodged at Prior's Kitchen, Durham.

6. Wyvill, *Political Papers* vol. v, p. 23.

7. Letter signed by Chauvelin, London, 23 May 1972, but in fact dictated by Talleyrand. Pallain, *La Mission de Talleyrand à Londres* p. 289.

CHAPTER 3

General Note: Principal sources: letters and reports on the reformers' activities in H.O. 102/5–6, also letters in the Grey Papers printed in the *Durham Historical Review* vol. xxv, No. 119.

1. *Caledonian Mercury*, 19 July 1792.

2. Ibid., 28 July 1792.

3. *State Trials* vol. xxiii, p. 147.

4. H.O. 102/8, 15 February 1793.

5. *Caledonian Mercury*, 13 October 1792.

6. Ibid., 22 October.

7. *Glasgow Mercury*, 19 October 1792.

8. Muir's trial, op. cit.

9. Anti-Reform pamphlets in British Museum, MS Nos. 231.e.46and 8133.bb.2.

10. *Caledonian Mercury*, 29 November 1792.

11. Ibid., 8 December 1792.

12. Ibid.

CHAPTER 4

General Note: Principal sources: minutes, notes, reports, and letters in H.O. 102/6–7.

1. *Caledonian Mercury* 12 December 1972.

2. *Memoirs and Trials of the Political Martyrs of Scotland, Tait's Magazine* (special supplement), 1837.

3. *Caledonian Mercury*, 27 December 1792.

4. *Glasgow Mercury*, 2 January 1793.

5. 8 January 1793.

6. The certificate was among documents seized on Muir when he returned to Scotland. Now in Scottish P.R.O. JC/26/276, 'Sedition trials'.

7. Grey Papers, in *Durham Historical Review*, vol. cit., 17 January 1793, p. 33.

CHAPTER 5

General Note: Principal sources: Alger, *Paris in 1789–1794*, papers, reports, and letters in H.O. 102/8–9, records of Muir's trial, and documents and articles in the Scottish Public Record Office, JC/26/276, 'Sedition trials'.

1. Mackenzie, *Reminiscenses* . . . p. 31 (footnote).

2. *Edinburgh Gazetteer*.

3. Spies' reports, H.O. 102/7, 16–21 February.

4. *Aberdeen People's Journal*, series of articles entitled 'Martyrs of Reform in Scotland' by A. H. Millar, July 1886. Millar had access to papers of a relation of Muir's, probably a descendant of his cousin William Muir.

5. Chief sources relating to Muir's capture are *Memoirs and Trials of the Political Martyrs of Scotland*, loc. cit.; 'The Convict and his Bible' (see the Australian section of the Bibliography); Millar, op. cit., in *Aberdeen People's Journal*.

6. *Caledonian Mercury*, 15 August 1793.

7. *State Trials* vol. xxiii: Gerrald's trial, p. 806.

CHAPTER 6

General Note: Principal sources: *State Trials* vol. xxiii, pp. 118ff., and Cockburn, *Examination of Trials for Sedition*.

1. *Memoirs and Trials of the Political Martyrs of Scotland*, loc. cit.

2. *Caledonian Mercury*, 10 November 1792.

3. Ibid., 7 September 1793.

4. H.O. 102/8, 3 September 1793.

5. Report on erection of Monument to Muir etc., *Scotsman*, 24 August 1844.

6. *Morning Post*, 22 March 1794.

7. *Morning Chronicle*, cutting in Place Newspaper Cuttings, vol. 36, p. 71.

CHAPTER 7

General Note: Principal sources: records of the trials of various Scottish reformers, and Minutes of the Convention in *State Trials* vol. xxiii; Cockburn, *Examination of Trials for Sedition*; records of parliamentary debates in *Parliamentary History* vols. xxx and xxxi; letters and documents in H.O. 102/9–11; Omond, *Arniston Memoirs*; Palmer, *Narrative* . . .; Belsham, *Memoirs of the late Theophilus Lindsay*; and J. T. Rutt's article in *Monthly Repository* vol. xii, May 1817.

1. *Altona Journal*, 1794.

2. Drew, article in *Old and New* vol. ix, 1894 (Boston), p. 7.

3. *Political Martyrs* . . . in loc. cit., based on 'information given by former friends and acquaintances'.

4. Northern Ireland P.R.O., 620/20, No. 73, 27 September 1793.

5. *Morning Post*, 9 December 1793.

6. The information in this paragraph is derived from *Monthly Magazine* vol. xvii, February 1806.

7. Arniston Papers, deposited in National Library of Scotland, Melville MSS, Lot 731. Lord Advocate to Dundas, 13 October 1793.

8. Veitch, *Genesis of Parliamentary Reform*, footnote 6 to p. 294. Evidence before Privy Council, 30 May 1794, l. 3., P.C.R. 22 Geo. II, 273, 275.

9. 'A Convention, the only means of saving us from mutiny', published in *A Letter to the People of England*, 1793.

10. *Morning Chronicle*, 12 November 1793.

11. *Edinburgh Gazetteer*, 9 November 1793.

12. *Historical Records of New South Wales*, vol. I, p. 826.

13. *Scots Magazine* vol. 55, 1793, p. 617.

14. Ibid.

15. Mackenzie, *Life*, p. 31, may not be correct about this.

16. *Caledonian Mercury*, 12 December 1793.

17. Letter in ibid., 2 December 1793.

18. Ibid., 12 December 1793.

19. Place Papers, B.M. Add. MS 27816.

20. *Morning Chronicle*, Place Newspaper Cuttings, vol. 38, p. 90.

21. Braxfield's judgment: H.O. 42/27, 508 and 741.

22. Kegan Paul, *William Godwin, his Friends and Contemporaries*, p. 121.

23. Cobbett, *A Bone to Gnaw for Democrats*, pt. II, p. 18.

24. Letter from Muir to Moffat from Sydney, 13 December 1794. Published *Morning Chronicle*, 14 July 1795.

25. Vol. 58, February 1794.

26. i. Until Union, punishment for leasing-making – 'uttering falsehoods against the King and his counsellors to the people' – had been death. By the Scots Act of 1703 punishment was in future to be arbitrary – fining, imprisonment, or banishment. ii. Braxfield argued that before 1688 convenanters had been transported to the plantations by order of the Privy Council but:

(a) to seek precedent in the Privy Council was very dubious;

(b) after the rebellions, transportation required the sanction of a statute, e.g. the Disarming Act of 1746, in which penalties for wearing highland dress were, for a first offence six months' imprisonment without trial, for a second seven years' transportation.

iii. Adams emphasized that owing to the lack of precision in the use of words in Scots law courts, their meaning must be construed by their context. When the Privy Council ordered transportation the term 'banishment' was employed, but care was taken to qualify the word. There was a totally different process of banishment by which a prisoner had to leave the Kingdom within a certain time and not return without licence. Braxfield contended that after the Act of 1703 men had still been sentenced to 'banishment forth to the West Indies' and imprisoned 'until transported to the plantations'.

iv. Braxfield and his fellow judges cited as authority for the sentence of transportation an Act passed in 1785 which authorized removal of Scottish prisoners to the hulks or outside Scotland. It was passed after the War of Independence when the American colonies ceased to take transported prisoners. In 1784 an Act was passed for the transportation of felons. This statute referred to prisoners convicted in England, Wales, and the County Palatine of Cheshire. Both Acts expired in 1788. The essential provisions of the English Act were continued in Section III of 28 George III C.24. The Scottish Act was not renewed. So in 1794 there was no statute in force to warrant Muir's and Palmer's transportation.

CHAPTER 8

General Note: Principal sources: *Historical Records of New South Wales*, vol. II; declarations taken on board the *Surprize* between 30 May and 24 October 1794 (bundle 19 of the *Supreme Court Papers* in the Mitchell Library, Sydney), and Place's examination of evidence in the Place Papers, B.M. Add. MSS 27808, 27816,, and newspaper cuttings vols. 36–8; Treasury Solicitors' files 11/952–959, 960, and J. T. Rutt's article in *Monthly Repository* vol. xii, May 1817.

1. 8 April 1794.

2. 22 February 1794.

3. Belsham, *Memoirs of Lindsey*, p. 355.

4. *Oracle and Public Advertiser*, 24 March 1794.

5. Cobbett, *Peter Porcupine's Gazette*, 1796.

6. *Archives des Affaires Étrangères, Corr. Pol. (Angleterre)* No. 588, f. 139.

7. *Oracle and Public Advertiser*, 24 March 1794.

8. *Morning Chronicle*, 10 July 1795.

9. Letter to Moffat, printed in *Morning Chronicle*, 10 July 1795.

10. This poem was later published in Tuckey, *Voyage to Establish a Colony at Port Philip*, reviewed in *Gentleman's Magazine*, April 1805, p. 333.

CHAPTER 9

General Note: Principal sources: Earnshaw, *Thomas Muir; Historical Records of New South Wales*, vols II and III; *Australian Historical Records*, vol. I; Collins, *An Account of the English Colony in New South Wales*; and other sources cited in the Australian section of the Bibliography.

1. To Joyce, 12 December 1794; published *Morning Chronicle*, 27 July 1795.

2. *Morning Chronicle*, 27 July 1795. Also in Place newspaper cuttings, B.M. Add. MS 27838, vol. 36, and Mackenzie's *Life*, p. 32.

3. 'T. D.' 'The Convict and His Bible.'

4. *Caledonian Mercury*, 28 January 1797; letter from Port Jackson, December 1795.

5. *Monthly Repository* vol. xii, May 1817, p. 265.

6. 16 October 1795, published in *True Briton*, 20 August 1796.

7. H.O. 102/12, 23 August 1796; acknowledged by Hunter, 25 June, 1797.

8. In fact written as a joke by Henry Carter. See H. H. Green, *A History of Australian Literature* (Sydney, 1966).

9. National Archives Washington D.C., P.G. 36; Records of Customs, Boston (Mass.), Reg. 227, 20 August, 1797.

10. Letter to George Washington, *A.G.I.* Seville, *Estado*. Guadalajara, leg. 1.

11. *Morning Chronicle*, 8 April 1797.

12. *The Friend* (London, 1809), Section I, Essay V.

13. Place MSS, B.M. Add. MS 27816.

14. 14 August 1797, *Monthly Repository*.

CHAPTER 10

General Note: Most of this chapter is based on Peron's Diaries. Peron was François Pierre, not François Auguste, the naturalist who went with Baudin on a French expedition to Australia 1800–1804 and wrote *Voyage of Discovery to the Southern Hemispheres*. See *Dictionnaire at Biographie de Maine et Loire* by Celestin Port. Other sources: documents and letters in the *Archivo General de las Indias* in Seville, and in the *Archivo Nacional* in Mexico City.

1. Meares, *Voyages made in 1788 and 1789. . . .*

2. *A.G.I.* Seville, *Estado*, Mexico, leg. 6 No. 340, Branciforte to Paz, 26 September.

3. The information in this paragraph comes chiefly from Tobar's *Testimonio*, ibid.

4. Written on July 14 and 15. All in *A.G.I.* Seville, *Estado*, Guadalajara, leg. 1.

5. Broughton, *Voyage of Discovery*; P.R.O. Admiralty Captains' log book 4490. *Providence* was at Port Jackson 25 August – 13 October 1795; left Nootka 21 May 1796; at Monterey 6 – 20 June.

CHAPTER 11

General Note: Principal sources: The *expedientes* sent with Muir between provincial centres, and other documents and letters, copies of which were sent to Spain and are in the *Archivo General de las Indias* in Seville, *Estado*, Mexico, leg. 6, leg. 23 No. 6, and leg. 26 Nos. 30 and 41; and *Estado*, Guadalajara, leg. 1.; also documentary material in the *Archives Nationaux*, Paris, *Affaires Étrangères, Corr. Pol.* 590 (relating to England) and 648–50 (Spain). See also Bibliography, America.

1. Tobar to Don Jacinto Caamono, *A.G.I.* Seville, *Estado*, Mexico, leg. 6; and Archives of California, State Papers, Sacramento vii.

2. Information on California is mainly derived from Bancroft, *History of the Pacific States*.

3. Callender to Jefferson 26 October 1798. N.E. Hist. Gen. Register L. 330.

4. For this paragraph see Archives of California, State Papers, Sacramento iv, 68; Morrison, *Maritime History of Massachussetts*, p. 60; *Arch. Gen.*, Mexico, Provincias Internas vi, exp. 16.

5. 22 October, in *Arch. Gen.*, Mexico, Californias, 37, exp. 3.

6. *Oracle and Public Advertiser*, 13 March 1797, *Edinburgh Advertiser*, 14 and 17 March.

7. For this paragraph see Capt. George Martin of *Irresistible*, 28 April 1797, P.R.O. Adm. 1:396, No. 71; Fernández Duro, *La Armada Española...* (Madrid, 1895–1903) vol. VIII, p. 141.

8. 28 April, printed in *Edinburgh Advertiser*, 1 June 1797, and *Caledonian Mercury*, 29 May.

9. *Caledonian Mercury*, 10 June.

10. *Scotsman*, 17 December 1842.

11. Cobbett, *Register* vol. vii, p. 162–266, 12 September 1790. M. Carey, *Porcupiniad*, 1799 (Philadelphia). Cited in *Notes and Queries* Series 4, iii, p. 365.

12. 2 May 1797, *Arch. Nat.* Paris, *Affaires Français*, iii 62, dossier 246.

13. August 1797; National Library of Scotland MS 1103, f. 37.

14. For this paragraph see *Gazette Nationale*, or *Moniteur Universel*, 7 December (17 Frimaire Year VI); Michel, *Les Écossais en France*, vol. I, p. 469.

15. *The Press*, 16 December; *Edinburgh Advertiser*, 15 December.

16. See in particular *Arch. Nat.*, Paris, *Affaires Français*, iii 88, No. 3600, 23 Frimaire (13 December).

17. 15 Frimaire Year VI. Letter published in *Edinburgh Advertiser*, 26 December 1797.

CHAPTER 12

General Note: Principal sources for this chapter:
W. Wolfe Tone, *Life of Theobald Wolfe Tone*, and Castlereagh, *Memorials and Correspondence*. Chief manuscript sources: H.O. 32/7; A.A.E. Corr. Pol. Angl. 588 f. 590, 592 ff. 164–5 and 171–4, 594 ff. 53 et seq, 596 ff. 321–2; A.A.E. Mems. et Docs. Angl. vol. 53, ff. 153–72, 215, and 361. See also Bibliography, France.

1. *Arch. Nat.*, Paris, *Affaires Français*, iii 579.

2. *Moniteur*, 4 January 1798 (15 Nivôse Year VI).

3. Reports on Sword brothers and letters in H.O. 102/16.

4. Hist. MSS. Commission, Dropmore MSS. vol. iv (1905), p. 69.

5. 7744b, *Dossier Br.* B 83–73, 7 Messidor Year VI (June 1798).

6. For Ashley see Place, *Autobiography*, p. 155 *et seq.*

7. Almost identical memorandum written in English. *A.A.E., Mems. et Docs. Angl.,* vol. 53 ff. 159–62. The date at the top of this – 1794 – is almost certainly incorrect.

8. Both Alger and Michel (*Les Écossais* . . ., p. 471) quote from the *Moniteur* of 10 Vendémiaire Year VI (October 1798) that Lord Walson [*sic*] had arrived at Nancy. Whether this refers to Watson or not, Watson had arrived in Paris in May: see *A.A.E., Corr. Pol. Angl.* 592, f. 220, 14 May 1798 (25 Floreal Year VI), and other documents in French archives. For Watson see *Dictionary of National Biography* and articles cited in it.

9. For United Scotsmen see Place MSS in B.M. Add. MS 27808. Reports of the Secret Committee of the House of Commons, *Parliamentary History*, Vol. XXXIV c. 641; H.O. 100/1, ff. 1 and 23–98.

10. *Aberdeen People's Journal*, 14 August 1886.

11. H.O. 108, 22 May 1802 (which shows inaccuracy in Watson's statements).

12. *Moniteur*, 24 November 1798 (4 Frimaire Year VII), P.C. 1/43, A 152.

13. Quoted by M. Donnelly in a booklet on Muir. Donnelly has unpublished letters of Muir's. His proposed biography will presumably throw more light on Muir's year in France.

14. *Glasgow Courier*, 26 August 1802.

15. Dr. J. A. Russell in *Bishopsbrigg News*, 12 March 1971.

CHAPTER 13

General Note: Principal sources: B.M. Add. MSS. 27808 vol. 16, 27816 ff. 79–82, 97, and 221.

1. *Scotsman*, 30 March 1831.

2. Corn Law poet Ebenezer Elliott, *Poetical Works* (Edinburgh, 1840), 'The Triumph of Reform'.

3. *Scotsman*, 11 August 1832; *An Account of the Edinburgh Reform Jubilee*, ed. W. Millar.

4. Trevelyan, G. O., *Life and Letters of Lord Macaulay*, (London, 1876) p. 468, letter to Macvey Napier.

5. Vol. xvii, 1 February 1804.

Selected Bibliography

<><><><><><><><><><><><><><><><><><><><><><><><><><><><><><><><><>

Books referred to in the text or with particular relevance to the subject.

GENERAL

Belsham, Thomas *Memoirs of the late Theophilus Lindsay, M.A.*, London, 1812.

Binns, John *Recollections of the Life of John Binns*, Philadelphia, 1854.

Brown, Philip Anthony *The French Revolution in English History*, London, 1918.

Campbell, Lord (Baron John) *Lives of the Lord Chancellors*, Volumes v–viii, London, 1845–69.

Cartwright, Miss F. D. *Life and Correspondence of Major Cartwright*, London, 1826.

Cecil, Lord David *The Young Melbourne*, London, 1939.

Christie, Ian *Wilkes, Wyvill and Reform*, London, 1962.

Cobban, A. B. C. (ed.) *Debate on the French Revolution 1789–1800*, London, 1950.

Cobbett, W., M.P., *A Bone to Gnaw for the Democrats*, Parts I and II, Philadelphia, 1795.

Cobbett, W., M.P., *The Works of Peter Porcupine*, Philadelphia, 1796.

Cobbett, W. (ed.) *Parliamentary History of England*, 1st series, Volumes xxxi–xxxiv: 'Committees of Secrecy 1794–9', London, 1819.

Colchester, Lord *The Diaries and Correspondence . . .*, London, 1861.

Conway, M. D. *The Life of Thomas Paine*, London, 1892.

Dyer, George *Slave and Famine Punishments for Sedition*, London, 1794.

Ellis, Grace A. *Memoirs, Letters and a selection from the Poems and Prose Writings of Mrs. Anna Barbauld*, Vol. I, Boston, 1874.

Field, William *Memoirs of the Life, Writings and Opinions of the Revd. Samuel Parr*, 2 vols., London, 1828.

Fox, C. J. *Memorials and Correspondence of C. J. Fox*, edited by Lord John Russell, London, 1853.

Goodwin, A. *The Friends of Liberty: the British Democratic Movement in the Age of the French Revolution*, London, 1980.

Hardy, Thomas *Memoir of Thomas Hardy, founder of . . . the London Corresponding Society . . . written by himself*, London, 1832.

Hill, J. E. C. 'The Norman Yoke', in Saville, J., ed., *Democracy and the Labour Movement*, London, 1954.

Howell, T. H. and T. S. (eds.) *Complete Collection of State Trials*, vols. xxiii–xxix, London, 1809–28.

Kegan Paul, C. *William Godwin, his Friends and Contemporaries*, London, 1876.

Masson M. Article on T. F. Palmer, in the *Scottish Historical Review*, Glasgow 1916.

Palmer, T. F. *A Narrative of the Sufferings of T. F. Palmer and W. Skirving during a Voyage to New South Wales on board the Surprise Transport, 1794*, Cambridge, 1797.

Place, Francis *Autobiography*, edited by M. Thale, London, 1972.

Roe, Maurice Article on Margarot, 'A Radical in Two Hemispheres', in *Bulletin of the Institute of Historical Research* London, 1959.

Romilly, Sir Samuel *Memoirs of the Life of Sir Samuel Romilly written by himself, with a Selection from his Correspondence*, edited by his sons, 3 vols., London, 1840.

Rose, John Holland *William Pitt and the National Revival: William Pitt and the Great War*, London, 1911.

Rutt, J. T. *The Memorials of J. T. Rutt* (for private circulation), Bristol, 1845.

Rutt, J. T. *Life and Correspondence of Joseph Priestley*, London, 1831.

Seaman, W. Unpublished thesis in the Institute of Historical Research, London University: 'British Democratic Societies in the Period of the French Revolution'.

Thelwall, Mrs. J. *Biography of J. Thelwall*, London, 1837.

Veitch, G. S. *The Genesis of Parliamentary Reform*, London, 1913.

Watson, J. Steven *The Reign of George III, 1760–1815*, Oxford, 1960.

Williams, J. *Memoirs of the late Revd. T. Belsham*, London, 1812.

Wyvill, C. *Political Papers and Letters respecting Reformation of Parliament 1794–1804*, 6 vols., York, 1805.

WITH PARTICULAR REFERENCE TO SCOTLAND

Beattie, William *Life and Letters of Thomas Campbell*, London, 1849.

Burnett, John *A treatise on various branches of the Criminal Law of Scotland*, London, 1811.

Chambers, R. *Life of Burns*, Edinburgh, 1851.

Cockburn, Lord Henry *Examination of Trials for Sedition*, Edinburgh, 1888.

Cockburn, Henry *Life of Francis Lord Jeffrey*, Edinburgh, 1872.

Cockburn, Henry *Memorials of his Time*, Edinburgh, 1872.

Coutts, James *A History of the University of Glasgow from its foundation in 1491 to 1909*, Glasgow, 1909.

Donnelly, Michael 'Thomas Muir' booklet issued by the Burgh of Bishopsbrigg, 1975.

Earnshaw, John *Thomas Muir, Scottish Martyr, some account of his exile to New South Wales*, Cremorne, 1959.

Elliott, Sir Gilbert *Life and Letters*, London, 1874.

Ferguson, W. *Scotland, 1689 to the Present*, Edinburgh, 1968.

Fergusson, Lt. Col. A. *The Hon. Henry Erskine, Lord Advocate for Scotland, with notices of certain of his kinsfolk and of his Time*, Edinburgh, 1882.

Fletcher, Archibald *A Memoir concerning the Origin and Progress of the Reform proposed in the Internal Government of the Royal Burghs of Scotland . . .*, Edinburgh, 1819.

Fletcher, Mrs. E. *Autobiography of Mrs. Fletcher of Edinburgh, with selections from her letters and other family memorials. Compiled and arranged by the survivor of her family* [Lady Richardson], Carlisle, 1874 (privately printed).

Fyfe, J. G. (ed.) *Scottish Diaries and Memoirs*, Stirling, 1928.

Galt, John *Annals of the Parish*, Oxford, 1967.

Galt, John *Autobiography*, London, 1833.

Hughes E. 'The Scottish Reform Movement and Charles Grey', in *Durham Historical Review* vol. xxv, No. 110.

Hume, David (Baron) *Commentaries on the Law of Scotland respecting the description and punishment of Crimes*, Edinburgh, 1797.

Kay, John *A Series of Original Portraits and Caricature Etchings*, Edinburgh, 1797.

Lehmann, W. C. *John Millar of Glasgow, 1735–1801*, Cambridge, 1960.

Lockhart, J. D. *Life of Burns*, London, 1838.

Lockhart, J. G. 'A Skeleton in the Cupboard', in *Blackwood's Magazine*, Edinburgh, July 1950.

Mackenzie, Peter *The Life of Thomas Muir*, Glasgow, 1831.

Mackenzie, Peter *Reminiscences of Glasgow and the West of Scotland*, Glasgow, 1865.

Mackie, J. D. *Short History of Glasgow University, 1451–1951*, Glasgow, 1954.

Macleod, Norman, M.P. *Two Letters to the Chairman of the Friends of the People at Edinburgh*, Edinburgh, 1793.

Marshall, W. Article on Thomas Muir in *Glasgow Magazine,* Glasgow, 1795.

Mathieson, W. C. *The Awakening of Scotland: A History from 1747 to 1797*, Glasgow, 1910.

Meikle, H. *Scotland and the French Revolution*, Edinburgh, 1912.

Meikle, H. 'Two Glasgow Merchants in the French Revolution', Edinburgh, January 1911, in *Scottish Historical Review* vol. 8.

Meikle, H. 'The Death of Muir', Glasgow, October 1948, in *Scottish Historical Review* vol. 27.

Millar, John *Observations concerning the Distinction of Ranks in Society*, with a *Life of Millar* by J. Craig, Edinburgh, 1806.

Murray, David *Memories of the Old College of Glasgow*, Glasgow, 1927.

Omond, G. W. T. *Arniston Memoirs: Three Centuries of a Scottish House*, Edinburgh, 1887.

Omond, G. W. T. *Lord Advocates of Scotland from the close of the 15th century to the Passing of the Reform Bill*, Vol. II, Edinburgh, 1883.

Phillipson, N. T. and Mitcheson, R. (eds.) *Essays in Scottish History*, Edinburgh, 1970.

Pratt Insh, Dr. Unpublished life of Muir, in National Library of Scotland.

'Senex' [Reid, Robert] *Glasgow Past and Present . . . the Reminiscenses of Senex*, Glasgow, 1851.

Smout, T. C. *A History of the Scottish People, 1560–1830*, London, 1969.

Strang, John *Glasgow and its Clubs*, Glasgow, 1856.

Tait's Magazine 'Memoirs and Trials of the Political Martyrs of Scotland', special supplement, Edinburgh, 1837.

WITH PARTICULAR REFERENCE TO AUSTRALIA

Abbott, G. J., and Nairu, N. B. (eds.) *The Economic Growth of Australia 1788–1821*, Melbourne, 1969.

Barrington, George (*wrongly ascribed to first edition, published anonymously*) *The History of New South Wales including Botany Bay . . . and all its dependencies*, London, 1802.

Bennett, Samuel *The History of Australian Discovery and Colonisation*, Sydney, 1867.

Border, Ross *Church and State in Australia 1788–1872*, London, 1962.

Britton, A., and Bladen, F. M. (eds.) *Historical Records of New South Wales*, vols. I–III, Sydney, 1895.

Clarke, C. M. H. *History of Australia* vol. I, London, 1962.

Clune, Frank *The Scottish Martyrs*, Sydney, 1969.

Collins, David *An Account of the English Colony in New South Wales*, London, 1798.

Gladstone, H. *Thomas Watling, Limmer of Dumfries*, Dumfries, 1938.

Greenwood, G. *Early American-Australian Relations . . .*, Melbourne, 1944.

Hainsworth, D. R. *The Sydney Traders: Simeon Lord and his contemporaries 1788–1821*, Melbourne, 1971.

Lang, J. D. *An Historical and Statistical Account of New South Wales*, London, 1834.

Mackaness, George (ed.) *Some Letters of the Revd. Richard Johnson . . .*, Sydney, 1954.

Mackaness, George (ed.) *Letters from an Exile at Botany Bay*, Sydney, 1945.

Paterson, George *The History of New South Wales*, Newcastle upon Tyne, 1811.

Royal Australian Historical Society, Journal, Sydney, 1901–   . Especially relevant articles, 1960–79.

Rudé, George *Protest and Punishment*, Oxford, 1978.

Rusden, G. W. *Curiosities of Colonization*, London, 1874.

'T.D.' 'The Convict and his Bible', published by the Scottish 'Monthly Visitor', Tract Society, Edinburgh, June 1910.

Tuckey, J. H. *An Account of a Voyage to establish a Colony at Port Philip, 1802–4*, London, 1805.

Watson, Dr. F. (ed.) *Australian Historical Records*, vol. I, Sydney, 1914.

White, Surgeon John *Journal of a Voyage to New South Wales*, London, 1790.

WITH PARTICULAR REFERENCE TO AMERICA

Bancroft, H. H. *History of the Pacific States of North America*, 34 vols., San Francisco, 1890.

Broughton, W. R. *Voyage of Discovery to the North Pacific Ocean . . .*, London, 1804.

Chapman, C. E. *A History of California, the Spanish Period*, New York, 1923.

Masson, M. and Jameson, W. 'The Odyssey of Thomas Muir', New York, October, 1923, in *American Historical Review* vol. 29, No. 1.

Mears, John *Voyages made in 1788 and 1789 from China to the North West Coast of America*, with a *Memorial to Grenville*, London, 1790.

Morrison, S. E. *The Maritime History of Massachusetts*, London, 1923.

WITH PARTICULAR REFERENCE TO FRANCE

Alger, J. G. *Englishmen in the French Revolution*, London, 1889.

Alger, J. G. *Paris in 1789–1794*, London, 1902.

Anon. *Histoire de la Tyrannie du Gouvernement Anglaise exercée envers le célèbre Thomas Muir Écossais*, Paris, 1798.

Castlereagh, Viscount *Memorials and Correspondence*, edited by the Marquess of Londonderry, London, 1848.

Desbrière E. *1793–1805, Projets de débarquements aux Îles Britanniques*, Paris, 1900.

Fitzpatrick, W. *Secret Service under Pitt*, London, 1892.

Michel, F. *Les Écossais en France et les Français en Écosse*, London, 1862.

Peron, Capitaine François *Mémoires du Capitaine Peron sur ses Voyages*, 2 vols., edited by L. S. Brissot-Thivars, Paris, 1824.

Pallain, G., (ed.) *La Mission de Talleyrand à Londres en 1792 (Correspondance Diplomatique de Talleyrand)*, Paris, 1889.

Williams, Helen Maria *A Tour in Switzerland*, 2 vols., London, 1798.

WITH PARTICULAR REFERENCE TO IRELAND

Drennan, Dr. William *Letters,* edited by D. A. Chart, Belfast, 1931.

Hamilton Rowan, A. *Autobiography*, Dublin, 1840.

Madden, R. R. *The United Irishmen, their Life and Times*, 7 vols., London, 1842–6.

Nicolson, Harold *The Desire to Please*, London, 1943.

Pakenham, Thomas *The Year of Promise*, London, 1972.

Wolfe Tone, W. T. W. *The Life of Theobald Wolfe Tone*, London, 1825.

PERIODICALS

Annual Register   Monthly Repository   Gentleman's Magazine   Scots Magazine   Monthly Magazine

Note: I have used more quotations from the *Caledonian Mercury* and the *Morning Chronicle* than from other newspapers because, on account of their political complexion, they gave more coverage to Muir and his fellow reformers.

MANUSCRIPT SOURCES

Archives of the Indies, Seville.
Arniston papers, deposited in the National Library of Scotland
California State Papers, in the Bancroft Library, University of California.
Court of Sessions Edinburgh: Minute Book, 1788–1795.
French Foreign Office Archives, Paris: files dealing with Spain and England.
Grey Papers, lodged at the Priors Kitchen, Durham.
Home Office Correspondence in the Scottish and English Public Record Offices.
Laing MSS, in the University of Edinburgh Library.
National Archives, Mexico City.
Place Papers, in the British Library, Additional MSS. 27808 and 27816. Also, Francis Place's collection of newspaper cuttings, vols. 36–40, in particular the volume entitled 'Libel, Sedition, Treason, Persecution'.
Treasury Solicitors' files, in the English Public Record Office.

Index